TITANIC

The Channel Island Connections

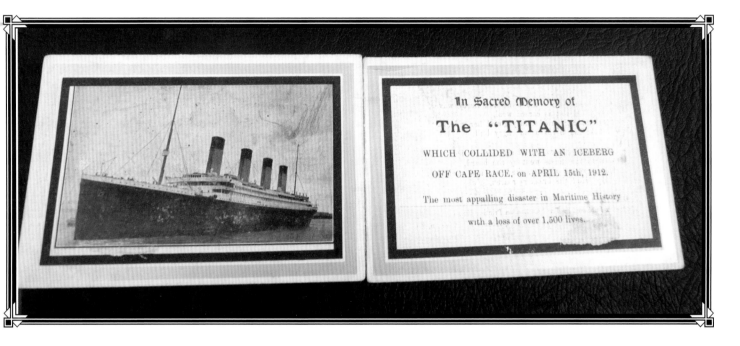

Memorial service, St Luke's, Jersey, April 1912 (John Ovenden collection)

This book is dedicated to the Channel Islanders who did not return

ALASDAIR CROSBY

CAPTAIN EDWARD SMITH

"When anyone asks me how I can best describe my experience in nearly forty years at sea, I merely say, uneventful. Of course there have been winter gales, and storms and fog and the like. But in all my experience, I have never been in any accident ... or any sort worth speaking about. I have seen but one vessel in distress in all my years at sea. I never saw a wreck and never have been wrecked nor was I ever in any predicament that threatened to end in disaster of any sort."

Edward J. Smith,1907
Captain, RMS Titanic,1912

Captain Smith was planning to retire after the maiden voyage of the Titanic.

Published in 2011
by
Channel Island Publishing
Unit 3b, Barette Commercial Centre
La Route du Mont Mado
St John, Jersey, JE3 4DS

ISBN 978-1-905095-37-7

www.channelislandpublishing.com

ACKNOWLEDGMENTS

I would like to thank the many people who have helped in one way or another, be it with material, pictures, information or by reading the draft manuscript:

Jersey:
Anna Baghiani of the Société Jersiaise Library
Heather Morton and Marco Campanini of the States Library
Alfie Barrett
Howard Butlin Baker
Doug Ford
Mary Jordan
Mandy Le Boutillier
Bob Olliver
Isobel Osmont
John Ovenden
Sue Renouf
David Gainsborough Roberts
Marion Rossler
Tony Shiplee
Michael Talibard

Guernsey:
Amanda Bennett and the staff at the Priaulx Library
Richard Digard, editor of the *Guernsey Press and Star*
Peter Burman
Hilda Carpentier
Denise Dekker
David Kreckeler
Roy and Elizabeth Northey
Ken Parker
Peter Quin
Jenny Ridley
Sally Thorneloe
Suzie Vowles
Malcolm Woodland

From outside the Channel Islands:
Günter Bäbler of the Titanic Verein Schweiz
Peter Engberg-Klarstrom (Swedish Titanic Society)
Philip Hind
Senan Maloney
Craig Sopin
Brian Ticehurst

And especially
My wife, Sara, for her help and understanding, without which the Titanic book project would undoubtedly have hit an iceberg and sunk, and my son, Edward, for being quiet - or at least quieter - while 'Daddy's on the computer again'.

FOREWORD
By
DAVID GAINSBOROUGH ROBERTS

Having just put down Alasdair Crosby's most informative book on the Channel Island connections with the ill-fated *Titanic*, which went down 100 years ago, I feel I was almost there on board.

I had no idea that Jersey and Guernsey had so many people on the ship as passengers and as crew members.

I have always been fascinated by the *Titanic* since reading Walter Lord's book, *A Night to Remember*, in 1955 and I was hooked by the time the film of the same name, starring Kenneth More, came out three years later. And what a coincidence that the star actor was educated in Jersey between 1926 and 1931!

What Alasdair has caught so perfectly in his book is the atmosphere on board: the ship was unsinkable and also British-made – and being British was very important in 1912. Britannia ruled the waves and Great Britain was the most powerful country in the world, where George V was the ruler of a quarter of the world's population.

I learnt a lot more of the *Titanic* than I could have imagined in Alasdair's book. I never knew that the *Virginian* was quoted in the first newspaper reports as towing the liner to safety – quite untrue, of course. But as the *Titanic* was both unsinkable and British, it was quite feasible that it would indeed be towed to safety.

On board there were heroes and villains, but as is so clearly pointed out, the powerful men who have been stigmatised as 'villains' - Sir Cosmo Duff-Gordon and Bruce Ismay - are not so villainous as they are popularly portrayed, and are given a fair consideration by the author (which is more than is given them in most biographies).

Another book recently published at the time of writing this foreword, on Ismay, the chairman of the White Star Line, shows that he was a rather boring, colourless individual. His reputation was badly damaged when he was accused of getting into a lifeboat whilst women and children were still waiting to be rescued. Ismay has also been accused (falsely) of forcing the ship's captain to go faster, and was thus responsible for the collision with the iceberg.

Sir Cosmo Duff-Gordon was also a survivor. But did he pay crewmen in his lifeboat to row away from victims of the disaster struggling in the icy water, in case they overturned the boat? I never knew that Lady Duff-Gordon was, at one time, a Jersey resident.

Around 63 per cent of first class passengers survived but only 25 per cent of third class passengers made it. Were doors locked as portrayed in Cameron's film of the *Titanic*? I think I agree with Alasdair on that one.

Rosalie Bidois, who lived in Jersey as a child and was on board the *Titanic* as personal maid to Madeleine Astor, survived with her, while her husband, the millionaire Colonel John Jacob Astor and his valet went down like gentlemen – so not all the rich and powerful people were saved.

Local heroes are mentioned here, in what I believe is the first time in book form. Joseph Duquemin lost both his legs eventually, as a result of immersion in the freezing water, and Alfred Olliver gallantly gave his own socks to a first class passenger in his lifeboat.

Alfred Olliver is buried in a Jersey churchyard in an unmarked grave, and I know that there are moves to erect a headstone to remember that gallant gentleman. I will be the first to subscribe to it. After all, Guernsey has a public memorial to its own *Titanic* people at the Fort Grey Shipwreck Museum.

The "Owen Gang" are reputed to have had Guernsey card sharps on board, which I had not heard before but like the author, I cannot go along with that one.

Did a German with a pistol force his way into a lifeboat? At the time, with the First World War only two years in the future, we British liked to believe that sort of detail – and of course, no British person would ever have behaved like that. Only a Brit could die in the heroic manner of Scott and Oates - as Gentlemen - in the Antarctic in the same fateful year. And did not the band on the *Titanic* go down as Gentlemen whilst playing 'Nearer, my God, to Thee'?

Did Noel Coward once say that he only travelled in foreign parts as there was 'none of this "Women and Children First" nonsense'? Well, perhaps he was misquoted.

I hope that several of my own *Titanic* pieces will appear in the Maritime Museum in St Helier in 2012, and I am so pleased that the Channel Islands and some of its residents will be remembered in this book – and not before time.

'Oh hear us when we cry to thee
For those in peril on the sea.'

This was the one hymn I was brought up with in my childhood, but my mother would never talk about the *Titanic*. Did she have any relative on board? Or perhaps a crew member? She came from a nautical background. I will never know for sure as she steadfastly refused ever to mention the name *Titanic*. However, it was the one hymn she requested we played at her funeral in 2001.

So, as I amble my way through life, one saying will keep me going: the reputed last words of *Titanic*'s Captain Edward Smith: 'Be British'.

DAVID GAINSBOROUGH ROBERTS

AUTHOR'S PREFACE

IN total, there were over 2,200 people on board the RMS *Titanic* when she sank in the early hours of 15 April 1912. Since then, the number of books that have been written about various aspects of that disaster must surely have exceeded that figure, and added to that in recent years there has been all the information that can be found on the Internet.

So, to produce yet another book about the *Titanic* needs, if not exactly an apology, at least a very good excuse. My own excuse is that although so many books have been written, none has yet dealt with the Channel Islanders and those with a clear association with the Channel Islands who were on board as passengers and crew.

There were many nationalities on board the *Titanic* apart from British and American. Among them were Canadians, Irish (especially emigrants), French, Italian and Swiss (many of them serving in the ship's grand restaurants), Eastern Europeans making their way to a Promised Land where they could live in peace – even Chinese stowaways. Some of these nationalities have been the subject of specialist works on the *Titanic*; this present book is, as far as I am aware, the first book to give some details of the Channel Island connection.

Although there has been no book written on this subject before now, there have been certainly plenty of articles in the two Island newspapers: the *Guernsey Press and Star* and the *Jersey Evening Post*. All newspapers love anniversaries, which usually perform the useful function of bulking out the features pages. In the past, various anniversaries of the *Titanic* disaster have been marked by carefully and thoughtfully written articles about the Jersey or Guernsey connection.

I feel that in my own work I am standing on the shoulders of several generations of journalists, and I am glad that at least I have been able to give their work and their research a wider and more easily accessible form.

From Guernsey there were about 19 people, passengers and crew, with a local connection; from Jersey there were about 10. That hackneyed quotation from innumerable politicians about Jersey or Guernsey 'punching above their weight' is accurate at least in the connection of the *Titanic* disaster – a total of 29 people with a Channel Islands connection is not an insignificant contribution from two such small areas of population, although understandable in the light of the strong maritime traditions of both Islands.

We will probably never know the exact number of those with a Channel Island connection who were on board; the figures given in the book are as near an approximation as is currently possible to give. In the aftermath of the tragedy there was considerable confusion about who was and who wasn't on board, who had and who hadn't been saved, and where exactly they came from. That confusion has persisted to the present day.

That there may be some mistakes and some omissions is something for which I apologise. As sure as eggs is eggs, this book will produce - doubtless within days of publication - communications about further family links, more artefacts and new information that has been omitted simply because of the ignorance of the writer.

Should an appreciable amount of further information come to light as a result of this book's publication, it is hoped to include this in a second edition. Any errors and omissions are my own, and not those of the many people who have kindly given me of their time and knowledge, and whom I list on the page of acknowledgements.

ALASDAIR CROSBY

CONTENTS

The Grand Staircase on the Titanic

Author's note:

Although the opening section of this book (Setting the scene) is fictional, only the two main characters are invented. Their experiences and impressions, however, are not invented: they are derived from many sources, recollections and stories of survivors. Those familiar with the story of the Titanic disaster will recognise the contributions of Margaretha Frölicher-Stehli, Edith Rosenbaum, Alfred Nourney and Lawrence Beesley. There are many other sources.

CHAPTER ONE

SETTING THE SCENE

'I cannot imagine any condition which would cause a modern ship to founder... shipbuilding has gone beyond that'

Captain Edward Smith of the White Star Line
speaking a few years before the Titanic disaster

Y ou are off to New York on the RMS *Titanic*, and you're looking forward to a happy and relaxing journey.

From the Channel Islands you and your wife are taking the steamer to Southampton, and from there sailing onwards on this amazing new liner. You have read unending press reports over the last year or so about the White Star Line's new 'Olympic' class of liners, especially all the publicity about the *Olympic,* which was launched in October 1910.

The *Titanic,* the *Olympic*'s 'younger sister', is supposedly even bigger (if just a bit) and better: the largest vessel the world has ever seen, with over 1,000 tons more in gross tonnage.

You couldn't open a newspaper without reading about the *Olympic,* and now, even if the *Titanic* does not have quite the novelty of the *Olympic,* it seems you still can't open a newspaper without reading all about it, its luxurious fittings and public rooms, amenities and grand restaurants, the novelty of having both a swimming pool and a Turkish bath on board... the publicity seems endless.

You were due to sail on the *Philadelphia,* but because of the current coal strike, the sailing has had to be cancelled. The agent sent you a telegram to let you know and at first you were most annoyed – yet another detail to confirm your belief that the country is going to the dogs. But then, when you realise that you have been transferred to the *Titanic,* you decide that there are some compensations after all.

It seems more like a floating luxury hotel than a ship, and it would be interesting, you think, to experience all this for yourself. Something to tell the grandchildren that you were on the maiden voyage of this wonder of modern shipbuilding technology.

Secondly, the *Philadelphia* was due to sail on Good Friday, 5 April. The *Titanic*'s sailing date is Wednesday 10 April, so at least you can have most of the Easter holiday at home, even though a lot of it will be taken up by packing and making final arrangements for your absence.

Your trip is a mixture of pleasure and business; it is not the first time you have made the trip to the USA, but this time you are travelling with your wife and treating the trip as much as a holiday as anything else – a chance also to visit relatives whom you have not seen for a long time, as they have made a new home for themselves over there. Your wife is also talking about the shopping opportunities in New York in a way that slightly alarms you.

Much as you expected, the Easter weekend passes in a whirl of packing and making final arrangements for your business to continue while you are away. Then, on Easter Monday morning, your lad loads up the wagon with your luggage, and off you go to the harbour in good time to catch the SS *Alberta* for Southampton.

Your wife is a little nervous about the forthcoming voyage, but cannot explain why. Although privately thinking that her 'premonitions' are quite ridiculous, you understand that some people might feel a bit apprehensive about boarding a steamer that replaced the ill-fated LSWR steamer SS *Stella* 13 years previously on the Southampton – Channel Islands run. She was wrecked on The Casquets reef with 112 fatalities. That was at Eastertime as well. Then there was the SS Hilda – also owned by the LSWR company - that was wrecked near St Malo at Christmas 1905, and in February 1907 it was the turn of the Great Eastern Railway to suffer the loss of the SS *Berlin* off the Hook of Holland, with 141 fatalities.

But, as you tell her, untold thousands cross from the Channel Islands to Southampton every year and vice-versa without mishap, and the same goes for crossing the Atlantic. And sea safety is improving all the time. She is still a bit apprehensive – as she points out, crossing the Channel can be a dangerous occupation. But of course, your own voyage on the bracing, cold but sunny April day is completely uneventful. You hope her fears have been put to rest – after all, the major leg of the journey is on the *Titanic*, and that's unsinkable.

At St Peter Port you observe a group of young passengers embarking and you murmur to one another with some apprehension that they look as if they might be noisy and a bit of a nuisance on the trip to Southampton. They are not drunk, but it's fairly obvious that they have had something to drink already. It seems to be the birthday of one of them, and it sounds as if they have been celebrating already. You quickly gather that they are all going to transfer to the *Titanic* at Southampton for the onward voyage.

It is evening by the time the *Alberta* docks at Southampton, and as soon as the gangway is put in place there is the usual scrimmage for porters. Eventually you find one, and a little later you arrive at the South Western Hotel, where you have reserved a room.

As you arrive, you have your first view of the *Titanic* at dock near the hotel: a fine sight, dressed overall, as she has been over the Easter weekend.

You both have a good night's sleep, and at

In berth at Southampton

breakfast the next morning you can see from the windows the four huge funnels of the *Titanic* towering above the buildings nearby. You quickly realise, as you overhear the conversation of some of the other guests, that many of them will be embarking tomorrow on the *Titanic*. At the next table, three passengers are discussing the chances of an accident at sea. You are not best pleased, as you can sense your wife's unease, but since glaring at them has no effect, you finish your breakfast quickly and stroll into the town for shopping and sightseeing.

Everywhere you see and hear '*Titanic*': mostly crew members out with their wives or girlfriends having a last day together before the voyage.

The shop assistants ask you if you are sailing on the *Titanic*, and when you say 'yes', they tell you that their husbands, boyfriends, or brothers will also be on board, as a sailor, or a steward, or a stoker... and how happy they are, because the unemployment situation is so bad at present.

For many, their employment on the *Titanic* is the first paid work they have had for a long time. Everyone in the town seems to have some connection with the ship, and most of the crew seem to come from there.

At dinner that evening it seems that almost everyone in the dining room is due to embark on the *Titanic* the next day. At one table is seated a party to which the waiters are paying special attention, and when you ask your own waiter who they are, you are told that this is the party of Mr Bruce Ismay, the chairman of the White Star Line, and Thomas Andrews, the shipbuilder.

Wherever you look there are passengers that are evidently travelling first class. You have booked second class, as you gathered that the standards are so high on this marvellous ship that travelling second class on the *Titanic* is equivalent to travelling first class on any other ship. But having made that decision, you are both now wondering if you have decided rightly and could be missing out – this trip is supposed to be part holiday, after all.

You decide to call at the purser's office on board tomorrow, and see whether there is a chance of converting your booking to first class. In the meantime, you observe your fellow diners with interest: it is undoubtedly only a perception, but you get the feeling that they all seem to know each other already.

Overhearing snatches of their conversations, they seem to have met earlier in London, in Paris, in Baden; there is talk of mutual friends, and parties or events where they met last… it seems more of a reunion than a chance meeting. Those with American accents in particularly seem absorbed in business conversations.

You feel a bit left out - is this really what you want as a backdrop to your voyage over the next week?

One of your favourite authors is the splendid 'Saki', with his richly comic stories of cosmopolitan socialites. Here, you think, they are in the flesh: deracinated to some extent, or at least without obvious ties to any specific locality, and, peculiarly to your way of thinking, not deriving an income from that traditional source of income, the land. You think of your own circle of friends and customers back home that together form the nucleus of social and commercial Island life: farmers, lawyers, military men both active and retired, colonial civil servants, usually making the best of their pensions in the Island's cheaper way of life - suddenly you feel both provincial and insignificant. You leave the restaurant and the bars to these loud, self-confident voices and go to bed.

The next morning you are up and having breakfast early as you want to get on board the *Titanic* in good time and look around it. As you are eating breakfast you see the long queue of stokers and stewards making their way on board to be assigned to their stations and their duties.

It is time, you think, to go on board yourself, so after breakfast you arrange for your luggage to be taken from your rooms and sent to your cabin. You settle your bill and stroll across to where there is already a constant stream of people making their way up the gangways: passengers and their well-wishers come to see them off, crew, press reporters and photographers.

Close too, the *Titanic* looks more like a fortress than a ship, with its side stretching high above you.

Almost the first person you see on board near the top of the gangway is Bruce Ismay again; he is treating his young children to a tour of the ship. Having found your cabin, you decide to wander about to see for yourselves what there is to be seen, and everybody is too busy and occupied to stop you from having a good look round.

It is everything you have imagined, truly more like a luxury hotel than a ship.

You quickly get lost, but every time you pause, there seems to be, at your elbow, another bellboy or steward, with a 'Can I help you, Sir?' and an unspoken but very clear suggestion that the information you are seeking is worth a tip. You feel that before too long this is something that could get quite annoying.

You make your way to the gymnasium, and the attendant suggests you have a go on the mechanical horse and the mechanical camel. You put your wife on the horse and you mount the camel; the attendant starts a small motor and they reverberate under you - enormous fun. You feel a bit foolish when some other visitors arrive and they watch you, chuckling as they see you being shaken up and down, but the attendant insists that you stay in the saddle for his 'friends' to take your photo. Luckily, you don't realise they are actually from the *Illustrated London News*.

Then you look into the Turkish baths, and go down by lift to look at the swimming pool, and up again to see what the first class dining room is like. In addition to the dining room there is the à la carte 'Café Parisien' that serves meals all day long. It gives you the impression that you have just stepped in from the Rue de la Paix. The prices on the menu also help to foster that illusion – you find both decoration and prices quite amazing.

You look into the squash courts, the tea gardens, the smoking rooms, a lounge bigger than the one when you stayed at a smart Paris hotel a couple of years before, a wood-panelled library...it is all the last word in opulent luxury.

But it is also a bit stiff and formal, not like your previous experience of crossing the Atlantic when, as you seem to remember, there was more of a cosy and friendly 'shipboard' feeling.

It is just after midday when you hear the whistles being blown to announce the ship's imminent departure and to warn visitors to go ashore.

Together with most of the other passengers you line the railings on the boat deck to see the departure. Just before the last gangway is withdrawn, a group of three stokers run along the quayside, their kit slung in bundles over their shoulders, and race for the boat. They are stopped by a Petty Officer at the shore end of the gangway, who refuses to let them board. You can see them obviously trying to explain why they are late and pleading to be allowed on board. But the Petty Officer refuses to let them on, and in a moment the gangway is withdrawn, and that puts an end to the argument. They move off down the quayside; from their demeanour they are obviously dejected at not being allowed to board the *Titanic*.

Very slowly the *Titanic* moves away from the side of the dock, and inches down the harbour, with friends and relatives ashore racing along the quayside to keep up with her. Then, to your horror, you witness an accident that could stop your voyage then and there.

As your ship moves abreast of the liner *New York* that is moored at the dockside, a rope on the *New York* seems to snap, for you hear a noise like a pistol shot, and see coils of thick rope fling themselves in the air before falling down on the quayside – the crowd races out of the way of the falling rope, and you hear afterwards from a sailor that he saw one woman on the quayside being carried away to receive medical attention.

The stern of the *New York*, no longer restrained by the rope, floats irresistibly towards the side of the *Titanic*. A collision seems inevitable, and you see sailors on board the *New York* hanging mats over the stern at the point where the collision seems about to take place. A tug, which a moment before had cast off from the *Titanic*, dodges round to the stern of the *New York* and makes fast, trying to drag the stern back and away from the passing stern of the *Titanic*.

At that moment an order from the *Titanic*'s bridge stops the ship dead in its tracks and the *New York*'s stern moves obliquely forward along the side of the *Titanic*, but fortunately a few feet away.

The stern swings instead in front of the bows of the *Titanic*... and instead of hitting

The near miss with the New York

her, hits the nearby liner, *Teutonic*. Fortunately the collision is very slight, but the ropes restraining the *Teutonic* become, in their turn, taut as the suction attracts the ship towards the *Titanic*. It looks, for the second time, as if a collision is about to happen.... but the *Titanic* passes by safely, and the *Teutonic* swings back towards her usual station, the tension on her ropes relaxing.

The crew and passengers on the *Titanic* also relax as she makes her way safely out of the harbour and into the river without further incident.

'That's your premonition explained,' you joke to your wife as the *Titanic* glides onwards. 'Now we can relax and enjoy the voyage.'

The *Titanic* drops down Spithead and past the shores of the Isle of Wight, looking beautiful in the spring sunshine. Watchers onshore wave to the ship as it passes, and you wave back. The *Titanic* exchanges salutes with a White Star tug stationed to await the arrival of one of the company's other liners, and sets off for the open waters of the Channel towards Cherbourg on the first leg of its journey. You reach there at dusk, and quickly it takes more passengers and mail on board before continuing her journey towards

Ireland, the final stop before the Atlantic crossing.

'Shall we, shan't we, see if there is space in first class?' you continue to debate, and after the *Titanic* leaves Cherbourg you decide that at least you can ask the Purser if there might be an opportunity to transfer to first class, and what the cost would be.

But as you wait to speak to him at his office, you find yourself in a queue just behind an arrogant youth, apparently German, who is shouting at the Purser, saying that his second class accommodation is quite disgusting and that he wants a first class cabin instead. He refers to himself so incessantly by his title, Baron von Drachstedt, that you cannot but help feeling that he is bogus. He is certainly unpleasant.

The Purser finds him accommodation in first class, but you look at each other, and there is no need to speak: you both turn away before taking the youth's place in front of the Purser's desk. You will be happy not to have the company of the 'Baron von Drachstedt' for the voyage; you will be happy not to be bothered so incessantly by bellboys wanting to perform unsolicited services for you; if you want to eat at an expensive 'Café Parisien' you will travel to Paris, thank-you,

Underway and passing the Isle of Wight

and do it there. In short, you decide to leave first class to the occupancy of the loud voices you saw yesterday. You will travel in your perfectly comfortable second class accommodation.

You enjoy a good supper, and turn in for your first night at sea. The next morning, after breakfast, you take a turn on deck, but the wind is too cold really, to sit out for long. Nevertheless, you stay on deck to watch the beautiful coast of Ireland pass by, the brilliant morning sunshine emphasising the greenness of the hillsides. At midday you reach Queenstown – last stop before New York.

The harbour is too small to take the *Titanic* and the ship stands out to sea, while the embarking passengers and the mail bags are transferred from the harbour to the ship on two lighters.

The passengers are mostly Irish emigrants, of course, travelling steerage. Despite the luxurious fittings of the *Titanic* for the first and second class passengers, it is the third class steerage passengers that pay the ship's way and cover the costs of the trip, explains a White Star official to whom you chat for a few minutes as you watch the new passengers embarking. That is why the *Titanic*'s steerage accommodation is also better than anything offered by competing lines: the White Star Line wants to attract as much of the 'emigrant trade' as possible. So the meals are well-cooked, the accommodation clean, and there are little touches provided, like having fresh fruit always available on the tables.

The Queenstown stop takes just over one and a half hours, and then the engines start, and off the *Titanic* sets again, sailing past the Irish coastline for the remainder of the afternoon. Gradually, by dusk, you move away from land, and the last thing you see is

First class lounge

the mountains of Ireland disappearing from the horizon as night falls and the ship moves off westwards to the Atlantic.

The next few days pass pleasantly and quietly on board. The sea is quite calm – no worries about seasickness – and the fresh sea air gives you both excellent appetites. It is too cold to spend much time on deck, so you spend a lot of the time in the library, reading and catching up on all those letters that you don't normally have time to write. These you post in the box on the library door, from where the letters will be collected and posted on arrival at New York.

Every day the *Titanic* makes good progress, but you gather that on this maiden trip she is not being pushed to her limits, and it is likely that you will make New York on Wednesday morning, rather than the Tuesday evening, as you first thought might be a possibility.

On the Sunday, you wake up and breakfast as normal. In the morning, the Purser holds a service in the Saloon, and that is followed by lunch. Afterwards you go for a turn on deck, but it is so cold that you quickly scurry back into the warmth again, and return to your usual haunt, the library.

First class White Star Line plate, knife and fork
(John Ovenden Collection)

The room is crowded because of the cold weather outside. During the course of the afternoon a Church of England clergyman approaches you and asks you both if you would like to attend a 'hymn sing-song' after dinner in the library, which he is organising. He is friendly and you don't want to give offence, so you agree, and after dinner you make your way back to the library, where you find yourselves two of about 100 passengers who have taken up his invitation.

The hymns are all well-known and well-loved favourites, played by a young Scotsman who accompanies the singing on the piano. Many of the hymns chosen have a maritime theme, especially the one with the tune you always enjoy: 'For those in peril on the sea'.

The meeting goes on until after 10pm, and then, as the stewards are evidently waiting to serve coffee and biscuits before going off duty, the meeting breaks up. You chat to some of your fellow passengers, including the clergyman's assistant, who hears that you are from the Channel Islands, and tells you that he ran a mission in Guernsey not too long before.

Then, at around 10.45 pm, you say your goodnights and retire to your cabin.

You change into your pyjamas, read for a short while in bed, and turn out the lights. You are looking forward to another peaceful night.

You are already asleep when you are woken, not too long afterwards, by a jolt – not a harsh one but enough to wake you up. At first, you suspect that there may have been some mishap in the kitchens. It is a bit as if (as you say to your wife) somebody had just drawn a finger nail down the side of the ship.

Your wife recalls a holiday of a few years back in Switzerland: the sensation, she says, was just like the shudder that happened when the paddle steamers that run on the Zurichsee came in to dock.

Curious, you get up, switch on the light, and put on your dressing gown. You open the door and look around for someone to ask – just in the same way as you see occupants of neighbouring cabins doing. Presently your steward comes along.

'Nothing to worry about ladies and gents,' he assures you all cheerfully. 'We've just hit an iceberg – or rather, an iceberg has hit us. On the steerage deck they are throwing snowballs! It might delay us a bit – but we'll know more in the morning. No reason to lose any sleep over it.'

You return to your cabin and look out of your porthole window. The iceberg has already slid astern, and there is nothing to see except a bright, starlit night. It all looks very peaceful, and very beautiful.

You tell you wife what has happened, and repeat the steward's reassurance to her: nothing to worry about.

You climb back into bed, turn off the lights and quickly drift off once again into sleep. You are blissfully unaware that only a very short time later, an urgent knocking on your cabin door will propel you into full wakefulness, and turn your dreams into a nightmare.

First class cabin B-58

TIME LINE • TIME LINE • TIME LINE

2 April 1912 6:00
Titanic began sea trials in Belfast

3 April 1912
Titanic arrived in Southampton

10 April 1912 9:30-11:30 a.m.
Passengers arrived in Southampton and began boarding the ship

10 April 1912 Noon
The Titanic set sail and began her maiden voyage

10 April 1912 18:30
Titanic reached Cherbourg, France and picked up more passengers

11 April 1912 11.30 am
Titanic reached Queenstown, Ireland

12 13th April 1912
The Titanic sailed through calm waters

14 April 1912
Throughout the day seven iceberg warnings were received

14 April 1912 11:40 p.m.
*Lookout Frederick Fleet spotted an iceberg dead ahead.
The iceberg struck the Titanic on the starboard (right) side of her bow*

14 April 1912 11:50 p.m.
Water had poured in and risen 14 feet in the front part of the ship

15 April 1912 12:00 a.m.
The captain was told the ship can only stay afloat for a couple of hours. He gave the order to call for help over the radio

15 April 1912 12:05 a.m.
The orders was given to uncover the lifeboats and to get passengers and crew ready on deck. There was only room in the lifeboats for half of the estimated 2,227 on board

15 April 1912 12:25 a.m.

The lifeboats began being loaded with women and children first. The Carpathia, southeast of the Titanic by about 58 miles, picked up the distress call and began sailing to rescue passengers

15 April 1912 12:45 a.m.

The first lifeboat was safely lowered away. Although it could carry 65 people, it left with only 28 on board. The first distress rocket was fired. Eight rockets were fired the whole night

15 April 1912 2:05 a.m.

The last lifeboat left the ship. There were now over 1,500 people left on the ship. The tilt of Titanic's deck grew steeper and steeper

15 April 1912 2.17 am

The last radio message was sent. The captain announced 'Every man for himself'

15 April 1912 2:20 a.m.

The Titanic's broken off stern settled back into the water, becoming more level for a few moments. Slowly it filled with water and tilted its end high into the air before sinking into the sea. People in the water slowly froze to death

15 April 1912 3.30 am

Carpathia's rockets were spotted by the survivors

15 April 1912 4:10 a.m.

The first lifeboat was picked up by the Carpathia

One of the lifeboats approaching the Carpathia

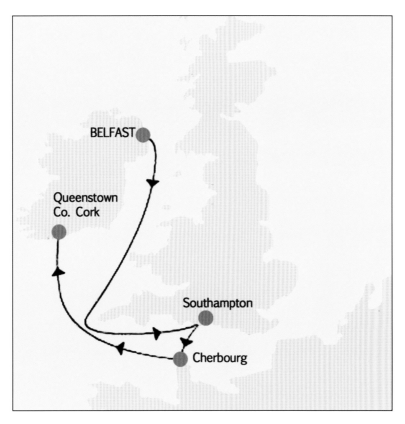

Maps of the route
(Queenstown now known as Cobh, Co. Cork, Ireland)

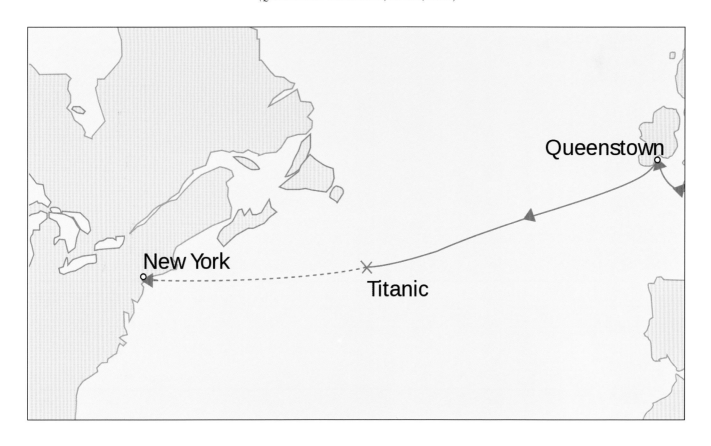

Getting ready to sail. The last picture taken of Captain Smith - seen top left.

TICKET COSTS
(one way)
Then as now, there was some variation in prices depending on availability, when booked, etc.

First Class (parlour suite) £870 (£57,333 today)
First Class (berth) £30 (£1,977 today)

Second Class £12 (£790 today)

Third Class £3 to £8 (£197 to £527 today)

From Wikianswers

One Pound GBP in 1912 had the purchasing power of about £65.90 GBP today.

NOTE - This historical conversion is the result of many calculations and considerations by a purpose designed program for which we take no credit.
The resulting answer should only be regarded as an approximation.

NUMBER OF PEOPLE ON BOARD & SURVIVAL FIGURES

Passenger Category	Number Aboard,	Percentage Saved,	Percentage Lost,	Number Saved,	Number Lost,
Children, First Class	6	83%	17%	5	1
Children, Second Class	24	100%	0%	24	0
Children, Third Class	79	34%	66%	27	52
Women, First Class	144	97%	3%	140	4
Women, Second Class	93	86%	14%	80	13
Women, Third Class	165	46%	54%	76	89
Women, Crew	23	87%	13%	20	3
Men, First Class	175	33%	67%	57	118
Men, Second Class	168	8%	92%	14	154
Men, Third Class	462	16%	84%	75	387
Men, Crew	885	22%	78%	192	693
Total	**2224**	**32%**	**68%**	**710**	**1514**

LIST OF THOSE ABOARD THE TITANIC WITH A CLEAR CONNECTION TO JERSEY OR GUERNSEY

'Millionaire and artisan – the occupant of the £850 staterooms and the £7 10s steerage passenger – have perished together and may at this very moment be locked in each other's arms "in the caverns deep of the ocean cold"' –

'The Jerseyman' (Weekly newspaper), 20 April 1912

JERSEY
Passengers

BIDOIS, Rosalie*
Saved
Aged: 46; single
Occupation: personal maid to
Mrs Madeleine Astor
First class; boarded Cherbourg
Travelled as part of the Astor's entourage
on one ticket: £247 10s 6d
Ticket number 17757
Lifeboat 4

DUFF-GORDON, Lucy Christiana,
Lady, (née Sutherland)*
Saved
Aged 48; married
Dressmaker, couturière and business
director. First class; boarded Cherbourg
Fare: £56 18s 7d
Ticket No. 17485
Lifeboat 1

ILETT, Bertha
Saved
Aged: 17; single
2nd class; boarded Southampton
Fare: £10 10s 0d
Ticket Number 14885
Lifeboat 12; transferred to 13 before
rescue.

JERSEY
Crew

AHIER, Percy Snowden
Lost
Aged 20; single
Steward (1st class)
Body not recovered

OLLIVER, Alfred C
Saved
Aged 27; married
Quartermaster
Lifeboat 5

POINGDESTRE, John Thomas
Saved
Aged 33; married
Able Seaman
Lifeboat 12

RATTENBURY, William Henry
Lost
Aged 36; married (separated)
Assistant boots steward
Body, if recovered, not identified

RYAN, Thomas
Lost
Aged 27; married
Steward, 3rd class
Body, if recovered, not identified

* Both Rosalie Bidois and Lady Duff Gordon were
resident in Jersey during their childhoods

VIGOT, Philip Francis
Saved
Aged 32; single
Able Seaman
Lifeboat 13

WILLIAMS, Walter John
Saved
Aged 28, married.
Assistant steward, second class
Lifeboat 13

GUERNSEY
Passengers

BAINBRIGGE, Charles Robert
Lost
Aged 23; single
Occupation: horse trainer
2nd class; boarded Southampton
Fare: £10 10s
Ticket number 31030
Body not recovered

BENTHAM, Lillian W
Saved
Aged 19; single
2nd class; boarded Southampton
Fare: £13
Ticket number 28404
Lifeboat 12

DENBUOY, Albert
Lost
Aged 25; single
Occupation: tomato grower
2nd class; boarded Southampton
Fare: £31.10 (for 3 passengers: also

Clifford and Ernest Jefferys)
Ticket number 31029
Body not recovered

DOWNTON, William Joseph
Lost
Aged 55; married
Occupation: quarryman
2nd class; boarded Southampton
Fare: £26 (with Peter McKane)
Ticket number 28403
Body not recovered

DUQUEMIN, Joseph Pierre
Saved
Aged 19; single
Occupation: Stonemason
3rd class; boarded Southampton
Fare: £7 11s
Ticket Number: 752
Collapsible Boat D

GAVEY, Laurence
Lost
Aged 26; single
Occupation: travelling oil rig fitter
2nd class;
boarded Southampton
Fare: £10 10s
Ticket number: 31028
Body not recovered

JEFFERYS, Clifford Thomas
Lost
Aged 24; single
Occupation: carter
2nd class; boarded Southampton
Travelled on Albert Denbuoy's ticket
Body not recovered.

JEFFERYS, Ernest Wilfred
Lost
Aged 22; single
Occupation: carter
2nd class; boarded Southampton
Travelled on Albert Denbuoy's ticket
Body not recovered

MITCHELL, Henry Michael
Lost
Aged 71; widowed
Occupation: retired businessman and
shopkeeper 2nd class; boarded
Southampton Fare: £10 10s
Ticket Number: 24580
Body not recovered

McKANE, Peter David
Lost
Aged 46; single
Occupation: quarryman
2nd class; boarded Southampton
Travelled on William Downton's ticket
Body not recovered

PARKER, Clifford Richard
Lost
Aged 17; single
Occupation: ledger clerk
2nd class; boarded Southampton
Fare: £10 10s
Ticket Number 14888
Body not recovered

RENOUF, Lillian Elizabeth
Saved
Aged: 30; married
2nd class; boarded Southampton
Travelled on husband's ticket
Lifeboat 12

RENOUF, Peter Henry
Lost
Aged 33; married (Lillian Renouf)
Occupation: carpenter/joiner
2nd class;
boarded Southampton
Fare: £21
Ticket Number 31027
Body not recovered

RUGG, Emily
Saved
Aged 21; single
2nd class;
boarded Southampton
Fare: £10 10s
Ticket Number 31026
Lifeboat 12

WHEADON, Edward Herbert
Lost
Aged 66; widower
Occupation: retired farmer and
businessman
2nd class;
boarded Southampton
Fare: £10 - 10s
Ticket Number 24579
Body not recovered

WILLIAMS, HOWARD HUGO
('Harry')
Saved
Aged 28; married
Occupation: driver for stone merchant
3rd Class;
boarded Southampton
Fare: £8 - 1s
Ticket Number 2466
Body not recovered

GUERNSEY
Crew

INGROUILLE, Henry
Lost
Aged: 21; single
Steward, 3rd Class
Body not recovered

MARTIN, Anne ('Annie')
Saved
Aged 33; married (separated)
Stewardess, 1st Class
Lifeboat 11

WHITFORD, Alfred Henry.
Lost
Aged 39; married
Steward, 2nd Class
Body not recovered

3rd class boarding ticket

Shop front in St Peter Port

St Helier Harbour

CORRECT FORM FOR DROWNING

'We read stories of heroism of the olden days; they appear like fairy tales to us, and we treat them of very little significance, but here today, in our own lifetime, are displayed acts of self-sacrifice and bravery such as the world has never known'

The Jerseyman (weekly newspaper)
Saturday 21 April 1912

Within a 10-month period there were, in 1912 and 1913, two memorial services held at St Paul's Cathedral, both of which drew enormous crowds that packed the cathedral and the surrounding area.

On 29 April 1912, a service was held in memory of those lost in the *Titanic* disaster. In February 1913, the Cathedral once again was crowded out for a memorial service for Captain Robert Scott and his four companions. They had died while on their way back from the South Pole, battling through snow and ice to win glory for King and Country.

When the tent containing the remains of Scott and his companions was discovered, letters he had written shortly before his death were discovered.

In one he had written: 'After all, we are setting a good example to our countrymen, if not by getting into a tight place, by facing it like men when we were there.'

In another: 'But we have been to the Pole, and we shall die like gentlemen.'

To the mother of one of his companions: 'We are very near the end of our journey, and I am finishing it in company with two gallant, noble gentlemen. One of them is your son.'

Earlier, when the feet of Captain Oates had turned gangrenous, Oates limped out of the tent, and walked off into the falling snow. He did not return.

Scott wrote in his journal: 'We know that poor Oates was walking to his death… it was the act of a brave man and an English gentleman. We all hope to meet the end in the same spirit and assuredly it is not far.'

In Scott's obituary in the Times, he was described as 'firm in his friendship and chivalrous in his conduct.'

The references to chivalry, to knighthood and to a knightly code of honour were pre-eminent in the contemporary public reaction to the failed expedition.

The western world in the early years of the 20th Century was truly a world of myth and legend, and of inspiring images – images, at times, sadly out of touch with reality – that reflected the High Mediaeval ideals of chivalry.

Knights might not win through to journey's end, nor survive their adventures to enjoy a comfortable old age. But knights *did* know how to die a noble death when circumstances called upon them to do so.

And in the same way as Scott and his companions were perceived, so also were the victims of the *Titanic*.

The American, 'Logan Marshall' (Logan Howard Smith), wrote shortly after the disaster in his 'instant disaster book', *The Sinking of the Titanic* (1912): '*Chivalry is a mild appellation for their conduct. Some of the vaunted knights of old were desperate cowards by comparison. A fight in the open field, or jousting in the tournament, did not call out the manhood in a man as did the waiting till the great ship took the final plunge.*'

And writing in a special issue of *Lloyd's Weekly News* that also appeared after the *Titanic* sank, titled: '*The Deathless Story of the Titanic*', the journalist Philip Gibbs wrote of the passengers: '*They had to think swiftly, to decide swiftly, to act swiftly. Without wasting time in dreadful doubt, in frightful hesitations, in the perplexity of despair, they made the most of the time allowed them by the harrying pursuit of death, and they filled it to the brim, and crowded it with valour, with sweet and noble acts. Men and women vied with each other in the courtesies of courage, in helpfulness, in renunciation, in loyalty, and in love. The "Titanic" became the shrine of many miracles, for there is no greater miracle than this, that a man should lay down his life for his friend; that weak women should suddenly be uplifted from their weakness and become strong to suffer and to dare; that men unused to hardihood, untrained to peril, born and bred in luxury, as many of them were, should rise above the temptations of fear and baseness, and obey to the last letter the great code of honour….*'

'*They helped the women into the boats with cheery words, with quiet discipline, with the*

FIRST EDITION.] [PRICE TWOPENCE.

The DEATHLESS STORY
OF THE
TITANIC
COMPLETE
NARRATIVE
WITH MANY
ILLUSTRATIONS
TITANIC
2d
FILMORE

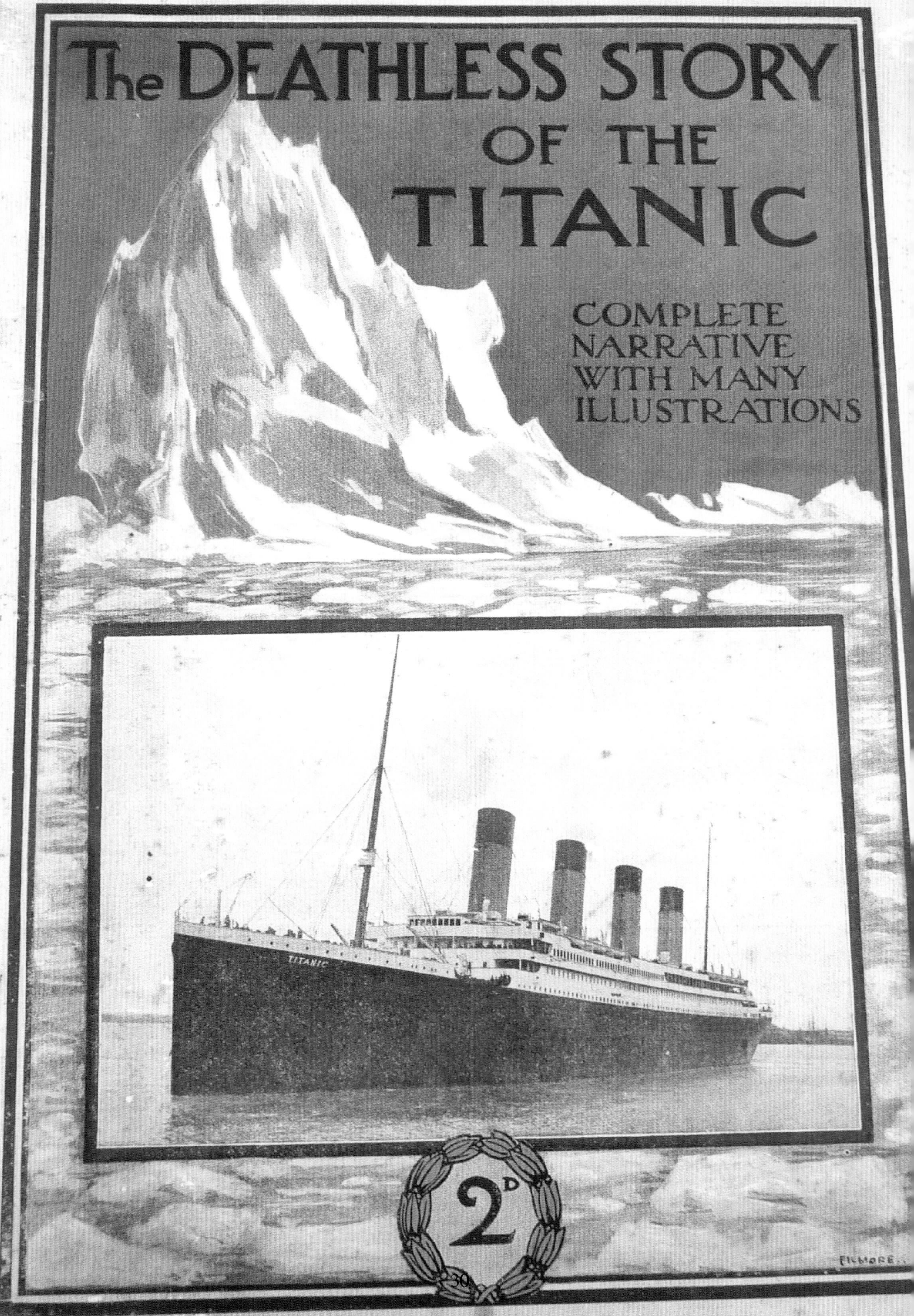

ISSUED BY "LLOYD'S WEEKLY NEWS."

spirit that lives in the fine flower of chivalry. They checked the least sign of panic, and then as they waved a last farewell to the women when the boats moved away like shadows across the water, they turned, and knew themselves to be within a little while of death.'

In such a manner were the accounts of survivors pieced together to form a shining and glorious tale of chivalry and knightly courage.

All was calm on that cold night that the *Titanic* went down. The huge liner blazed with light, and the band played ragtime music at the head of the grand staircase. The lifeboats were filled, but the order had gone out: 'Women and children first', and so gentlemen escorted ladies to the boats as to their carriages, and helped them courteously in. After that they stood back, and waved farewell as the boats were lowered.

Colonel John Jacob Astor, reputedly the richest man in America, handed in his new young bride to the lifeboat. He asked permission to join her – she was, he explained, in a delicate condition. Permission was refused. He made no protest: he stood back, smiled and touched his cap. Then he turned back to his place among the men.

'Walter, you must come with me' begged the wife of the American millionaire industrialist, Walter Douglas.

'No,' he replied, turning away.'I must be a gentleman.'

The English writer and journalist, W T Stead, was last seen quietly reading; death by drowning was just a trivial annoyance. The American businessman, Benjamin Guggenheim, having seen the women in his party into a lifeboat, returned to his cabin with his valet, Victor Giglio, to change into evening dress.

'We've dressed up in our best and are prepared to go down like gentlemen,' he informed a surprised steward as they re-emerged. He also gave a survivor a message saying, 'Tell my wife, if it should happen that my secretary and I both go down, tell her I played the game out straight to the end. No woman shall be left aboard this ship because Ben Guggenheim is a coward.'

The two men were last seen seated in deck chairs, sipping brandy and smoking cigars.

The crew behaved wonderfully. They remained at their posts until the very last minute. The stewards were unfailingly courteous and helpful. The PT instructor in the gymnasium continued to instruct passengers on the mechanical horse and the parallel bars.

The engineers stayed by their engines; not one of them would survive. The band went on playing ragtime until just before the end; just before the ship went down, they changed the tune to the hymn: '*Nearer My God To Thee*'.

The wireless operator, John ('Jack') Phillips, stayed at his post, even when given permission by the Captain to leave and save himself if he could, continuing to tap out calls for assistance at his wireless set in the hope that a ship might hear and come to the rescue; the postal clerks spent the last hour of their lives in trying to rescue the mailbags.

The last words of the Captain, Edward Smith, megaphoned from the bridge were: 'Be British.' Then, following the noble traditions of the service, he went down with his ship. But there were stories that he was last seen swimming in the icy waters afterwards. He was carrying a little girl, whom he placed in the arms of the occupants of a lifeboat. He was urged to climb in to safety, but he refused. He asked: 'Where's Murdoch?' (the First Officer). When told that he had been lost in the disaster, he let go of the boat, and was never seen again.

There was indeed some panic on board, it was admitted. One of the stewards reported afterwards that there were attempts to rush the boats, by 'various men passengers, probably Italians or some foreign nationality, other than English or American'.

The wretched creatures were unaware that the correct way to meet death by drowning was an attitude of calm indifference.

Similarly four years later, in the midst of the

Opposite: Lloyd's Weekly News (John Ovenden Collection)

First World War, Lord Kitchener, on board the armoured cruiser *HMS Hampshire* when it struck a German mine in the course of a Force 9 gale, was last seen, composed and dignified, dressed correctly in his uniform, standing on the deck.

That was how Britons faced the trivial annoyance of sudden death at sea.

However, even as the first reports of golden heroism, self-sacrifice and devotion to duty were being filed in newspaper offices around the world, a darker, more discordant note was also being struck.

Within hours of the initial news of the loss of the *Titanic* came the first reports that there was grossly insufficient lifeboat space for the total of the crew and passengers that needed them. The *Titanic* had 2,227 aboard, and lifeboats for only 1,100.

The Jerseyman encapsulated the millions of words that were written, then and since, on the failure to provide adequate lifeboat capacity. On 4 May the leading article stated:

'In our opinion, it was the duty of the managers and directors of the White Star line to protect the lives of the people entrusted in their care. They failed to protect them. A great multitude of precious lives were sacrificed. Mr Bruce Ismay himself, the managing director, on board, was saved – with the women and children.

'The simple fact is ground enough for bitter indictment of the White Star Company. It took charge of 2,200 human lives and it made no adequate provision for their safety.'

Ismay himself was excoriated in the press both then and afterwards.

Adverse comment on the 'Women and children first' orders also quickly appeared. It was said, certainly with reference to the Second Officer, Charles Lightoller, that there was greater insistence on preventing men from entering the lifeboats than on trying to save them. As a result, many of the lifeboats left the ship with a spare capacity of unoccupied seats. Only 711 people approximately escaped from the disaster in spite of the calm sea; had all the seats been filled, another 450 people might have been saved.

As it was, the lives of 1,513 people were lost.

But apart from any other fault, there had been no boat drill; no crews and no passengers had been allocated to particular lifeboats. The launching of the lifeboats and the evacuation of passengers from the *Titanic* was done without any forethought or pre-planning.

A glaring example of the 'unscientific' use of the available lifeboats was the escape of Sir Cosmo and Lady Duff-Gordon and Lady Duff-Gordon's secretary: in their boat there were 12 people only on board (of the nine others seven were crew) but there were spaces for 40. This is aggravated by the subsequent allegation that Sir Cosmo had bribed the crew not to return to pick up any more people struggling in the water, for fear of swamping the lifeboat.

This brings us to the other great issue that has rolled on over the past century: the fact that a greater proportion of first class passengers were saved than second class or steerage passengers; fewer children survived from the steerage class than children in the first or second classes. 63% of the people in the first class were saved; 42% in the second class were saved, only 25% in third class, and only 22% of the crew.

For women and children, the survival rate for second class was 81%, and only 37% in third class.

This has been interpreted, especially in the 1997 film *Titanic*, almost as a deliberate policy to favour first and second class passengers and as a result this enjoyable entertainment seems at times more like a propaganda film on behalf of the Communist party. More accurately, despite such well documented events as doors being locked – and even guarded – so as not to allow steerage passengers easy access to the upper decks, one cannot transpose the social attitudes of modern times on to events that happened a century ago. It is only the unconscious application of the then contemporary attitudes that we see in these percentage statistics of persons saved from first class, second class and steerage.

In addition, there are the stories of panicked stewards racing down the corridors and forcing their way on to lifeboats. The Captain is alleged to have been to a dinner party earlier in the evening, and was drunk by the time of the collision, and the band had given up playing anything by the end; they did not play *Nearer, My God, to Thee* nor anything else: they were

slinking into one in order to escape. It is perhaps unfortunate for his subsequent reputation that he wore a handlebar moustache – correct facial wear for any villainous 'Sir Jasper'.

Already, by the time the rescue ship, the *Carpathia*, had arrived in New York with Ismay and the other survivors, his conduct was being called into question.

Much of this opprobrium was whipped up against him by the American newspaper

The Daily Telegraph breaking the news

milling about hoping for rescue, like all the other people stranded on board.

Finally, there is the conduct of the White Star chairman, Bruce Ismay. He is portrayed, especially in the flawed *Titanic* film, almost as a pantomime villain, bullying Captain Smith into trying to break the speed record to New York so as to gain the resultant newspaper publicity, arrogantly decrying the need for extra lifeboats during the voyage, but after the collision

magnate, William Randolph Hearst, one of the richest and most powerful men in America.

They had first met years before, when Ismay was the White Star's agent in New York. Ismay, a private man, had always disliked talking to the press, a habit which although might be morally neutral and often prudent, invariably tends to make journalists cross. Hearst was no exception. Twenty years later, following the *Titanic* disaster, he prosecuted a vicious campaign against him.

It was Hearst who instigated the countless stories that Ismay had manipulated the *Titanic's* captain into driving his ship faster than he wanted; of cowardice in taking the place of a passenger in one of the lifeboats; and of resigning from the company after the disaster rather than face the public. None of these allegations were true, but that didn't worry Hearst, who never ever allowed the truth to get in the way of a good story.

The image created by Hearst and his 'yellow press' survives largely to this day.

J. Bruce Ismay did not order or put pressure on the commander or chief engineer to make a record passage to New York for the *Titanic's* maiden voyage, and there is no evidence that he told passengers that the *Titanic* was out to 'make a record.'

The newspapers, particularly in the United States, expected Ismay to sacrifice his own life in the sinking. The story of a cowardly ship-owner jumping into the first available lifeboat to save his own skin while passengers lost their lives was just too irresistible.

True, Ismay did escape in a lifeboat, but only after he had helped with the loading and lowering of several others, and only when he was sure that no women were in the vicinity of the collapsible lifeboat did he get in. When the boat reached the water he helped to row it. In every respect he acquitted himself far better than many other passengers and crew members.

Nor did he afterwards, as a result of the shame and opprobrium from which he suffered, retire and spend the rest of his days reclusively on his estate in Ireland, as is often claimed.

He had already, in January 1912, announced his impending retirement as president of the White Star's holding company, International Mercantile Marine. He did so in June 1913.

However, he continued to be involved as chairman and director of several important companies in Liverpool and London. One of these companies dealt with the huge number of insurance claims resulting from the *Titanic* disaster.

Although it is high time for Ismay's reputation to be rehabilitated, unfortunately the actions of Captain Smith need to be questioned. He had been given plenty of information about icebergs in the area. Some of these messages may not have been sent on to him, but some certainly were. His only response was to push on, without slackening speed, unlike the *Californian*, for example, the nearest ship to the *Titanic*, which had shut down its engines and stopped in the face of the ice floes surrounding it.

It will never be known exactly where the balance of probability lies between the 'shining and heroic' version and the 'dark' version of the story of the *Titanic* disaster. The general rule is that truth lies midway between the two opposing ends of a controversy, greyer than we might have hoped for, but whiter than the darkest interpretations put on it.

Certainly there was much heroism displayed; the tragedy was – perhaps both with Scott's South Pole expedition as much as with the *Titanic* disaster – that there was a lack of intelligent forethought that would have rendered heroism unnecessary.

First Officer William Murdoch

Close up of starboard side plating

(II)

A TITANIC IMPACT

'Mr A.S Franklin, Vice-President of the International Mercantile Marine, in a statement this morning, says: - "No message has been received reporting the accident and if the collision occurred, the vessel is in no danger, since she is absolutely unsinkable. There is no cause for serious anxiety"

Evening Post (Jersey) report
15 April 1912.

The impact of the *Titanic* disaster, as a news story, was similar, in its day, to any of the most riveting or dramatic stories of our own generation. The attack on the Twin Towers in New York, the so-called '9/11', for example, is an irresistible comparison to make in our own time, in respect of column inches in the immediate aftermath, and the volume of analysis and comment that followed, which still follows a decade later, and which will doubtless continue into the far future as notable anniversaries occur.

The anniversaries of the loss of the *Titanic* have regularly produced features in the Channel Islands' newspapers. The one that follows, reproduced with permission from the *Guernsey Press and Star*, was written in 1992 for the 80th anniversary of the disaster. It is commendable for describing how a similar incident at the time of its writing might have caused similar shockwaves worldwide. To make its point it draws on the soon to be opened Channel Tunnel (which in fact took place two years later):

'The date is September 1993. The occasion is the first commercial use by train of the Channel Tunnel. Amid vast publicity, the celebrities and lesser folk sink into their luxurious seats.

'On the television screens, the public see the Queen and the President of the French Republic read messages of goodwill. The President of the US, the Emperor of Japan and other world leaders offer congratulations.

'Newspapers and television stress that safety is absolute, and that every possible precaution has been taken.

'News fanatics collect special supplements, which detail the engineering triumph represented by the construction of the tunnel.

'Yet again, Man has conquered Nature.

'In the train's sumptuous first-class dining car, which is hung with original paintings by David Hockney, fabulous meals are served, and gallons of champagne are drunk.

'Driver F. K. Smith sets off from London. Halfway across the Channel, the train is *consumed by fire after a collision. Two-thirds of the passengers are killed, including Sir James Goldsmith, David Frost, Jacques Delors, Edith Cresson and Ian Botham.*

'Several senior travel officials escape. They are later blamed for getting away and for negligence. Numerous railway employees are accused of cowardice. Britain and France hold controversial inquiries. Anglo-French relations sink to a new low....'

The news of such an horrific incident in this 'alternative history' would have reverberated around the world, just as did the loss of the *Titanic* in 1912.

The famous South American explorer, Colonel Percy Fawcett, was in an isolated upriver settlement on the Amazon at the time of the *Titanic* disaster. The news reached even there, and a local resident, who had never seen the Atlantic Ocean nor could envisage it, told him with all seriousness that in his opinion the *Titanic* should have stayed out in the middle of the water, and not tried to follow the banks, where it was well-known that there were shoals, submerged logs and other perils.

Everybody at the time probably had his own opinion on what caused the disaster, and some theories about it that have gained currency are about as equally well informed as Fawcett's 'expert' informant.

In both Jersey and Guernsey, the first reports were carried by the *Evening Post* and *Guernsey Evening Press* respectively. At that time they were still evening papers, and so could scoop the morning papers by carrying the breaking news on the evening of Monday 15 April.

As in all the news reports of the *Titanic* tragedy, it is fascinating to compare the early troubling reports - in which the ship is said to be sinking, but perhaps slowly, and 'no cause for serious anxiety' (in the words of a senior company official) - with the reports of a day or so later, as the full horror of the disaster became clear.

The initial headlines in the *Evening Post*

announced the *'Titanic Disaster'* and that *'The Leviathan hits an Iceberg'*. The information was received by wireless from the Allen Liner, *Virginian*, that had left Halifax to assist the stricken vessel and even take off the passengers 'if necessary'.

Other headlines reported that the damaged liner was slowly making for Halifax, and that the passengers were safe.

'We have heard nothing direct from the *Titanic*, but are perfectly satisfied that the vessel is unsinkable,' was the confident first quoted statement from Philip Franklin, then vice-president of the International Mercantile Marine company, the parent company of the White Star Line.

'The fact that the Marconi messages ceased means absolutely nothing. It may be due to atmospheric conditions or the coming up of the ships or something of that sort.

'We are not worried about the possible loss of the ship, as she will not go down, but we are sorry for the inconvenience caused to the travelling public.'

The remarks were to haunt him for ever after.

Later reports, such as detailed in the following day's *Morning News*, stated that she was sinking by the head and that women and children were being taken into life rafts. The last signals were said to be 'blurred and ended abruptly.'

The next day's issues of both papers on the evening of the Tuesday and morning of the Wednesday adopted a very different tone, with headlines of 'Vessel reported sunk' and 'Great Loss of Life feared', although they still held out for 'rays of hope'.

Messages reported that 20 boatloads of passengers had already been taken on board the *Carpathia*, and that the *Parisian* and the *Olympic* were drawing near.

By Wednesday a fuller story emerged with headlines of *'The World's Greatest Shipping Disaster'* and some eyewitness accounts, but the details were only finalised that Friday after the *Carpathia* had docked in New York with its

Titanic survivors.

The exact particulars of those who escaped from the *Titanic* with their lives are difficult to specify for reasons given above. In addition, the passage of time has blurred details, as also the fact that the outbreak of the First World War two years later quickly eclipsed the *Titanic* as a compelling newspaper 'story'.

The final factor is that, with some notable exceptions, many of the *Titanic* passengers and crew had previously led perfectly ordinary or mundane lives, and most of the survivors would continue to do so once they reached dry land. Their voyage on the *Titanic* was their only moment in which the ordinariness of their own lives became, for a few days, perfectly extraordinary, and they touched history.

The difficulty is exacerbated in respect of those who were travelling second class or in steerage, and for the rank and file of the crew, where information about their lives was of little interest to the White Star Line and even fewer details were noted.

After the initial stunning news of the disaster, the Island's charitable instincts quickly came to the fore, with appeals opened by the *Evening Post,* the Constable of St Helier, and many collections at events held to raise money for the families of crew members where the bread-winner had perished in the disaster.

At the Opera House the management put on a 'startling' film of the disaster – 'its cause fully explained and actual icebergs shown floating south from Labrador towards the track of the ill-fated liner *Titanic*.'

Showing with this picture was another one, rather less serious, entitled 'Tommy becomes a Toreador.'

Special football matches, fêtes, whist drives and theatrical performances – anything that might raise money - were arranged in both Islands to help the Mayor of Southampton's appeal and the Mansion House fund in aid of *Titanic* survivors and bereft dependants.

On the Sunday following the disaster special

services and prayers were held in places of worship around the Island. From the pulpit of the Town Church, the Dean of Jersey, Samuel Falle, assured his congregation: 'Out of this unparalleled disaster, good will comes.'

In so far as that passenger-carrying ships thereafter ensured there were actually enough lifeboats for all on board, he was right.

In Guernsey, the *Evening Press* reported on 15 April: 'The *"Montreal Star"* reports from Halifax that the *Titanic* is still afloat, and is making her way slowly to Halifax.'

Also: *'A message from Montreal timed 8.30 a.m. says that the Titanic is heading towards Halifax with her own engines. It is thought the bulkheads will prevent her sinking. A further message says wireless telegraphy brings word that two vessels are standing by the Titanic.'*

However, in Guernsey the focus was very quickly on the number of Islanders and relations

The Arcade in Guernsey where the ticket office was situated

of Islanders who were known to be on board and who would have been affected. The Monday issue of the newspaper carried the names of 11 Islanders on board. Another four names were added to the list the following day.

In fact the total number of those with a Jersey and Guernsey connection known to be on board was 10 from Jersey: 3 passengers and 7 crew; a total death toll of 0 passengers and 3 crew. Of the three passengers, two had a birth or childhood connection only, and only the third one was a Jersey resident.

There were 19 people aboard from Guernsey: 16 passengers and 3 crew; a death toll of 12 passengers and 2 crew. It is more difficult to divide the surviving passengers into 'locals' and 'non-locals', since many of them had very strong Guernsey connections, but had previously emigrated to America. They had returned to Guernsey on a 'home visit' a few months previously and were returning to their new homes in the USA.

The figures given above cannot be absolutely confirmed, because in the immediate aftermath of the disaster there was confusion as to who was and who was not on board, with misspellings of names and subsequent corrections – something that added to the misery of the unfortunate relatives waiting for news of their loved ones.

The list of Guernsey passengers was high because a dozen of them comprised a loose group of friends and relations travelling together. They were all from Guernsey or the offspring of Guernsey parents. Some, as we have said, were returning to their new homes in the USA after a visit 'back home', others were young Islanders off to the USA to seek fame and fortune – or least better opportunities for work than existed in Guernsey.

The existence of the Guernsey colony in New York and its surrounding area is less celebrated than that, for example, of the Irish, Italian or Puerto Rican colonies. But, if smaller in scale, it performed the same function of providing a 'home-from home' and a welcoming local community of their own countrymen for new immigrants just arrived.

On the morning of their departure from Guernsey, the group of friends held a party to bid farewell to all their friends. It was also a continuation of the day before of a birthday party: one of them, Laurence Gavey, was celebrating his 26th birthday.

One of those who had gathered to say good-bye to the group was a columnist in the *Guernsey Evening Press.* Writing about three weeks later in his column - *Quens j'y pens* (While I think of it) - he stated: *'The unforeseen, the unexpected, really the undreamt of – has befallen the little group of Islanders who, on Easter Monday, so full of joy and hope, assembled at the Half-Way Station and bade a cheerful 'au revoir' to the many neighbours who had there gathered to God-speed the parting contingent.*

'The writer himself on that Easter Monday morning chatted with all but two of the whole party, and the recollection of their happy faces and cheerful anticipations points vividly the reality of the phrase: "In the midst of life we are in death".

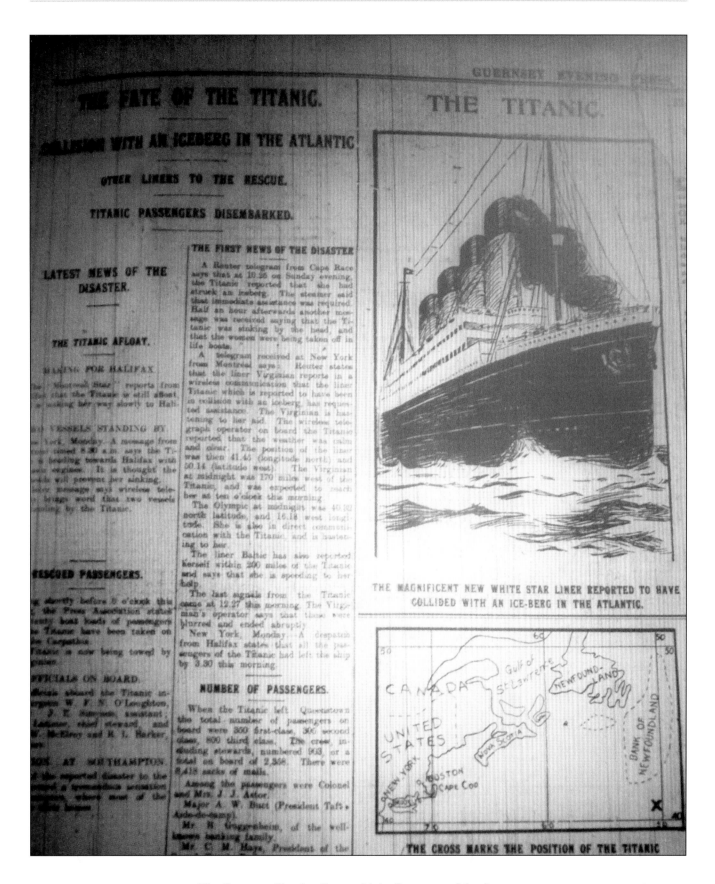

The Guernsey Evening Press with its first story of the disaster

THE GUERNSEY CONNECTIONS

'The tragedies of this wreck can never all be told'

Stewardess on the Titanic, Anne Martin, from Guernsey,
quoted in a newspaper interview, April 1912

Guernsey passengers:

Bainbrigge, Charles Robert   †
2nd class

Bentham, Miss Lillian W
2nd class

Denbuoy, Albert   †
2nd Class

Downton, William Joseph   †
2nd Class

Duquemin, Joseph
3rd class

Gavey, Lawrence   †
2nd Class

Jefferys, Clifford Thomas   †
2nd Class

Jefferys, Ernest Wilfred   †
2nd Class

Mitchell, Henry Michael   †
2nd Class

McKane, Peter David   †
2nd Class

Parker, Clifford Richard   †
2nd Class

Renouf, Mrs Lillian Elizabeth
2nd class

Renouf, Peter Henry   †
2nd Class

Rugg, Miss Emily
2nd class

Wheadon, Edward Henry   †
2nd Class

Williams, Howard Hugo 'Harry'   †
3rd Class

Guernsey crew:

Ingrouille, Henry   †
Steward, 3rd Class

Martin, Anne
Stewardess, 1st Class

Whitford, Alfred Henry   †
Steward, 2nd Class

The list of passengers omits the name of Rosalie Bidois. Although she is invariably claimed to be from Guernsey, this seems to originate in one article in an American newspaper, the New York *Evening World*, which stated that she was 'a Guernsey girl'; in fact she was born in St Helier.

The name of 'Mr H Robilliard, of Bon Enfant, Vale' is given as a steward in an early list of Guernsey people on the *Titanic*, contained in the *Evening Press*. However, this name is not repeated and no details are given about him, so it is very probably a mistake.

The name of a barber, 'Mr G Rousseau, formerly of the Pollet' was given initially as being among the victims. He had stopped working in St Peter Port, and it was believed that he might have taken a job working on the *Titanic*. However, the report seems to have been based on the fact that the chef of the *Titanic*'s à la carte restaurant was also named Rousseau. On the night of the disaster Pierre Rousseau (49) refused to jump into a lifeboat – he said he was too fat. Having originally published 'G Rousseau's' name, the *Guernsey Evening Press* later informed its readers: 'Mr. J. Sweetland writes from Dorking to inform us that he has met Mr. Rousseau at Paddington since the disaster. '

In addition, Stuart Collett (25), a student of divinity from North London, had previously conducted a mission at Cobo, where he was known as 'the boy preacher'. An uncle of his, Mr D Nicolle, lived in Castel. He was on his way to visit his brother, who was then in the USA. On the night of the *Titanic* crash, he helped the officiating clergyman at a hymn concert held in Second Class, and after the collision, he was able to obtain a seat on a lifeboat by claiming to be in charge of two young women. After his rescue, he returned to England, married and had three children. He died on 8 May 1941.

TITANIC
The Guernsey Passengers

On Easter Monday 1912, eighteen Guernsey people boarded the ferryboat "Alberta" at White Rock bound for Southampton, where they joined the "Titanic" for her maiden voyage to New York.

Only six of the eighteen survived the "Titanic" disaster. The other twelve were amongst the 1502 lost.

On the night of 14th/15th April 1912 in the North Atlantic, (latitude 41°46' N; longitude 50°14' W) the "Titanic" foundered. It was the most horrific shipping disaster ever to occur in peacetime.

The White Star liner "Titanic", the largest and most luxurious ship in the world, was making her maiden voyage from Southampton to New York, when she struck an iceberg and sank two hours forty minutes later with great loss of life.

The tragedy of the collision was that there were not enough lifeboats to save the 2207 people on board, and of the twenty lifeboats available, few were filled to capacity. Only 705 survivors were picked up by the Cunard liner "Carpathia" when she arrived on the scene four hours later.

THE GUERNSEY LIST

1st Class Passengers

Miss Rosalie Bidois. SAVED
Maid to Mrs. Astor, whose husband Colonel J.J. Astor was amongst the victims.

2nd Class Passengers

Edward H. Wheadon   LOST
Aged 67, the head of the agricultural firm, E.H. Wheadon & Sons of La Couture. A St. Peter Port douzenier. Travelling to New York to visit his married daughter.

Henry Mitchell   LOST
Aged 73. In the boot trade in Mill Street. An ex - douzenier. A widower, he was travelling with Mr. Wheadon.

Charles Bainbrigge   LOST
He was returning to Savage's International Stock Farm, Minnesota, where he had lived for some years. He had been visiting his family at Rohais Manor.

Laurence Gavey   LOST
Aged 26. He had lived in USA for 5 years, and was an oil rig fitter for Rockefeller & Hawkins. His family lived at Bas Courtil, St. Sampson.

Clifford R. Parker   LOST
Aged 19. Son of Richard Parker, grower, of Les Huriaux, St. Andrew. He was a clerk with Les Riches.

Peter Renouf   LOST
Aged 35. The son of William H. Renouf of Les Banques, he had emigrated in 1907 to New Jersey and worked as a carpenter. Married to Lillian Jeffrey. They had been staying with a relative, Mrs. Falla, of Rosslyn, Halfway.

Mrs. Lillian Renouf   SAVED
Nee Jeffrey, the wife of Peter Renouf.

Clifford Jeffrey   LOST
Aged 22. Brother of Mrs. Lillian Renouf. He was a carter for William Bird the coal merchant. He was emigrating to the USA where he was to live with the Renoufs.

Ernest Jeffrey   LOST
Aged 22. Brother of Mrs. Lillian Renouf. A carter for Mowlem the stone merchant. He was also going to live with the Renoufs in New Jersey.

Albert Denbuoy   LOST
Aged 26, of Les Sauvages, St. Sampson. A grower with his father and a keen footballer. He was travelling with the Renoufs and Jeffreys, and was going to live with the Renoufs.

William Downton   LOST
A quarryman, who had lived in the USA for 25 years. Married with 2 children. He had been staying with his brother in law, Mr. Domaille near Vale Church.

Peter McKane   LOST
A quarryman in Rochester N.J. An old friend of Downton, he had travelled and stayed with him in Guernsey.

Miss Lillian W. Bentham   SAVED
Aged 19. She was born in USA, but her parents were natives of Guernsey. She had travelled and stayed with Downton and McKane, and a young American, John Perrin who had decided to stay in Guernsey.

Miss Emily Rugg   SAVED
Of St. Sampson. She was travelling to New York for her wedding.

3rd Class Passengers

Howard H. Williams   SAVED
Aged 28, of La Rochelle, Vale. A driver for Manuelle the stone merchant. Leaving for Boston and a job at a shipyard. Married to Emily Crabb

Joseph Duquemin   SAVED
In his early twenties, and a quarryman -mason from Port Grat, St. Sampson, he was seeking work in America. He survived by swimming through icy water to a lifeboat.

Titanic Crew

Henry Ingrouille   LOST
A steward. He had been visiting his family at La Turque, Vale.

Titanic plaque at Fort Grey, Guernsey

Period picture in Guernsey

(I)

THE PARTY OF FRIENDS

'Sitting by me in the lifeboat were a mother and daughter. The mother had left a husband on the Titanic, and the daughter a father and husband, and while we were near the other boats those two stricken women would call out a name and ask, 'Are you there?' 'No,' would come back the awful answer, but these brave women never lost courage, forgot their own sorrow, telling me to sit close to them to keep warm... The life-preservers helped to keep us warm, but the night was bitter cold, and it grew colder and colder, and just before dawn, the coldest, darkest hour of all, no help seemed possible'

Liz Shutes, Governess.
Travelling in first class, aged 40

There was a party atmosphere on that Easter Monday morning in April 1912 as a dozen or so passengers for Southampton gathered at the Halfway tram stop, Les Banques, to bid a cheerful farewell all together to friends and relations.

They were due to catch the LSWR *Alberta* railway steamer to Southampton, and there connect with the new liner, the *Titanic*, that would take them, in one loose companionable grouping of friends, friends-of-friends and family, to New York.

Some of them had already made the big move to the New World, settled there, and late the previous year had made a trip back 'home' to visit friends and relations. Now, their visits completed, they were returning to the new homes they had made.

Others were doing the trip for the first time, perhaps to emigrate, or at least to look about and see something of America. One member of the group who had travelled back to Guernsey in December 1911 had now decided that he wanted to stay longer in the Island, so he was also paying his farewells to his departing friends; for another member, this was a continuation of his 26th birthday celebrations of the day before.

Seven days later, only four of those dozen friends would still be alive; the others had perished with the *Titanic*.

They were due to take an earlier sailing, on the Good Friday, on the American liner, the SS *Philadelphia*. But there was a national colliers' strike taking place, and it had badly affected the shipping schedules. And so the travellers were transferred to the *Titanic*. Probably they were delighted to have their Easter in Guernsey with their friends and families before setting off – and they would doubtless have been happy to experience the maiden voyage of this new giant liner.

In this period before the First World War, the economies of both Channel Islands were not exactly vibrant. There was a lot of emigration and travel to and fro, and there were communities of Channel Islanders already settled in the States that would welcome new arrivals and provide a home-from-home for them until they had established themselves. Many of those in the group were connected with quarry work – still an economically important part of Guernsey life. Quarrying in the northern parishes supplied granite to London and other mainland cities.

Most of the group were travelling 2nd class; a couple of them chose to go steerage.

Lillian ('Lily') Bentham (19), (pictured) who lived in Holley, New York, had been travelling in Europe for the past few months. Her deceased father and her mother had been born in Guernsey, and she had relations and friends there. She was staying in Guernsey in early April, at the end of her tour, before setting off back home to the USA.

She and another Guernsey-American, John Perrin, had been accompanied by her godfather, William Downton (55). He had been born in Guernsey and had emigrated to the USA 25 years previously, where he worked as a quarryman.

His name is sometimes spelled, wrongly, 'Douton'. His wife, Esther, was born a Le Monnier. She stayed at home in Holley with their two children, while her husband accompanied Lily Bentham on her European holiday.

Lillian ('Lily') Bentham in later years

Before leaving Guernsey for the return trip he had been lodging with his brother-in-law, Mr Domaille, near Vale Church.

John Perrin, who had travelled with Lily Bentham and William Downton from New York, decided, when the time came to return, to stay on in Guernsey and not to make the return voyage with his friends.

Two friends of William Downton were travelling on the boat with him and Lily for the return journey: Peter McKane and Laurence Gavey. Peter was aged 45, and was travelling back to Rochester, NY, near where Downton and his wife lived. Peter was an old friend of Downton and had also travelled back to Guernsey with him from the States; he stayed with Downton at the home of Mr and Mrs Domaille while he was in Guernsey.

Laurence Gavey (pictured) celebrated his 26th birthday the day before sailing. He was returning to America, his destination was Elizabeth, New Jersey, where for the past five years he had been working as a travelling oil rig fitter for the company of Rockefeller and Hawkins. He had travelled to over 48 different towns in the USA in the course of his work, and, according to details given after the *Titanic* disaster in the *Guernsey Evening Press*, 'was much esteemed by all who knew him for his unfailing bonhomie and cheerful spirit'.

His family lived at Bas Courtil, St Sampson. His younger sister, Daphne, wanted to travel back with him, but their mother considered her too young to go on such a long trip far away from home – so, much to her disgust, she had to stay behind in Guernsey when her brother and the others departed.

Albert ('Bert') Denbuoy, a friend of Laurence Gavey, was making the trip to the USA for the first time. He was a keen footballer, and was captain of his club's second team for the 1911-1912 season. On the night the *Titanic* went down he was two days short of his 26th birthday.

Bert was the second son of Alfred Denbuoy, who was a grower with his home address at Les Sauvagées, St Sampson; he worked for his father on the farm.

He was travelling to the USA to work, and planned to stay with the Renouf family (see below) at Elizabeth, New Jersey.

His great friend, Joseph Duquemin, (pictured page 50 & 51) was also on board, travelling steerage. Aged 19, he was the son of Joseph Duquemin and Louise Quentin, and lived at Port Grat. He worked as a stonemason and quarryman, and had been employed at Manuelle's stone merchant company. His destination was Albion, NY.

Travelling steerage with him was Joseph's friend and work colleague, 'Harry' Williams. He was a married man, aged 28; his wife was Emily (née Crabb) and they lived at La Rochelle, on the Vale Road. Like Joseph Duquemin, Harry had been employed at Manuelle's, and he was leaving for Boston and a job in a shipyard. He planned to live with the son of another Guernseyman who had emigrated earlier, William West.

A couple making the return crossing after a stay in Guernsey were Peter and Lillian ('Lily') Renouf, aged 33 and 30 respectively. They had emigrated from Guernsey in 1907 and for the past two years had been living in Elizabeth, NJ. During their return visit to Guernsey they stayed with a relative, Mrs Falla, of Rosslyn, Halfway.

Peter, who was the son of William H Renouf of Les Banques, was working as a carpenter in Elizabeth and had made a settled life for himself; he was a member of a local church and a keen athlete – a member of the Hawthorne Athletic Club.

Their visit to Guernsey had been prompted by the death the previous December of Lillian Renouf's mother. She was taking back to the USA her two brothers, Ernest and Clifford Jefferys - both intended to work there; her third brother, Fred, lived next door to them in Elizabeth, but hadn't joined his sister and brother-and-law on the visit back to Guernsey. Ernest and

Clifford both lived at Rosslyn, Halfway, Banques in Guernsey, and both worked as carters for a stone merchant and a coal merchant respectively.

The Jefferys family had seemingly a talent for working with animals; they were carters and other relations travelled with cattle in the then prominent cattle export business.

The Jefferys brothers planned to live initially with the Renoufs. They too had intended to sail on 5 April, Good Friday that year, on the *Philadelphia*.

Also in the party was Emily Rugg (pictured) 21, who was born in Guernsey; her father, William Rugg, was one of the Island's pioneer bus drivers and owned his own small bus company at Nocq Road, St Sampson. She bought her ticket from the White Star agency in the Arcade, and had originally intended to travel steerage, but something led her to upgrade her ticket from third class to second class. That may have saved her life, since the survival rate for second class passengers was much higher.

She was on her way to New York to spend at least one year in the USA to see whether she wanted to settle there. She would live with cousins at Wilmington, Delaware, where her uncle, F W Queripel, ran a grocery store at which she planned to work.

Of that kinship and friendship circle, only the three girls - Lillian Bentham, Lillian Renouf and Emily Rugg - and one man - Joseph Duquemin - were to reach journey's end.

The experiences of Lillian Bentham are the most fully documented of the survivors of that travel group: she survived, gave an interview to her local newspaper once she reached home and then gave several other interviews on anniversaries of the sinking during the course of her life.

The interview for an article for the anniversary in 1950 described her as 'a shy and gentle lady', illustrating the truism that it is the shy and gentle ones that are often the ones to watch out for. Certainly she showed amazing courage and compassion on the night of the disaster.

The stories of the travelling companions in that group are all, to some extent, intermingled. To avoid confusion, they are, as far as possible, treated separately.

Lillian Bentham and William Downton

Born on 23 July 1892 in Holley, NY, Lillian lived, after the death of her father, with her widowed mother, Mary J Bentham. She left for Europe at the turn of 1911-1912 for a four-month holiday tour with her godfather, William Downton, on hand for at least part of that time so as to keep an eye on her. Also in the party travelling to Europe were Downton's friend, Peter McKane, and her own friend, John Perrin.

Her final stop was Guernsey to look up relations, and she booked her return voyage at the White Star agency in the Arcade, St Peter Port; her ticket cost her £13.

Travelling back to America with her was the party of Guernsey-born friends that included her godfather.

On board, she shared a cabin with Emily Rugg, and both were sleeping peacefully at the time of the collision.

It was Bert Denbuoy who rushed down eight flights of stairs from the deck to their cabin to ensure that both girls were properly awake and to hurry them up on deck ready to get into lifeboats. It was only when he burst into their cabin and told Lillian Bentham to hurry on deck that she accepted the seriousness of the situation.

In later years she would credit her survival to him.

As Lillian got out of her bed, she put on a hooded 'steamer coat' over her nightclothes, and before Bert hurried her out of the cabin, he also grabbed her fur coat which was draped over a chair.

On deck, like so many other passengers, she was reluctant to exchange the apparent security of the giant liner for a small open boat. After all, the *Titanic* was unsinkable.

'It was so big, so magnificent, that I did not think it possible. We all felt safer on the 11-storey-high ship than on the cold ocean in a tiny eggshell,' she declared in a later interview.

She reached the deck with Bert just in time to get into a boat before it was lowered from the davits and her godfather had to push her forcibly into it. Emily Rugg and Lily Renouf were bundled into the same lifeboat.

She recalled: 'The officer on deck shouted to the seaman in charge of the lifeboat to pull away quickly, that the *Titanic* was going down, and the suction would pull us under. A man jumped from an upper deck and landed in our boat just as we pulled away.'

'Joseph Duquemin'

The seaman in charge was a Jerseyman, Able Seaman Jack Poingdestre.

'It was just as our boat was being lowered that the awful realization seemed to hit everyone: the impossible was happening, the *Titanic* was going down.

'We had just moved a few yards from the giant ship when it was broken by the explosion of her boilers and sank in two sections. The suction did pull us back toward the great hole in the water the ship left as she plunged. But we kept afloat, a frail craft loaded with women and children with the exception of the seaman in charge and the man who had jumped.'

This man was very probably Gurshon (Gus) Cohen, an 18-year-old printer-compositor from Whitechapel, out of work and off to America to seek his fortune. According to his own account, he saw a lifeboat with plenty of space on board, and so 'lowered himself' on to it via a rope. He would also later state that the band was not playing 'Nearer, my God, to Thee' – or any other hymn or music - while the boat went down. They had stopped playing and were standing about in the hope of being saved, just like everybody else.

Lifeboat Number 12 left at 1.20 am; and was picked up by the *Carpathia* just over seven hours later at 8.30 am.

'The greatest horror of the experience was the eight hours we spent floating about until we were picked up. At first the sea was as smooth as glass but it was literally dotted with human forms swimming, clinging to wreckage, fighting to climb into the lifeboats. Most of them were lost.

'Towards morning the wind freshened, and the boats, which had been lashed together, tossed dangerously and crashed against one another, so they were cut apart. Then the lifeboats separated and drifted in all directions.'

She said the women and children in her boat suffered extremely from cold and exposure and that most of them were hysterical.

It was very cold, and afterwards she said that if it hadn't been for her fur coat, she would not have survived.

'For my part, I began to realize that I had lost nothing compared to others, who had been compelled to see their relatives and friends go down with the *Titanic*. There was a Frenchwoman there, too, who was very much possessed. I helped the seaman with the oars and did what I could to comfort the others.'

Later the survivors in the boat heard the sound of a whistle being blown; they rowed towards the sound, and found a half-submerged and overturned collapsible boat, with 20 survivors clinging to it. This was Collapsible Lifeboat B, under the command of Second Officer Charles Lightoller.

She recollected: 'They were huddled together, stiff and cold, absolutely helpless. In their midst was an apparent millionaire, dressed in evening clothes and a fur coat and wearing a life preserver. He had been to a gay party in a first class cabin the night before and was gloriously intoxicated. He did not seem to realise the situation and was having the time of his life.'

Another had died from the cold, and his body was put back into the sea. Some accounts suggest that this was the *Titanic*'s wireless operator, John ('Jack') Phillips.

'I helped the seamen pull those 20 men into our boat, which already had more than 30 in it. We had to pile them on the bottom of the boat, like so many sacks of flour, because they were unable to do anything to help themselves. The boat was very much overloaded when the task was finished.

'I had the privilege of helping to pull the men in our boat. If you recall it was a whistle that saved the lives of the men and I have the honour of being the proud possessor of the whistle, also five pieces of silver taken from the pocket of a man who died in our boat, given to me by a steward. One of those men was virtually dead when we pulled him into our boat. Seven of them died from exposure.'

The young steward, Clarence Fitzpatrick, who had saved himself and the others by blowing the whistle, was shivering uncontrollably, and so she

'Joseph Duquemin'

wrapped her fur coat around him. It was Fitzpatrick who later, in gratitude, gave her that tiny Scout whistle from his belt. He had blown it all night in an effort to call some other boat to their aid.

'I will never, never forget any part of that nightmare, she said.'

The boat was now very crowded; so much so that a stoker, who was only wearing a uniform jumper, had to sit with his feet dangling in the icy-cold water. As time went on, the sufferings of the man from cold became apparent, and Lillian arose from her place - the keel beneath where she was sitting was dry - and insisted that the man exchange places with her. She took his place, and sat with her feet in the water instead.

News dispatches of the time cited her as one of the heroines of the disaster, and her sacrifice in taking off her coat and giving it to an unprotected man has been mentioned in a number of books.

'I had two coats and could spare one,' she said modestly.

They might have escaped from the *Titanic*, but in the cold and with many of them scantily dressed, it was not so obvious that they would survive the night.

The boat drifted on with the wind, which had kicked up a considerable sea, until sunrise.

'That was the most beautiful sunrise I have ever seen,' she continued. 'The sun came up like a great ball of fire, casting its rays on a large iceberg behind us, causing the berg to glisten like gold. And then, far off in the distance, we saw smoke, thin and indistinct at first, but gradually coming nearer. Then we made out what it was. It was a ship, answering the SOS call. It was the *Carpathia*.

'Talk about your thrill of a lifetime. To me, and

I guess to all of the others in that boat, that was the most wonderful ship in the world.

'Then our hearts sank with terrible fear as the ship disappeared. We were sure we were lost. But it came into view again and hope revived. Several times it did that. We did not know at that time that the *Carpathia* was steaming about the ocean, picking up the survivors from the different lifeboats that had been so widely scattered.

'It finally came to our boat and we were lifted on deck. They used ropes with a seat on it for the adults. The children were pulled up in rope baskets. We were given every care on the *Carpathia*, and it must have been a task for that ship to get us all back to New York, for the *Carpathia* is a small boat and was greatly overcrowded.'

When the *Carpathia* docked in New York, Lillian Bentham was to find out that because her brother had contracted typhoid fever, neither he nor their mother had been able to meet the boat.

Her mother had spent many anxious hours after the sinking of the *Titanic*, as news dispatches had reported her daughter both as a survivor and as a victim.

St Peter Port

Although her mother could not come to collect her, eight friends did come to meet her at New York, including Fred Jefferys, another Guernsey-American friend, Molly Moles, and Esther Downton.

"The first person I saw on the dock was my godmother, Mrs. Downton, and her first words were,"Where's William?" '

'The chill strikes me today that struck me that midnight, when I had to reply, "He's gone." '

Emily Rugg

On the early evening of Sunday 15 April, Emily had spent time with her friends, William Downton and Peter McKane, and then went to bed in the cabin she shared with Lillian Bentham at around 9 pm.

A couple of hours later, she was sleeping soundly but was awoken by the jarring noise of the collision. Looking out, she saw a mass of ice.

What happened next depends on which of the slightly contradictory nature of other accounts the reader might prefer. On the one hand, it is stated that she threw a coat about her, went on deck and saw lifeboats being lowered. Returning to the cabin, she dressed, and then aroused 'two women friends in the adjoining cabin.'

Another report says that she was woken up by the sound of water rushing into cabins. On deck a member of the crew dragged her forward to a lifeboat and lifted her into it.

Alternatively, she stayed in her cabin with Lillian Bentham, convinced that all the noise and shouting could safely be ignored ('The *Titanic* is unsinkable – no need to panic') until both girls were collected by Bert Denbuoy, and then taken by him to the deck. There, they met up with William Downton, who pushed them, much against their wishes, into the lifeboat (number 12) that was just about to be lowered.

It is perhaps feasible to suggest that the exact sequence of events is a combination of these versions: she was awoken by the jar of the collision; she threw on a coat and went on deck, where she was probably reassured by a steward that there was nothing to worry about, so went back down to her cabin. She then at least lay on her bed, perhaps dozing, until she heard the sound of water rushing into cabins. At about the same time Bert Denbuoy arrived; she returned with him and Lillian to the deck and the lifeboats.

Later, she said that the boat 'was

overcrowded' – which it was not, at least initially, as later on it was able to take on board some 20 survivors from the overturned collapsible boat.

As she was climbing into the lifeboat, a panic had started among those who remained on the *Titanic*. An Italian jumped from the steerage deck and fell into a lifeboat, landing upon a woman who had a baby in her arms.

In her own boat, along with Lillian Bentham and Lily Renouf, she saw the *Titanic* go down. According to an interview she gave shortly after she arrived in the USA: 'She declares but for the horror of it all, it might have been termed one of the grandest sights she ever saw. The boat seemed to have broken in half, and with all the lights burning brightly, the stern arose into the air, the lights being extinguished as it did so. A moment later the ship plunged beneath the surface.'

Eight hours later they were rescued by the *Carpathia*, and when it docked in New York, she was awaited by her uncle, Mr F.W. Queripel of 119 South Van Buren Street, Wilmington, Delaware.

Lillian ('Lily') Renouf, Peter Renouf, Ernest and Clifford Jefferys

Lily Renouf, the third survivor who was in the same lifeboat as Lillian Bentham and Emily Rugg, was visited by the press almost immediately she arrived in America. She was met by her brother, Fred Jefferys, and taken by him to the home of friends, Mr and Mrs Henry Paul, who lived nearby in Elizabeth, New Jersey. Mrs Paul had crossed to Guernsey with the Renoufs the previous December, but had returned to Elizabeth several weeks before the Renoufs' own trip.

And no sooner had she arrived at their home than the representatives of the press were at the door. The interview, when it appeared a day later, consistently referred to the husband and wife as 'Mr and Mrs Reniff'.

Her own account, below, has been extracted from this interview: :

'I had just gone below when the crash came. It must have been just after 11 o'clock, as all of the

women are ordered off the deck at that time and I had been on the port side of the boat talking to my husband and brothers. It was a beautiful, clear night, the stars appearing like glittering steel points against the dark sky.

'When the watch ordered women off the decks, I went down into my stateroom and I was partially undressed when the collision occurred. The shock was awful. Not fully realising what had happened, I was dressing myself again when my husband and brothers burst into the cabin.

'They had been in the smoking room, and had seen the iceberg as it bore away from the vessel and told me to dress hurriedly although they thought there was little danger. Nearly all of the passengers thought that the *Titanic* could not sink. Some of them took the collision as a joke and others were annoyed at the jouncing which they had received. My husband and brothers, who were fully dressed, helped me to put on my wraps and hurried me to the deck.

'There for the first time the passengers saw their peril and the utmost confusion prevailed. People were hurrying back and forth. Orders were being shouted in all directions and the crew was busy, getting ready to launch the lifeboats. The first and second-class passengers were calm in the face of the disaster but when the steerage passengers burst up from below, the scramble for places in the boats and the bedlam of noise was awful. I saw no flagrant instances of cowardice. Everyone was terribly excited and people forgot everything but their eagerness to get off the sinking ship. It was trembling from stem to stern. The foreigners from the steerage were like animals, but an officer with a revolver stood by every boat and ordered the women to go first.

'The boats filled up rapidly, and cast off. I was in one of the last boats. My husband pushed me forward and he was standing there on the deck as the lifeboat went over the side. Rocket after rocket was shot from the deck of the *Titanic*.

'For a few minutes the boats were grouped together near the sinking ship while the officers watched the last loads of passengers come over the side.

'The ship was just starting to settle when the last boat went into the water. The halyard of one of the dories snapped as it was being lowered and the boat with its load of passengers fell fifteen or twenty feet into the water. It landed right side up and I do not think that any of the passengers went overboard.

'Just as the boats were leaving the side of the steamer the chief steward of the second-class cabins jumped off the *Titanic* into one of them. The impact nearly capsized the boat but it righted itself. The steward was allowed to remain in it. The big boat could be plainly seen. She parted in the middle. There was an awful roar followed by violent explosions. The whole steamer seemed to rock and steady herself for the final plunge. Then she went down. The screams of those who had been left on board were frightful. I shall hear them to my dying day.

'I remember hardly anything after the sinking of the ship. We floated around for hours, it seemed. It was bitterly cold and all of the passengers in our boat suffered. I do not know how many there were. I think that they all survived. I remember hearing someone say that several men had been shot by the officers while trying to escape with the women and children, but I saw no acts of violence. We suffered horribly. Although the sea was smooth waves broke frequently over our boat and we were drenched through. Some of the women were scantily clothed.

'I was dreadfully cold and was confined to a berth on the Cunard liner until we landed. There were two doctors on board and they did great work. It was a frightful experience and the only wonder of it is that so many escaped alive. The seamen kept up their spirits. One of them told me that when the *Titanic* sank he was drawn down into one of the funnels and that he was shot out again when the air rushed from the ship. He said that he swam sixteen miles before he was picked up.

'I did not see the captain of the *Titanic* after the collision nor had I seen him during the evening. The officers and men performed their work nobly and only praise can be given them.'

The last she had seen of her husband and brothers was when they had cajoled her into the lifeboat. The printed interview stated: 'Mrs. Reniff's condition is so serious that it was deemed unsafe to tell her of the loss of her husband, brothers and friends. She thinks that they were picked up by another ship and has not given up hope of seeing them again.'

On top of everything else, she had to endure and counter a rumour, already printed in the New York papers, that the Jefferys brothers were not so unremarkably normal as might have been supposed.

The newspaper interview of Lily Renouf continued (with variations of the spelling of Jefferys as written): 'Mrs. Reniff and Fred Jeffrey, her brother, both deny absolutely a story published in New York evening papers last night to the effect that Ernest and Clifford Jefferies, second class cabin passengers, who went down with the *Titanic*, were members of the notorious "Doc" Owen gang of card sharps who live by fleecing passengers on trans-Atlantic liners.

'The only two second-class cabin passengers by the name of Ernest and Clifford Jefferies who were on board the *Titanic* were the brothers of the local woman [Lily Renouf]. They left Southampton on the *Titanic* for their first trip to this country, according to Fred Jeffrey and he cannot account for their names being mixed up with the Owen gang.

'Mr. Jeffrey was so incensed over the story that he declared he would sue those who were responsible for its publication.'

The story in which the names of the Jefferys brothers had appeared stated that the Owen gang had planned to fleece the multimillionaire, Colonel John Jacob Astor IV, who was one of the most notable victims of the *Titanic* disaster.

To suggest that the two young men from Guernsey, making their first trip to the US, were in any way connected with urbane card sharpers capable of insinuating themselves into a card game with the formidably rich Colonel Astor, seems preposterous It is interesting to note that the journalistic habit of not letting the truth interfere with a good story is by no means a modern phenomenon.

An interview with Lillian Renouf, contained in the Guernsey Evening Press of 8 May 1912, is contained in Chapter 5 of this book.

Bert Denbuoy, Joseph Duquemin

Bert Denbuoy, who had rushed down eight flights of stairs from the deck to the cabin of Lillian Bentham and Emily Rugg to bring them up to the lifeboats, was among the other men of the party who said a hurried goodbye to the three ladies as they propelled them into the lifeboat. Laurence Gavey was not to be found; Bert thundered on his cabin door, but there was no answer and it was locked.

We do not know how William Downton, Laurence Gavey and Peter Renouf met their ends. We do know that Bert Denbuoy continued to help passengers into boats until he was waist deep in water.

With him was his friend from Guernsey, Joseph Duquemin, who had been travelling third class. At one point Joseph took off his overcoat and wrapped it round a shivering seven-year-old girl.

Right at the end, when all the boats had left and there was no more to be done, Duquemin said 'I'm off', and swam away from the deck for Collapsible Boat D. Denbuoy hesitated for a moment and when he started to follow the suction from the sinking ship pulled him under. His screams as he was dragged under by the current gave Duquemin nightmares for years. Time and time again he would hear his friend crying out as the current pulled him to his death.

Eventually Joseph reached the collapsible boat. At first he was refused permission to board and it was only after he told the seamen that he could pull an oar as well as they could (he was a Guernseyman, after all), that they dragged him to safety. He joined the oarsman in the battle to pull the crowded boat away from the suction of the sinking ship.

He also helped another survivor out of the icy water. Hearing a cry for help, he dragged another swimmer on board. The rest of the passengers were so angry that they threatened to throw him back in the sea. The man saved turned out to be one of the Jersey crew members, Walter Williams.

Duquemin survived the cold, was rescued by the *Carpathia* and landed at New York. It is said that he was first reported as a stowaway, as nobody could spell his name correctly. On landing, he resumed his journey to Albion.

The news of his safety was conveyed in a message from the White Star Line at Southampton in a telegram to his parents in Guernsey.

His younger brother, Gerald, told an interviewer from the *Guernsey Evening Press and Star* in 1967 (at the time he owned Capelles Building Stores) about how the loss of the *Titanic* was received at home: 'I was only ten years old at the time the *Titanic* went down but I can remember very well what results the sinking brought home.

'We heard about it on the 15th or 16th of April but there was no news of my brother. I remember my mother (Ann Louise Duquemin) was shocked and worried, and we had to have the doctor – he used to come on horseback – and he confined my mother to bed. We all waited for news. Mother said she had a feeling Joseph was all right but time went by, and we began to fear the worst.

'Then, on April 20th – my mother's birthday – Mr Veal of the Vale Post Office arrived in father's building yard. Mr Veal came himself with the telegram. He wouldn't send one of the boys. I remember my father coming towards the house with the telegram in his hands. They were shaking so much he couldn't read the words. He called to my sister to read them out. There were only five words:

'Joseph Duquemin reported safe. Ismay.'

The envelope remained in the possession of Gerald Duquemin in Guernsey; the telegram was given to Joseph Duquemin's family in the USA.

Joseph's later story was that on arrival in USA he settled for a while in Albion, NY, and then later moved to Stanford, Connecticut. His move there from Albion was probably influenced by Frederick Hoyt, a survivor from first class who also escaped in collapsible boat D. The Hoyt family were prominent in Stanford. It is possible that Duquemin assisted him in some way – perhaps pulling him on board, and in return Hoyt felt obliged to offer him assistance, and found a job for him in Stanford.

Joseph married Marion Flanagan, a Connecticut native, who was born 14 Nov 1900. They had a daughter (d 1985) and a son, also called Joseph ('Joe').

He was a stonemason for Yale and Towne Manufacturing Company in Stanford and served in Supply Company 42nd Infantry USA in the First World War.

In later life he suffered badly from the effects of frostbite contracted by exposure to the icy water. He complained of pains in his legs, and he had to have first the right leg and then the left leg amputated.

He died on 1 Jan 1950, at Stanford Hospital stated cause of death was pulmonary embolism. He is buried in Spring Grove Cemetery in Darien, Connecticut. His wife died 25 February 1979.

His mother, four sisters and two brothers continued to live in Guernsey,

Years later there was a sequel to his story: A Justice of the Peace, called Eva Hart, from Becontree Heath in Essex, came on holiday to Guernsey twice – in 1955 and 1957 - and visited Joseph's younger brother, Gerald, and the other members of his family. She wanted to tell them about the night Joseph had handed her his overcoat when she stood shivering on the deck of the *Titanic*, as a girl of seven. She had come to say 'Thank-you'.

His son, 'Joe', visited Guernsey in 1991. In an interview with the *Guernsey Evening Press and Star*, he said that his father never spoke about the *Titanic* tragedy, but often mentioned his home island, which he missed very much. He stayed in Guernsey with his uncle, Gerald

Duquemin, who still kept pieces of the lifejacket worn by his brother when he swam away from the ship. The late Mr Gerald Duquemin for many years was the proprietor of Capelles Building Stores.

When Laurence Gavey's younger sister, Daphne, heard the appalling news of the *Titanic* and the death of her elder brother, she was wearing green. Never in her life did she ever wear that colour again.

Of the three women survivors, there is little more to say – at least about two of them. Lily Renouf re-married, but had no children.

For Emily Rugg, her experience on the *Titanic* stood out in a life that was otherwise perfectly normal and un-sensational. Her parents initially had to assume her probable death, but then heard by telegraph that she had survived.

Like many other survivors, she made a claim against the White Star Line for the loss of her property, which she valued at around £100. In terms of modern purchasing power, the value equates to around £6,000. And like the others, she probably didn't get much of it back.

It was, understandably, many years before she wanted to make another trans-Atlantic voyage. Her first one back home was in 1930, and she made a second one in 1937. On her return to America she worked for the Nowland family of Wilmington, looking after their children and then as a housekeeper; Barbara Allison (née Nowland) remains in touch with Emily's family in Guernsey.

Emily made a final trip to Guernsey in the early 1950s, travelling on the *Queen Elizabeth*. She was met at Southampton by her brother, William, and her uncle, Ernest, and then she travelled on with them to Guernsey, staying in the Island for two months with her brother at Hillside, Nocq Road.

It was an amazing coincidence that the taxi that met them at the Harbour and drove them to St Sampson was driven by a former *Titanic* steward – unfortunately the newspaper report of her visit did not mention his name.

She kept in friendly contact with Lillian Bentham throughout her life; she died in 1958.

Lillian Bentham suffered no ill effects of her experience, and was all right a few hours after she had shaken off the effects of the cold and exposure.

In 1918 she married John Black and continued to live at 11 Kay Terrace, Rochester. She died on 15 December 1977 in Rochester, and is buried in Hillside Cemetery, Holley. There were no children.

In one of her later interviews she remarked: 'I would not care to go through it again - perhaps next time I would not be so fortunate.'

Cabin B-60

(II)

THE OTHER GUERNSEY
PASSENGERS

'Anxiety of local people.

The news caused the gravest anxiety to many Guernsey people who have relations and friends on board. All the morning our notice-board was scrutinised by eager crowds, and enquiries were constantly received by telephone from all parts of the island. Our 2 o'clock Edition was quickly bought up'

Guernsey Evening Press report
Monday 15th April 1912

Charles Bainbrigge

Charles Robert Bainbrigge was born on 19 October 1889, to Reginald John Bainbrigge and his wife, Matilda (née Platts) at Rohais Manor, St Andrew.

The Bainbrigges were a distinguished military family, prominent in 18th and 19th Century Guernsey history. Lieut-Colonel Philip Bainbrigge commanded the garrison in Guernsey in the 1780s and later fell in 1799 at Egmond aan Zee, a battle in which many Guernseymen took part. Two sons, Philip and John, became Generals, and a grandson fell at the Battle of Sebastopol. General John Bainbrigge settled at Rohais Manor, a property located near to the present St Pierre Park Hotel. In St Andrew's Church there is a monument erected by him to his son, Captain Robert Bainbrigge, who fell in action at Kotah in 1858 during the Indian Mutiny, aged 34.

Charles Bainbrigge's father, Reginald, was General John Bainbrigge's grandson.

Charles had an affinity with horses, and he had begun working as a trainer in the USA at Savage's International Stock Farm in Minnesota. From there he had travelled home to Guernsey to visit his widowed mother at Rohais Manor.

He was 23 when he made his return trip to New York, travelling on the *Titanic*, second class.

Charles first travelled to the States in April 1905 as a tourist, together with his elder sister, Ethel. She seems to have stayed behind there, and in 1912 was living in St Paul, Minnesota.

Charles visited her there on a second trip to the States in March 1909, and then stayed in Minnesota to work.

For his return trip after visiting his mother in Guernsey, he was supposed to travel on the *Olympic* on 3 April 1912, but delayed it so as to travel on the *Titanic* instead. The national coal strike may have had something to do with his altered travel arrangements just as it

did with many other passengers who found themselves transferred to the *Titanic*.

He died in the sinking; his mother received a grant of £85 from the *Titanic* Relief Fund.

After the death of her only son, his mother sold most of the extensive Rohais land to a Catholic institution, located near Rohais. This was Vimiera College, a de la Salle foundation that was used for some time as a Jesuit seminary. It had been grafted on to a home owned by another notable military Guernsey family, named Brock. The institution was being extended in the early 20th Century and a chapel was built in 1908; the farmland of Rohais also became part of the property after its sale to them. From 1946 to 1971 the leasehold of the farm was held by the Quevatres family. It was a mixed farm, with a dairy herd and cider apple orchards.

By the 1970s the buildings had fallen into decay. A directory of notable buildings in St Peter Port published by the National Trust for Guernsey in the 1970s described it disparagingly as 'a dreary Jesuit seminary… very forbidding… in dark grey rendering…would make a good haunted house setting for a film.'

After it had been left empty for several years, it was taken over by the Jersey-based Ann Street Brewery, which was looking for a suitable location for a luxury hotel – and it was developed into the present luxury 'St Pierre Park Hotel'.

The stables and farm buildings of Rohais Manor were converted into the present golf club, and the golf course now occupies the site of the manor's farmland and apple orchards.

Henry Mitchell

Henry Mitchell was born in 1841 in England, but had lived in Guernsey for nearly all his life.

In 1912 he was living at 4, Upland Road, St Peter Port, with his married daughter, Ellen Grut. He was, by trade, a coach builder, and had also run a successful boot business in Mill Street. He had also been a St Peter Port Douzenier. By 1912, when he was aged 73, he was living in retirement. His wife had died the previous July.

He was travelling to the States on pleasure: he planned to visit his sister, Mrs Anna Jeffrey, who was living in Toledo, Ohio, and his brother, John Mitchell, who had settled in the States about two years previously, and now lived in Montclair, New Jersey. The brothers planned to spend several months in touring America.

Originally he had purchased a ticket for the *Philadelphia*, which was to have sailed on 6 April. Coal was not available because of the colliers' strike, and the voyage was cancelled; he was transferred to *Titanic* just before it sailed.

He left the island in the company of his friend, Edward Wheadon, with whom he had arranged to travel.

Both friends died in the disaster; those waiting for him knew that he had taken the *Titanic* only when the lost and saved lists were published.

Clifford Parker

Clifford Parker (17 years and 11 months)) was a son of Richard Parker, a grower at Les Huriaux, St Andrew, with whom he lived at the family farm, Fernleigh. He had been working as a ledger clerk in Le Riche's Stores.

He was the youngest of five children. His father had been head gardener to Victor Hugo, who had a house close to St Peter Port, and Clifford's elder brother Victor, was a market gardener and tomato grower.

Clifford was not yet 18 when he set off from Guernsey to 'seek his fortune in America'. Tragically that was the last his family heard from him.

The family grave in St Andrew's Churchyard mentions his name and his demise on the *Titanic*, but the present poor state of the headstone makes the inscription almost illegible.

Edward Wheadon

Edward Henry Wheadon (66) was accompanying his friend, Henry Mitchell. Like Henry, Edward had lost his wife, Caroline, and he was also travelling to the States to see family. He had planned to pay an extended visit to his married daughter, Carrie Bourgaize, and to see his grandchildren.

Carrie and her husband, John Bourgaize, lived at Edgewood, Rhode Island. They had emigrated from Guernsey some years before. The Bourgaize family had been growers in Guernsey, and John Bourgaize moved to the United States to buy farmland and continued as a grower on a more major scale than was possible in Guernsey.

Edward Wheadon was the head of the agricultural company of E.H. Wheadon and Son, of La Couture; his home was Grenada, Fosse André. He had an extensive business as a flower grower, and he commissioned paintings from the Guernsey-resident painter William Caparne, who specialised in horticultural subjects. Among the paintings of Caparne were Edward Wheadon's chrysanthemum field and packing house. His farm holding is now largely built over and is part of suburban St Peter Port.

Edward Wheadon was described in a Guernsey Press article written after the sinking as: 'a man of most kindly nature and charitable disposition. Among the members of the family and their very wide circle of

GEP advert, Wheadon's manures

Edward Wheadon

friends his loss has come as a tremendous blow, which is also felt in a very real sense by the large staff of workmen and women.'

He was also a St Peter Port Douzenier, and for many years he sat on the council of the Royal Guernsey Agricultural and Horticultural

States Member 'Edward T Wheadon' who instituted a social security system in Guernsey and after whom the States Social Security Department in St Peter Port is named.

There were also two daughters, Annette and Carrie, both married – the latter whom he set

Another GEP advert, Wheadon's manures

Society and the committee of the Growers' Association. He was a trustee of Ebenezer Wesleyan Chapel.

There were three sons, Edward, George and Herbert. His son, Edward, was the Guernsey

out to visit when he left home; doubtless full of pleasurable anticipation of a relaxing holiday and seeing his daughter and grandchildren, together with his friend, Henry Mitchell.

An earlier picture of Edward Wheadon and family

(III)

THE GUERNSEY CREW

"Their Majesties made the acquaintance of a stewardess, Mrs. Robinson, one of the Titanic survivors. The King was immediately interested, and plied the stewardess with questions, but Mrs. Robinson seemed disinclined to speak of the calamity".

"It is the sort of thing one doesn't like to talk much about afterward," she said to him. "It was too terrible."

"But do tell me this," persisted the King, "do you think more lives could have been saved?"

"Among the third-class passengers I certainly think so," was the reply. "But they appeared to think more of their belongings than they did of themselves."

King George V and Queen Mary meet a surviving Titanic stewardess, Annie Robinson, 1913
As reported in New York Times

Ingrouille, Henry

It was the death of Henry Ingrouille's father in January 1912 that brought his son back to Guernsey for the funeral. He was in the Merchant Navy, and had already worked on liners: his previous ships had been the White Star's *Teutonic*, and the *Olympic* - from the latter he transferred to the *Titanic* when he left Guernsey again in the spring of 1912.

Henry had been born in 1891 in Vale, and was the son of Frederick Alexander Ingrouille, a carpenter, and Mary Ellen Bourgourd, who lived at La Turque, Vale. He was the seventh of eight children.

When signing on the *Titanic* he gave his address as 15, Floating Bridge Rd, Southampton. As a third class steward, he expected to receive wages of £3 15s a month.

He died in the sinking.

Martin, Anne (Annie)

Annie Martin (Pictured) was a woman in a man's world: making her living as a stewardess on liners. She was 39 at the time of the *Titanic* disaster, and had been working previously for the White Star Line – she was transferred from the *Olympic*. On the *Titanic*, she was one of 23 women crew members in a total complement of some 900.

She had been born Anne Woodland on 17 November 1872. Her family had moved to Guernsey some generations before, from Dorset. It was a farming family, both in Dorset, where cousins lived in the Bridport area, and in Guernsey.

Aged 21, she married William Henry Martin, a soldier of the King's Yorkshire Light Infantry stationed at Fort George, at St Martin's Church in 1893.

What happened then? One can only assume that her husband was posted away from the Island, and possibly died – or else they drifted apart - if he was still alive, they were certainly not living together. One can only speculate: a farmer's daughter, left for one reason or another to make her own way in the world unassisted, chose to work on liners. She may well have had personal qualities that made her a natural success as a first class stewardess; she certainly possessed initiative.

Members of her family are still living in Guernsey today, among them Malcolm Woodland, her great-nephew. He said: 'Divorce was not so easy in those days, and I think that something must have happened to her husband.'

There were seafarers in her family, and he believes this would have led Annie to work afloat if she needed to earn her own living.

When she signed up on the *Titanic* on 6 April, she gave her address as Postbrook Road, Portsmouth. It appears that she had been working at sea for some time before becoming one of the 23 women of the *Titanic*'s crew.

Shortly after her return to England she was interviewed by the *Daily Mirror* together with a friend, fellow stewardess Kate Gold – the interview, which was republished in the *Guernsey Evening Press*, is printed in full in Chapter 5. One of the saddest aspects of her own story is the harsh treatment she and the other surviving stewardesses received after they had been rescued and were on board the *Carpathia*.

In her words: 'We were very severely abused by women passengers, because we had been saved and we were told that we ought to have given our places in the boat up to women passengers. Women asked us rudely what business we had to be there, and one woman went to a stewardess and told her we ought not to be carried as passengers, but ought to be made to work.'

Mr Woodland said: 'Annie was friendly with Kate Gold, who had already been involved in a maritime collision a few years before, when she was working on the White Star's *Suevic*. The stewardesses were popular with the crew, who would probably have made sure that their shipmates got away.'

Her salary was £3 10s a month, but because (as was the case for all surviving crew, on the time-honoured naval principle 'No ship, no pay') it was deemed that she stopped working for the company at the moment the ship foundered, she was only paid the pro rata amount of her monthly wage: 14 shillings.

As she explained in her interview with the man from the *Daily Mirror*, she entered the lifeboat carrying her fur coat, but in the boat it fell to the bottom, underneath everyone's feet, and it was too crowded to get it back. She reclaimed it once she was on the *Carpathia*, but she feared that, because of the hostility towards the surviving stewardesses, she would be accused of stealing it. Once she was back in England, she returned to Guernsey for a while, swearing that she would never go to sea again. But it appears that she did. By the time war started in 1914, she had left Guernsey once again, this time for good. The war disrupted family communications, but she remained in correspondence with relations in Australia until contact ceased in around 1947.

But the rest of her life is a closed book to her present day relations, until by chance some records can be found that might throw some light on it.

*Mr Woodland is doubly connected to the *Titanic* tragedy: he is both the great-nephew of Annie Martin and also his mother's sister married Albert Jefferys, who lost two brothers in the disaster.

Whitford, Alfred Henry

Aged 39, he was born in Guernsey and had a home in Southampton at 33 Richmond Street. He had been transferred from the *Olympic*. As a second class steward he received monthly wages of £3 15s. He died in the sinking; no further details of his life or experiences have been found.

St Peter Port during that time

Grave in St Sampson's Churchyard of the Denbuoy family which includes the name of Albert Denbuoy

Birthplace of Albert Denbuoy

4 Upland Road, St Peter Port – home of Henry Mitchell

Grave of Parker family, St Andrew's Churchyard, includes name of Clifford Parker

Fernleigh, Les Huriaux, St Andrew – home of Clifford Parker

Rohais Manor, St Andrew, home of Charles Bainbrigge

Corner of golf course, former farm buildings and Rohais Manor in background

St Pierre Park golf course, formerly farmland of Rohais Manor

Catholic institution formerly on site of St Pierre Park Hotel

Capelles Building Stores, formerly in possession of Duquemin family

The Duquemin's house

Le Pollet, Guernsey

HOW THE NEWS WAS REPORTED IN GUERNSEY

'Even this picture of tragedy and gloom has its relief in the thought that nobility of character has not departed from the English-speaking race'

Guernsey Evening Press,
Leading article 19 April 1912

The following reproduction of articles are taken from the 'Guernsey Evening Press' coverage of the Titanic disaster. Lack of space has dictated that only the first news stories on 15 April 1912 are reproduced, followed by references to local connections or events. The other local newspaper, 'The Star', also contained news of the Titanic, but carried only the national news, not stories with a Guernsey dimension.

Monday 15 April 1912

THE FATE OF THE TITANIC

COLLISION WITH AN ICEBERG IN THE ATLANTIC

OTHER LINERS TO THE RESCUE

TITANIC PASSENGERS DISENBARKED

THE FIRST NEWS OF THE DISASTER.

A Reuter telegram from Cape Race says that at 10.25 on Sunday evening, the Titanic reported that she had struck an iceberg. The steamer said that immediate assistance was required.

Half an hour afterwards another message was received saying that the Titanic was sinking by the head, and that the women were being taken off in life boats.

A telegram received at New York from Montreal says: Reuter states the liner Virginian reports in a wireless communication that the liner Titanic which is reported to have been in collision with an

The Guernsey Evening Press

iceberg, has requested assistance.

The Virginian is hastening to her aid. The wireless telegraph operator on board the Titanic reported that the weather was calm and clear. The position of the liner was then 41.45 (longitude north) and 50.14 (latitude west). The Virginian at midnight was 170 miles west of

the Titanic, and was expected to reach at ten o'clock this morning.

The Olympic at midnight was 40.32 north latitude and 16.18 west longitude. She is also in direct communication with the Titanic, and is hastening to her.

The liner Baltic has also reported herself within 200 miles of the Titanic and says she is speeding to her help.

The last signals from the Titanic came at 12.27 this morning. The Virginian's operator says that these were blurred and ended abruptly.

New York, Monday. - A despatch from Halifax states that all the passengers of the Titanic had left the ship by 3.30 this morning.

LATEST NEWS OF THE DISASTER.

THE TITANIC AFLOAT. MAKING FOR HALIFAX.

The "Montreal Star" reports from Halifax that the Titanic is still afloat, and is making her way slowly to Halifax.

TWO VESSELS STANDING BY.

New York, Monday – A message from Montreal timed 8.30 a.m. says that the Titanic is heading towards Halifax with her own engines. It is thought the bulkheads will prevent her sinking.

A further message says wireless telegraphy brings word that two vessels are standing by the Titanic.

RESCUED PASSENGERS.

Wiring shortly before 6 o'clock this evening, the Press Association states that twenty boat loads of passengers from the Titanic have been taken on board the Carpathia.

The Titanic is now being towed by the Virginian.

GUERNSEY PASSENGERS ON BOARD THE TITANIC.

Among the passengers on board the Titanic were the following Guernsey people: -
Mr. Peter Renouf
(Golden Villa, Banques).
Mrs. Renouf
(Golden Villa, Banques).
Mr. L. Gavey
(Bas Courtil, St. Sampson's).
Mr. H. Williams
(La Rochelle, Vale-rd).
Mr. E. Jeffrey
(Vale-rd).
Mr. C. Jeffrey
(Vale- rd).
Mr. A. Denbuoy
(Les Sauvagés, St. Sampson's).
Miss Emily Rugg
(St. Sampson's).
Mr. C.R. Bainbrigge
(Rohais Manor).
Mr. E.H. Wheadon
(La Couture).
Mr. H. Mitchell

(Upland-road).

All these Guernsey passengers left the island on Easter Monday by the Alberta for Southampton.

Mr. and Mrs. Renouf and Mr. L Gavey are returning to New Jersey after a visit to relatives in Guernsey, and are being accompanied by Mr. N. Williams, E. and C. Jeffrey, and Mr. A. Denbuoy.

Mr. E. H. Wheadon was crossing to America on a visit to his daughter, Mrs. Bourgaise.

We understand that the passengers also included a number of Jersey people.

ANXIETY OF LOCAL PEOPLE.

The news caused the gravest anxiety to many Guernsey people who have relations and friends on board. All the morning our notice-board was scrutinised by eager crowds, and enquiries were constantly received by telephone from all parts of the island. Our 2 o'clock Edition was quickly bought up.

A JERSEY PASSENGER.

There was but one Jersey passenger on board the Titanic, a Miss Stett. One of the crew, a steward named Williams, is also a native of Jersey.

Tuesday 16 April 1912

[The same list of passengers, addresses and other details given on the Monday is repeated on the following day, with the following additions]:

Messrs. W. Downton and P. McKane have resided in America for some years, and were returning after a visit to relatives in Guernsey.

Miss Bentham, we

A lifeboat along side the Carpathia

understand, was born in America, but her parents are natives of Guernsey.

Another Guernseyman on board the Titanic was Mr. H. Robilliard, of Bon Enfant, Vale, who occupied a position as a steward.

It was announced that Mr. Eric W. Sharp, a son of Mr. W. Sharp, Principal of the States Intermediate School for Boys, was the wireless operator on the Titanic. This rumour is incorrect, for Mr. Sharp is on the troopship Roholla.

Wednesday 17 April 1912

NEWS OF MISS RUGG

Mr. William Rugg received at 7.30 this morning a cable from a relative in America, stating that his daughter, Miss Emily Rugg, was amongst the passengers saved, This confirms the news received from other sources.

Friday 19 April 1912

Leading article:

THE GREAT DISASTER

On both sides of the Atlantic a period of great suspense has been gone through, while full and authentic news has been awaited of the way in which the Titanic and so many of her passengers met their fate. Unhappily the earlier conflicting reports gave rise to wrong impressions, and the news was spread that all on board were safe and that the great liner, crippled, was making slowly for port. Not many hours later the terrible news was known that of the 2,358 souls known to be on board, about one-third had been saved. From time to time rays of hope have lightened the gloom, because of the possibility that other liners called to the scene of the disaster might have picked up survivors, but one by one these hopes have had to be given up, and the hard fact accepted that the survivors on

Survivors on board the Carpathia

the *Carpathia* appear to number all the saved of the Titanic's living freight.

When it was known that comparatively few were of a certainty survivors, there was anxiety on the part of relatives and friends ashore to ascertain whether those near and dear to them were included in that list. In this connection the gravest anxiety has been aroused in this island, for sixteen among the Titanic's passengers and crew had left Guernsey not many days before to embark for America, some of these passengers on a pleasure trip; others to take up new careers in the United States; others, too, who had already made their homes there, and were returning thither after a visit to the island of their birth. Deeply shocked by the news of the disaster, their relatives and friends were eager to learn whether they were among the survivors. Most, if not all, of the names of survivors on the Carpathia were transmitted, and among them could be recognised the names of Mrs. Renouf, Miss Rugg, and Miss Bentham, of the Guernsey party. The last hope that remained was that, when the ship reached port the fuller and clearer reports might reveal the fact that some names had been omitted, or badly transmitted, and that one mourned as lost might be among the saved. These have been the emotions of the past few days, and the anguish of mind which so many people have endured has won for them the deep sympathy of the whole community, and widened everyone's sense of the bereavement this terrible calamity has caused.

From the first fragmentary and conflicting messages that reached shore by wireless telegraphy brought home to everyone the great fact that the discipline of the sea was faithfully kept by the officers, the crew and the men passengers. The first chance it was evident was given to the women and children – to those who could least help themselves, though any man's chance in so dire a calamity was tragically slight. Could there be a higher testimony to human character than was contained in the few words of the Carpathia's message, after her arrival on the scene was recorded? All around was wreckage and the boats which had been launched from the sinking liner – and in the boats were mostly women and children. It is a great grief to both England and the United States to find so few of their citizens' names in the list of those picked up by the Carpathia, yet that very gap in the list must thrill everyone with a realisation of the heroism that implies. Among the missing are officers and members of the crew, prominent Englishmen and Americans, men of vast wealth, and the poorer English emigrant. Even this picture of tragedy and gloom has its relief in the thought that nobility of character has not departed from the English-speaking race.

First impressions of the heroism displayed are fully supported by the knowledge that is now available of the tragedy of the Titanic. The tale is a terrible one, brightened only by the record of the courageous way in which a terrible fate was met by so many noble men and women.

Saturday 20 April

THE GUERNSEY SURVIVORS
MR J. DUQUEMIN

REPORTED SAVED. MRS RENOUF SAFE.

Anxiety about Mrs. Renouf was allayed this evening when a cabled messaged was received from Elizabeth, New Jersey, reporting her to be safe. The fact that she had not sent a message to Guernsey on landing gave rise to the fear that she might have been rescued, but had succumbed on the Carpathia. These fears were proved groundless by the following cablegram:

"Lillian Renouf safe."

The cablegram was signed: "Rugg, 227, Baltic-street, Elizabeth, New Jersey."

MR. JOSEPH DUQUEMIN

At noon today news was received by telegraph from Southampton that Mr. Joseph Duquemin, who had been regarded as missing, was among the saved. The message was as follows: "Joseph Duquemin officially reported saved."

The news of Mr. Duquemin's safety may revive hopes of the safety of other missing Guernsey people, but such hopes may be based on a slender foundation. We presume that Mr. Duquemin's name was included in a list of forty which it was said last night had yet to be transmitted. Had any other Guernseymen been included in that list presumably their names would have been cabled.

Knowledge of the safety of Mrs. Renouf, and the addition of Mr. Duquemin to the list, made the following list of Guernsey survivors up to the time of going to press:
MRS. RENOUF.
MISS EMILY RUGG.

MISS LILLIAN BENTHAM.
Mr. JOSEPH DUQUEMIN.

THE OTHER GUERNSEYMEN.
The other Guernseymen were:
Mr. E. H. Wheadon.
Mr. H. Mitchell.
Mr. Charles Bainbrigge.
Mr. Peter Renouf.
Mr. C. Jeffry.
Mr. E. Jeffry.
Mr. A. Denbuoy.
Mr. H. H. Williams.
Mr. L. Gavey.
Mr. H. Ingrouille.
Mr. W. Downton.
Mr. P. McKane.
Mr. C.R. Parker.

THE RESCUED / LOST. OFFICIAL FIGURES.

New York, Friday. – The White Star Company has issued the following statement, giving the number of persons rescued from the Titanic: -

FIRST CLASS	202
SECOND CLASS	115
THIRD CLASS	178
CREW	206
OFFICERS	4
Total:	703

In all 1,635 persons lost their *lives.*

Monday 22 April

THE TITANIC SURVIVORS.

SOME UNFOUNDED RUMOURS
We were able to announce on

Saturday evening that anxiety about Mrs Renouf was allayed. A cablegram was received from New York announcing her safety in the following terms: "Lillian Renouf Safe."

On Saturday we were able to announce, too, that Mr. Joseph Duquemin was among the saved. His name was included in a list despatched after the bulk of the names had been received, and it had been supposed that no more were to be sent.

Knowledge of Mr. Joseph Duquemin's safety revived hopes that news might be received of others. It was reported that a French paper, the "Figaro" or the "Journal" had given the names of Messrs. Denbuoy and Downton in a list of survivors. Investigation proved that the list was of passengers who had embarked at Southampton, and therefore the report of their safety was proved groundless. Inquiry by cable of the White Star Line officials in New York confirmed the report that they are missing.

The Guernsey survivors, so far as is at present known are:
MRS. RENOUF.
MISS EMILY RUGG.
M. JOSEPH DUQUEMIN.

Various rumours have been in circulation in the island with regard to members of the Guernsey party still missing, but inquiries fail to prove these rumours of any value.

A cablegram was received last evening by Mr. Thomas Renouf of the Banks, from relations in America, thus:

"Mrs. Lillie Renouf quite well. Staying with Mrs. Paul, Baltic-st., Elizabeth, New Jersey."

It is believed that Mrs. Renouf landed practically penniless, for the funds of the party were to be carried by Mr. Renouf.

A TITANIC SURVIVOR.

One of the lady passengers saved was Mrs. A. Martin, formerly of Guernsey. We had not previously included Mrs. Martin among the Guernsey people. Mr. H. Woodfield, nephew of Mrs. Martin, signed on as a steward on the *Titanic*, but was taken ill and did not join her. He is going on the Olympic.

MR. STUART COLLETT.

Mr. Stuart Collett, the Boy Preacher who conducted a mission at Cobo some time ago, was among the survivors. A telegram announcing his safety was received by his uncle in London, and a copy of it was transmitted to Mr. D. Nicolle, Gélé, Castel.

REPORTED MISSING

MR. E.H. WHEADON.

Mr. E.H. Wheadon was in his 67th year. He was the head of the agricultural firm of E.H. Wheadon and Sons, Couture. He was a man of most kindly nature and charitable disposition. Among the members of the family and their very wide circle of friends his loss has come as a tremendous blow, which is also felt in a very real sense by the large staff of workmen and women.

Mr. Wheadon was a member of the Central Douzaine of St. Peter-Port and was for many years on the Committee of the R.G.A. and H.S., and the Committee of the Growers' Association. He was also intimately connected with the activities of Ebenezer Wesleyan Chapel, of which he was a Trustee.

Mr. Wheadon had three sons, Messrs Edward T., George, and Herbert Wheadon, and two daughters, Mrs J. W. Spiller and Mrs. J. Bourgaize. He was crossing on the *Titanic* to pay an extended visit to Mr. and Mrs. Bourgaize at their home at Rhode Island, U.S.A., and left the island on Easter Monday for Southampton.

MR. H. MITCHELL.

Mr. H. Mitchell, who was aged 73, was on the way to pay a visit to his brother and other relatives. He was an ex-Douzenier of Canton No. 1 and was for some years in business in the boot trade in Mill Street. He was a widower and resided with his daughter, Mrs. H. Grut, in Upland-road. He left the island in company with Mr. Wheadon, as they had arranged to travel together.

MR. PETER RENOUF.

Mr. Peter Renouf was the son of Mr. William H. Renouf, who resides with his brother, Captain James Renouf, of Golden Villa, Half-Way. Mr. Peter Renouf, who was 35 years of age, emigrated with his wife to America some four and a half years ago, and settled in New Jersey, where he had continued to practise his trade as a carpenter. Mr Renouf married Miss Lillian Jeffrey, a daughter of Mr. William Jeffrey, of Rosslyn. Mrs. Peter Renouf is included in the list of survivors. Both had been staying since Christmas with Mrs. Falla, a relative, at "Rosslyn," Half Way.

MESSRS. C. AND E. JEFFREY.*1

Messrs. Clifford and Ernest Jeffrey, aged 22 and 20 respectively, were brothers of Mrs. Renouf. Mr. C. Jeffrey was a carter in the employ of Mr. William Bird, coal merchant, St. Sampson's, while Mr. E. Jeffrey, also a carter, was in the employ of Messrs. John Mowlem and Co., stone merchants. Both brothers were proceeding to New Jersey, intending to take up residence with the Renoufs.

MR. A. DENBUOY.

Mr. Albert Denbuoy, the second son of Mr. Alfred Denbuoy of Les Sauvagées, St. Sampson's, travelled with the last mentioned party. Mr. Denbuoy would have celebrated his 26th birthday next Wednesday, and had been employed on his father's estate as a grower. Mr. Denbuoy will be remembered as an old

member of the Pelican's Football Club. Later he played with the Northerners, and then with the Belgrave Wanderers. Mr. Denbuoy had been a member of the Belgrave Wanderers for three years, and this season was appointed captain of the second team. Mr. Denbuoy was to take up his residence with Mr. and Mrs. P. Renouf at New Jersey.

MR. H. H. WILLIAMS.

Mr. Howard Hugh Williams, aged 28, resided at La Rochelle, Vale Road,. Mr. Williams was a driver in the employ of Messrs. A. and F. Manuelle, stone merchants, from where he obtained an excellent testimonial on leaving their employ for America. Mr. Williams, who is the son of the late Samuel Williams (of Valnord Hill, St. Peter Port) married Miss Emily Crabb. He was proceeding to the home of Mr. William West, of St. Sampson's.

MR. GAVEY.

Mr. Laurie Gavey, son of Mrs. A. Gavey of the Bas Courtils, Banks, also travelled by the *Titanic*. Mr. Gavey was returning to Elizabeth, New Jersey, where he first settled exactly five years ago. As a travelling fitter for the great firms of Rockefeller and Hawkins Mr. Gavey had visited over 48 different towns in the United States in the pursuit of his calling, and was much esteemed by all who knew him

for his unfailing bonhomie and cheerful spirit. Mr. Gavey was a member of the "Sons of St. George," and as we understand that the annual fête has been postponed on account of the disaster to the *Titanic*. The day before Mr. Gavey left he reached his 26th birthday, and a number of friends and relatives met at the Bas Courtils to celebrate the event, as well as to wish "God-speed" to the one who was leaving.

MR. H. INGROUILLE.

Mr. Henry Ingrouille was one of the stewards of the *Titanic*. Mr. Ingrouille, who was formerly a steward on the Teutonic, crossed at the end of January to Guernsey, owing to the death of his father, Mr. Frederick Ingrouille, of La Turquie, Bordeaux. During his stay in the Island Mr. Ingrouille resided with his brother, Mr. Frederick Thomas Ingrouille, of La Turquie.

MESSRS. DOWNTON AND McKANE.

Included among the passengers from Guernsey were Messrs. William Downton and Peter McKane, and it was only by the merest chance that they were not accompanied by their former companion, Mr. John F. Perrin. All three returned to Guernsey last November after an absence of over 25 years. They were quarrymen engaged in Rochester,U.S.A.

Accompanying them was

Miss Lillian Bentham, a young lady aged 19, who was saved. During his stay on the island Mr. McKane, who is unmarried, resided with a brother in Trafalgar Square, St. Sampson's. Mr. Downton, who was married and has two children, stayed with his brother-in-law, Mr. Domaille, near the Vale Church. Mr. Perrin, who is staying at Sous les Hougues, Bordeaux, at the last moment decided not to accompany his comrades, but to settle down to business in Guernsey. Naturally while relieved at his narrow escape from almost certain death, he is deeply affected by the fate of his former companions.

MR. C. R. PARKER.

Mr. C. R. Parker, formerly employed as a ledger clerk in the offices of Messrs. Le Riche, Ltd., is also included among the missing. Mr. Parker, who is 19, is the son of Mr. Richard Parker, grower, of Fernleigh, Les Huriaux, St. Andrew's, and was held in esteem by the large staff at Le Riche's Stores, Ltd.

MR. CHARLES BAINBRIGGE.

Mr. Charles Bainbrigge was a son of Mrs. Bainbrigge of Rohais Manor. He was returning to Savage's International Stock Farm, Minnesota, U.S.A., where he had spent some years.

The London "Globe" contained the following paragraph on Saturday:-

Mr. Charles Bainbrigge, a member of a well-known Guernsey family, was a second-class passenger on the *Titanic*, his name having been published as Mr. Bainbrigge. So far, his name has not been announced among the saved.

Tuesday 23 April

THE LOSS OF THE TITANIC

A steel-blue sky for the brilliant stars,
A city is on the sea,
A floating palace in sparkling light,
Oh, who would in it be?
Men plough the main and catch the breeze.
Of the chilling northward ice.
But "ha, ha," laugh they, "we are safe this night."
And sleep all eyes entice.

Sharp golden notes of alarm clash out,
As shimmering through the night,
A sheeted ghost of the north shore vast
Climbs tow'ring blue to white.
A cruel stab and a shriek of steel.
As the city's walls fall out,
And the men look dark, the women pale.
Afar is the master's shout.
But the sea is blue, its bosom calm.
Save where the waters pour,
As up the jagged heights ahead
Remorselessly they roar:
"To the boats" the cry – as Britishers
They sought the women first;

Like unto drills in port they ride.
To the deep, where no man durst.

The lady clings to her husband's arm,
The emigrant's wife her own,
While the great seas sob the awful thing.
That responds to the human groan.
Then deep down to the surgeless tide.
Which flows to Nirvana's shore.
Wives pass beyond the grasp and the kiss:
A kerchief waves – and no more.

As a spectre curls the foam at the bow.
The ocean in white play
In eddying waves o'er the wooden street.
Reflects the electric ray.
Then blackness comes as the sea creeps in.
And floods the hissing wheels:
There's a whisper of death thro' the shortened decks.
Where the ship's band music steals.

Deep reels the great ship to her wound,
(Now buried beneath the tide).
The Captain speaks the trumpet command.
A fathom from it wide.
Then, all things done, he meets the sea.
A hero with the best:
Men jump from out the plunging hull:
Men jump – we know the rest.

And now the silent tread past doors.
Where whitened shadows show.

And now the whispered word and deed.
To those who weeping, know
That in that one dread hour of death.
Where character is tried
Their own kin bravely helped the weak.
And, for their living, died.

OUIAM.

Wednesday 24 April

JEREMIE CUP FINAL

It was proposed and c a r r i e d that this Final be played on Monday, 29th inst., at the Cycling Ground, at 5 p.m., when H.E., the Lieut.-Governor had kindly consented to present the cup. Should the match, after extra time, terminate in a draw, it was agreed that if the Delancey ground was obtainable, the match would be played there on Saturday, May 4, when a collection for the *Titanic* Fund would be taken up and gross proceeds handed over.

TITANIC FUND MATCH

It was decided that should the Jersey Cup Final not terminate in a draw, the Royal Irish (subject to their approval) and an Island XI play on May 4 at Delancey if ground is obtainable. The Priaulx and Jackson Cups, also the Junior Shield be presented on this occasion and a collection taken up, gross proceeds to go to the *Titanic* Fund, Match to start at 3pm, usual charges and all to pay.

PERMISSION GIVEN

The local Inter-Insular delegates granted permission to the Council to make a collection at the Cycling Ground on the occasion of the Muratti Final, for the *Titanic* Fund. A sub-committee of four members, vix., Messrs. W. Middlevick, W. Broadhurst, G. Torode, and H. F. Sallin, were

Guernsey Weekly Press 20.4.12

Carpathia

appointed to carry out the necessary arrangements in conjunction with Mr. H. G. Bentley, Inter-Insular Competition Secretary. It was decided that Mr. Bowden announce the amount collected the same evening at St. George's Hall.

Thursday 25 April

NEWS OF THE TITANIC IN SARK

News was first received of the disaster to the *Titanic* on Monday evening, when the cutter arrived from Guernsey. The news soon spread, but nothing further was heard till Wednesday, when the Alert arrived. Much sympathy is felt for all the relatives of those who went down in what is the most terrible wreck in history.

TITANIC MEMORIAL SERVICE

A Memorial service was held last evening in St. Sampson's Church, and there was a fairly large congregation.

The service was based on the funeral service for King Edward VII. The organist, Mr. Auger, opened the service with Chopin's Funeral March which was followed by the singing of the opening words of the service for the burial of the dead, by the choir. Then followed special Psalms, preceded by the antiphon "Make Thy way plain before my face" (Merbecke). The anthem "O rest in the Lord" was beautifully rendered by the choir boys, whose purity of tone and clear enunciation were almost perfect. A very impressive address was given by the Rev. P. H. Kelly.

The concluding voluntary was Beethoven's March from the Pianoforte Sonata, the rendering of which testified to the ability of the organist and the fine qualities of the organ.

Monday 29 April

LETTERS TO THE EDITOR
GUERNSEY TITANIC

RELIEF FUND.

Sir, - As some of your correspondents seem to have an erroneous idea with regard to the above Fund, we carve a small space in your paper to explain the object in view.

The suggestion made at the public meeting held on the 25th was to raise a fund to be sent either to the Lord Mayor of London or the Lord Mayor of Southampton as the contribution of the Island of Guernsey.

On Friday last the Committee definitely decided in favour of the Mansion House Fund. The magnitude of the disaster was deemed such as to require an appeal to the nation by the Lord Mayor, and we trust that a sum befitting the Island will be sent by Guernsey in response to the national appeal, if only as a token of respect to our dear fellow Islanders, who went down with the *Titanic*, standing aside in favour of the women and children, and doing their duty to the last, like men.

Subscription lists have been placed at the banks and various shops.
"Bis dat qui cito dat."
Yours, etc,
For the Committee of the Fund,

J. ESTEN DE JERSEY.
Hon. Sec.

Wednesday 1 May

THE EXPERIENCES OF GUERNSEY PEOPLE ON THE TITANIC

Letters are beginning to reach the island relating to the experience of the Guernsey people on the *Titanic*. Letters have been received by members of the Denbuoy, Rugg, Jeffreys, and Gavey families, and we have been permitted to make public some of the particulars given therein.

Mrs. A. Falla, of "Rosslyn," Banks, has received a letter from Miss Molly E. Moles, who had accompanied the Renouf party to Guernsey from America, and in that letter are given details as described by Mrs. Renouf. At the time of writing Mrs. Renouf was scarcely able to give a connected account of her experiences, owing to grief and shock. She was staying with Mrs. Paul, Baltic-st., Elizabeth, New Jersey.

According to her story, when the *Titanic* struck the iceberg Mrs. Renouf was in her berth, lying down. She was called by her husband, and he and her brothers, Messrs. C. and E. Jeffreys, helped her to dress and get ready to leave the vessel. She did not wish to be parted from her husband and brothers, but was forced into the boat, which was then lowered. She never saw her husband and brothers again. In the boat with Mrs. Renouf were Misses Lillian Bentham (of Jersey) and Miss Emily Rugg.

When the boat left the ship's side there were 30 on board, but later 30 men were taken from a raft, of whom one died later from exposure.

Messrs. C. and E. Jeffreys, L. Gavey, and A. Denbuoy shared the same cabin, but only Gavey was in the cabin at the time of the collision. Later when the party proceeded in search of Gavey, it was found that the cabin door was locked. Nothing more was seen of him.

Miss Moles and Mr. Fred. Jeffreys describe the scene of the landing of the survivors at New York as vey pathetic and moving. The weather was bitterly cold and rain was falling heavily. Mrs. Renouf is stated to have been much bruised and in a state of collapse, but she hopes to write a fuller account of her experiences, herself, later on.

Mr. A. Gavey, of the Bas Cortils, Banks, received a letter from a friend, but no full details bearing on the disaster were included.

Another letter was that received yesterday by Mr. A.L. Denbuoy, of the Sauvagées, This was sent by Mr. Charles Cann, of New Jersey, who proceeded to New York to meet the survivors. Mr Cann only saw Mrs. Peter Renouf, whom he describes as looking fairly well after her awful experience, but naturally in a very excited condition.

Mr. William Rugg received a letter from his daughter, Miss Emily Rugg, who is staying with relatives at Wilmington, Delaware, stating that she was alright and promising further details by another mail.

Rosalie Bidois, the subject of this article, in fact came from Guernsey (see page 113)

MRS ASTOR'S MAID
"MISS BIDOIS, AN ISLE OF GUERNSEY GIRL."

The above headlines are abbreviations of the headlines in the New York "Evening World" of April 18. The article describes how Colonel Astor and his valet were lost in the *Titanic*, and Mrs Astor, her nurse and maid were saved.

We make the following extracts from the article:

"Among the stories that come creeping from seaward is one that Mrs. John Jacob Astor found herself in one of the *Titanic*'s lifeboats, perhaps dressed only in her nightclothes and a raincoat, and yet attended by her French maid and her trained nurse.

"The maid is Rosalie Bidois".

Rosalie Bidois came from the Isle of Guernsey, in the English Channel. She is trim and chic and has been in the service of Mrs. Pierre Lorillard and Mrs. Joseph Stickney. She was furnished to Mrs Astor several months ago by a fashionable Fifth Avenue Employment Agency that caters for the domestic needs of wealthy people.

Mrs. A. J. Dickinson, the head of the agency said to-day: "Just as soon as I heard that Rosalie was saved with Mrs Astor, I knew the Colonel's bride was in safe hands. I would rather have that little Frenchwoman beside me in an emergency than many a man. She is absolutely reliable. I don't believe she ever lost her head in her life. Most French maids are flibbetty-jibbety creatures, with brains that don't go much further than a knowledge of how to lay out an evening gown and how to dress her mistress's hair, but that isn't Rosalie's sort.

"It is my belief that Rosalie did more to help Mrs. Astor than anybody knows now. From the first she must have been at Mrs. Astor's side. Probably Mrs. Astor was wearing an evening gown – of course she would have had to dress for dinner on a boat like the *Titanic*. They say she had on only a raincoat, but I doubt that. If Rosalie had time to get anything at all for her mistress, it can be depended on that she found the warmest coat obtainable and the clothing best suited for such an emergency."

"Miss Bidois has been in America about ten years. Practically the whole time she has been in the service of wealthy women.

"The master and the man went down; the mistress and the maid were saved - a striking commentary on the democratic rule that puts the salaried maid above the millionaire master, and the millionaire mistress above the wage-earning valet."

LETTERS TO THE EDITOR
THE TITANIC RELIEF FUND

Sir, - I have failed to see

any real need for establishing a second fund in our small community for *Titanic* Relief, excepting, perhaps, as an outlet for the good people assembled at the Guille-Allès Library last week. If this latter thought be correct, then I suggest the following alternative for them. Let them think out how the claims of the distressed would be met in this island, where there is no form of compensation, if this disaster was to befall one of our local passenger steamers. In our desire to appear optimistic we must not ignore the fact that such disaster is more probable along our coasts than that of liners colliding with icebergs. An examination would reveal the fact that lifeboat accommodation is only provided for about one third of the complement of passengers. Yours truly,

O. B. Kairful.

Thursday 2 May

GUERNSEY SURVIVORS' STORIES. THE STEWARDESSES

The "Daily Mirror" has published reports of interviews with two stewardesses of the *Titanic*, Mrs K. Gold of Liverpool, and Mrs. A. Martin of Portsmouth (formerly of Guernsey).

The Interviewer wrote: -
Before the train left Plymouth an hour and a half later, Mrs. K. Gold and Mrs. A. Martin of No. 11 boat, told me their thrilling story.

They had been intimate friends for years and have served on the Adriatic and Olympic with Captain Smith. They are both first saloon stewardesses.

"One of the stewards came to us a little before midnight," began Mrs Gold, "and said: 'Are you awake, girls? Come on deck as quick as you can and get to the boats."

"We had heard or felt nothing of the collision, and were sleeping in the same cabin. We hastily put some things on over our nightclothes.

"On our way up to the boat deck we met an officer, who said, 'Hurry up, girls.' We replied: 'We have only just been called. It was then a long time after the collision there was hardly anybody in bed in our section except Mr. Ismay. We heard him being called and met him afterwards in his pyjamas, with an overcoat over them.

"Most people had been up late for suppers and entertainments.

"We were sent down again to help passengers find their lifebelts, which were kept on a shelf in the berths, and most passengers never think about them.

"They were awfully good lifebelts, or many of us would not be alive."

"Until after we had left the ship most people did not want to go in the boats at all. Women had to be pitched into them anyhow. The first boat that got away was nearly full of firemen, but that was mainly because nobody could at that time be persuaded to enter the boat.

"I saw many women refuse to enter my boat. It looked so dreadful to go into a little boat like that."

CHIEF STEWARD'S OVERCOAT

Mrs. A. Martin. Mrs. Gold's friend, went on with the narrative.

"The first-class barber, who was flung into the sea was picked up," she said, "and told us on the Carpathia that all the heads of department were on the deck when the ship broke.

"He said that Lambert, chief steward, had just remarked to him when he was urged to take off his heavy overcoat, 'Oh, no; this ship will not break in two.'

"If he had taken off his overcoat he would have had a better chance.

"The ship was almost underneath the water before the great explosion, which must have killed most of those remaining on board. From our little boat we could see nothing then but the lovely starlit sky and great clouds of steam and smoke.

"Mrs. Gold had a little steerage passenger woman in her arms all night. The woman had lost her husband and nothing could stop her crying.

"I was wearing my alpaca uniform, a thin jacket and my

lifebelt. I had brought my fur, but it was at the bottom of the boat and too crowded for anyone to look for things, but I got it afterwards.

"We were terribly cold in the boat – everyone was blue with cold, and another hour or two would have killed many.

GERMAN WITH A PISTOL

"I saw dead people taken from one of the boats afterwards. It was one into which a German passenger, like the scoundrels in ours, had forced his way brandishing a pistol and threatening to shoot anyone who forced him out.

"We stewardesses all feel very sore at the way Mr. Ismay has been treated in America. He put two of our girls into a boat and said, when they wanted to stand back and make room for passengers, 'You are women anyhow.'

"We saw him taken on board the Carpathia. We recall him sitting on his haunches on the stern of the boat that was cleared by the Carpathia just before ours. He just sat there like a statue, blue with cold, and neither said a word nor looked at us. He was nearly dead when taken on board, for he was wearing only nightclothes and an overcoat.

"It was about 6.30 in the morning. We had no lantern in the boat, and had to make a flare every ten minutes or so by lighting the end of a piece of rope.

"We had nothing to eat. We saw a steward throw a box of biscuits into a boat on thinking he was going into it himself, but he was moved on to our boat, where there were no biscuits.

GRIM TIME FOR JESTING

"People could joke even in these awful hours. There was a very slender moon, and a seaman cried out cheerily: 'Turn your money over, ladies: it's the proper thing to do when there's a new moon.' All laughed, for we had no money, of course.

"As the sun rose in the east we could just discern the lights of the approaching Carpathia. We were afraid we should not reach her, and as we could see no other boats from the *Titanic* feared she was going away. Four men rowed hard, but were exhausted, and could not go fast – the boat was very heavy, too.

"The older children never made a murmur, but were all stiff with cold when we went aboard the Carpathia.

"Two *Titanic* passengers, Mr. and Mrs. Ryerson, had come over to America by the last boat after hearing that their son had been killed in a motoring accident. Mrs. Ryerson was in our boat; her husband was drowned.

"I saw one of Mrs. Carter's beautiful dogs running about the deck of the *Titanic*, and afterwards swimming in the water.

"We had got fond of him on board. He used to come into our cabin and 'How do you do' to us each morning.

"The tragedies of this wreck can never all be told.

"I saw one poor soul in the New York hospital quite distracted because she had lost her husband and children.

WOMEN ABUSED FOR BEING ALIVE

"We are very seriously abused by women passengers on the Carpathia because we had been saved, and were told that we ought to have given our places in the boat up to passengers.

"Women asked us rudely what business we had to be there. One woman went to a stewardess and told her we ought not to be carried as passengers, but ought to be made to work.

"We did work hard, looking after our people on board the Carpathia. Everybody did their best for us, but the 700 survivors of the *Titanic* crowded the Carpathia dreadfully.

"I and the other saved stewardess slept on the deck each of the four nights till New York was reached, and never had anywhere even to sit down and rest. We had nowhere to wash ourselves even, but we knew the captain, officers, and crew of the Carpathia did their utmost.

"I had a mackintosh under my lifebelt. There was one

boat which overturned as it was leaving the *Titanic*, and I think many of the 156 women and children who were lost must have been on that boat. We know we lost three of our stewardesses shipmates in it.

"Mrs. Bliss, of London, who went with seventy other persons in boat 15, told me:-

"Mrs. Wallis, a steerage matron, came out to see two boats away, and said to me, 'I am not going on that boat. The ship is safer than that.,' and I saw her go into her cabin and lock her door."

MR. J DUQUEMIN

The relatives of Mr. Joseph Duquemin, reported to be one of the survivors of the *Titanic* Disaster, have not yet heard from him direct, but yesterday a letter was received from the White Star Line's Southampton office, confirming the telegram sent on the 28th April with respect to the safety of Mr. Duquemin.

GUERNSEY CLAIMS

The following appears in a communication to the Editor of this paper from the Mansion House, London:

"The Lord Mayor will be very glad indeed, if you will ascertain whether there are any sufferers in Guernsey, and, if so, their number and circumstances."

The Editor of the "Guernsey Evening Post" will be glad to hear from anyone having a claim upon the Fund, in order that the wishes of the Lord Mayor may be carried out.

Wednesday 8 May 1912
MRS. RENOUF INTERVIEWED BY A REPRESENTATIVE OF THE "G.E.P."

Guernsey Weekly Press 20.4.12

View down the port side

We have received a letter from New York, from a representative there of the "Guernsey Evening Press." In accordance with our cabled instructions he proceeded to Elizabeth, New Jersey, where Mrs. Renouf went after leaving the Carpathia. He writes:-

On arriving there I found the home where Mrs. Peter Renouf was staying. She is, as is only to be expected, terribly prostrated by the awful ordeal which she has passed through. The doctor who has been attending her would not allow any reporters by whom she had been besieged to see her, but, on hearing that I came on behalf of the "Guernsey Evening Press," she very kindly consented to see me.

It will have been noticed that the various survivors' stories do not agree in many ways, but this is easily understood when one takes into account the state of the minds of these people when a calamity of this kind occurs.

After questioning Mrs. Renouf, I gleaned the following facts: She was in her cabin in bed when the accident happened, and hurriedly throwing on a coat over her night-dress she went on deck. There, with other passengers, she was told that there was no danger of the vessel sinking, but was advised to go down and fully dress. This she did and a lifebelt was placed around her.

During this time various officers and stewards were assuring everyone that the *Titanic* was unsinkable, so that when the time came for her to say good-bye to her husband and brothers before entering the lifeboat, she, with the rest, did not for one moment imagine that she would not see them again. It was the general idea of those in the lifeboats, in whose minds the impression was firmly rooted, that the ship could not possibly sink, that they would put off for a time and await developments; but as is only too well known now, the *Titanic* was far from being unsinkable, and after being on the water for some time (it was impossible for Mrs. Renouf to give an idea how long) she witnessed the sinking of this great vessel. The *Titanic* seemed to part in half, there was a terrible explosion, and the remaining ones on the vessel were washed off the decks as she disappeared from view. After this happened, Mrs. Renouf has only a dim recollection of what happened.

The Sea front, Guernsey. Note the tram.

She just remembers that two or three men, who were struggling in the water, were taken aboard with difficulty and great danger to the already overloaded boat. There were no seats available, and it was necessary to stand all night in the freezing temperature until rescued by the Carpathia in the morning. After being given restoratives, Mrs. Renouf came to, and then realised for the first time that she probably was the only one saved of the party who came out together from Guernsey.

The party consisted of Mr. and Mrs. Peter Renouf, Clifford and Ernest Jeffery, (brothers of Mrs. Renouf), Laurence Gavey and Ernest Denbuoy; and also Miss Rugg. Mrs. Renouf, however, learned later that Miss Rugg had been saved.

The White Star Line have made arrangements to ship any identified bodies to any part of the world, but it is very much feared that a very small percentage of bodies will be recognisable, owing to the severityof the weather in the Atlantic just now.

The Guernsey party were originally booked for passage on the ss Philadelphia, but were transferred to the *Titanic*, owing to the strike in England.

Mr. and Mrs. Peter Renouf had been five years in this country, but returned home to Guernsey on Dec. 9 last for a vacation; the rest of the party were on their first trip to America. Miss Rugg, the other survivor, on arriving at New York, immediately went to her cousins at Willburton, Del. Mrs. Renouf has one brother

out there who went home for the Coronation. Much sympathy has been expressed in Elizabeth for Mrs. Renouf. On next Sunday, the 29th, a special memorial service was to be held at the Grace M.E. Church, the Brothers of the Order of the Sons of St. George, of which Mr. Renouf was a member, were to attend.

It will be a great consolation to the people of Guernsey, whose sympathy will go out with Mrs. Renouf, to know that in her great trial she is surrounded by people from her home, there being quite a number of Guernsey people located in Elizabeth.

Footnotes

[1] The surname is often wrongly misspelt; the correct spelling is Jefferys, but to preserve the authenticity of the reproduced newspaper articles, the misspelling is maintained here.

Period picture of Le Pollet

THE JERSEY CONNECTIONS

'I think it is foolish to speak of the heroism displayed. There was none that I witnessed. It was merely a matter of waiting your turn for a lifeboat, and there was no keen anxiety to enter the boats because everybody had such confidence in that wretched ship. The officers told us that they had wireless communication with seven vessels, which were on the way to relieve us, and the men believed themselves as safe on board as in the boats. It seemed the vaguest possibility that the ship might sink before one of the seven vessels arrived'

Mrs Ruth Dodge, from San Francisco.
(First class passenger)

Names marked thus - † - were lost in the Titanic disaster

Passengers with a Jersey Connection

Bidois, Rosalie	1st class
Duff-Gordon, Lucy Christiana, Lady	1st class
Ilett, Bertha	2nd class

Jersey crew

Ahier, Percy Snowden †   1st class
Steward.

Olliver, Alfred C
Quartermaster.

Poingdestre, John Thomas
Able Seaman.

Rattenbury, William Henry †
Assistant Boots Steward.

Ryan, Thomas †   3rd class
Steward.

Vigot, Philip Francis
Able Seaman

Williams, Walter John   2nd class
Steward.

This is a much shorter list than many that have been given in the past, some of which have estimated a total number of 16 people 'at least' with a Jersey connection on board the *Titanic*.

The other names given in previous lists are there because in the few days following the *Titanic* disaster there was considerable confusion in establishing a list of survivors and victims, sometimes due to misspellings or misunderstandings of hard-to-decipher or intercepted wireless messages. It was an added torture to relatives and loved ones waiting for news, with some names of those lost being given initially as survivors, and then having to be corrected. Some survivors' names were also initially given out as being drowned.

Other names that have been included in Jersey lists:

Henry James Beauchamp †   2nd class

Research has established that there is no Jersey connection; Henry Beauchamp was born in Hampshire. He and his business partner and brother-in-law, Percival Sharp (with whom he was travelling), both lived in London.

Mrs H Parlett and Miss Parlett

The names are mentioned once in the *Evening Post* as Jersey passengers, but no further details of this couple are repeated, nor are these names on the passenger list.

Albert Mallet † his wife Antoinine and infant son, André.

The names of this family, like those of Mrs and Miss Parletts, were given once in a listing of Jersey passengers by the *Evening Post* at the time, and have occurred in most lists since then as a result.

There is no other record of a connection to Jersey, and he is described as a French national. It is reasonable to suppose that, like Beauchamp and the Parletts, his inclusion in a Jersey list was the product of the confusion and many erroneous messages sent in the aftermath of the disaster.

Albert Mallet (31) was a wine and spirits merchant, born in 1881. There is no mention of him in the Jersey census of that year or in the 1891 census.

He was working at the time of the *Titanic* disaster for a Canadian firm of cognac importers and liquor company, Laporte, Martin & Co, Montreal. The family address was 210 Hutchison Street, Montreal.

He and his wife Antoinine (24) and their 18-month-old son, André, were returning to Montreal after visiting relatives in Paris.

The Mallets had planned to sail on the *France*, but exchanged the tickets they had bought so as to return on the *Titanic*. They boarded the ship at Cherbourg, travelling 2nd class.

Albert perished in the disaster, and his body was never recovered.

Antoinine Mallet (sometimes called Antoinette), was clearly French. She was aged 24, born in Paris on 16 December 1887. She survived the *Titanic*, and she and her infant son were rescued by the Carpathia, possibly from lifeboat 10.

She returned to France, and in 1918 married a Leonivas Rodamanowski. She died near Paris, 22 October 1974.

The son, André Clement, had been born on 11 June 1910 in Montreal. He survived with his mother, and with her was rescued by the Carpathia.

After arriving in New York, he and his mother were first sent to St Vincent's Hospital, then they went to their home in Montreal. Eventually they would return to France. He died in Paris on 22 September, 1973.

The details of Albert Mallet's family and relations, French connections, his occupation and address all strongly suggest a French background rather than a Jersey background, despite the incidence of 'Malet' or 'Mallet' as a Jersey surname – something that is liable to have caused the confusion in the first place.

Miss Stett

This is assumed to be a transmission error for 'Ilett' (see above) from the wireless of the rescue ship, *Carpathia*, since there are no other details about her except for one mention of her name.

However, the name Rosalie Bidois is generally included in the lists of Guernsey people on board.

It is often stated that she originated from Guernsey – erroneously. The first mention of her 'Guernsey connection' appeared in American newspaper reports following the *Titanic* disaster, such as the article that appeared in the New York *Evening World* describing her as 'Miss Bidois, an Isle of Guernsey Girl'. This was picked up upon by the *Guernsey Evening Press*, and so the error has continued. Her name, for example, appears in lists of Guernsey *Titanic* people, such as on the plaque at the Fort Grey Shipwreck Museum in Guernsey – wrongly.

Records show that she was born on 10 May 1865 in St Helier, Jersey. She is shown as living in Jersey in the 1871 census, but the family is not mentioned in either the Jersey or Guernsey censuses of 1891. It is possible that she and some of her family returned to Normandy. Although other relations remained in Jersey, she always thought of herself as French, born in the Channel Islands coincidentally by the fact of her parents' residence there for work purposes.

Lillian Bentham is likewise sometimes said to have been from Jersey, and that she was visiting Jersey before leaving for Southampton to catch the *Titanic*. This name is included in the Guernsey section, since she was part of the same friendship and family-related group of a dozen people that left Guernsey in a group to travel to America.

The confusion may well derive from the fact that her home was stated to be in New Jersey.

Not passengers on the *Titanic* were W G Le Brun and family – who had booked on the *Titanic*, apparently, but then fortunately transferred to the *Olympic*.

There were many such stories making the rounds in the aftermath of the disaster; some of them were undoubtedly genuine, others less so – most probably the result of a desire to make known to friends and neighbours that the lucky 'escapee' had some peripheral association with an event of world importance – or even, in the case of 'premonitions', an hitherto unsuspected psychic talent.

Roger Marie Bricoux (20), the cellist in the *Titanic*'s band, was to have come to

Jersey in May 1912. He would have joined 'Mr A Romaine's orchestra' – the orchestra that played at the Opera House.

A further connection with the Channel Islands is the name of the commander of the second of four ships chartered by the White Star Line to search for bodies after the sinking.

The *Minia* was owned by Western Union and sailed under the command of Captain William George Square de Carteret.

It left Halifax, Nova Scotia, on Monday 22 April and arrived in the search area on the Friday. Bad weather hampered the search and 17 bodies were recovered in a week.

Captain Square de Carteret was born in St Helier on 10 March 1860. His father was George Frederick Square, a tin plate worker, born in Jersey in 1830; his mother was Patty Mary Fleming, born in Sark where her parents originated and who later moved to Jersey. Her father, John Fleming, was a sea captain.

There was a strong 'Sark – de Carteret' descent through his mother: the Island had

A tot, raised in the arms of her elder sister, places a coin in one of the "Titanic" disaster collecting boxes, placed by the St Simon's Troop of Boy Scouts outside Messrs. C. Le Masurier and Co.'s establishment at Number 7, Charing Cross. (Morning News)

been colonised in 1563 by Helier de Carteret from St Ouen, Jersey. Later in life William Square added the surname 'de Carteret' to his birth surname.

George and Patty Square lived in Broad Street, St Helier; William was the second of their three children. Like his grandfather, he became a seaman, going to sea first on the Seaflower under his uncle, Captain Thomas Le Dain (the husband of his mother's younger sister, Jane).

He is shown in the UK Census of 1881 living with his (by then) widowed mother and his 18-year old younger sister, Alice, at 22 Chichester Terrace, Southampton. He passed his master's certificate of competence in London in 1887.

He married, in 1897, Annette Trot, and they had three children: Hélier, Norman and Phyllis Square de Carteret. He may have already moved to Canada at the time of his marriage.

He seems to have retired from the sea shortly after being the master of the *Minia* in 1912. There are a couple of patents issued in North America to a William George Square de Carteret in 1919.

He died in 1945 in Halifax, Nova Scotia.

Jersey passengers boarding in St Helier for Southampton

New North Quay

A busy St Helier Harbour

(I)

COUTURIÈRE IN A CATASTROPHE

'Like everyone else I was entranced by the beauty of the liner. I had never dreamed of sailing in such luxury... everything about this lovely ship reassured me'

– Lucy Christiana, Lady Duff-Gordon

Lucy Christiana, Lady Duff-Gordon

LUCY Christiana, Lady Duff-Gordon, was one of the most famous of the *Titanic*'s survivors. She was a leading fashion designer of the late 19th Century and early 20th Century. Her famous fashion houses in London, Paris, New York and Chicago – the business was known as 'Maison Lucile' - attracted customers from royalty, nobility and the world of the stage (and in the later years, films). Among her customers were Lillie Langtry, Daisy, Countess of Warwick (both of them mistresses of Edward VII), Margot Asquith, the wife of the future Prime Minister, the future Queen Mary (wife of George V) and the Queen of Spain.

She was the first British designer to achieve international renown. Her styles were innovative, as well as her use of what would these days be called 'public relations'. She is reputed to have originated the modern-day fashion show, with its cat walk parades and professional models. She launched slit skirts and low necklines, popularised less restrictive corsets, and promoted alluring lingerie. She costumed many theatrical productions including the London première of Franz Lehár's operetta *The Merry Widow.*

Her gift to the English language is the word 'chic', which she is supposed to have invented to describe her own dresses.

No less a successful woman in her own way was her younger sister, Elinor. She was the author of a succession of mildly erotic books, which, at that time, were considered very risqué. One of them, *Three Weeks,* scandalised Edwardian society, although that didn't prevent it from selling two million copies. Even that notorious rake, King Edward VII, forbade the book to be mentioned in his presence. It was found particularly shocking that the female lead character seduced the male character – not the other way round – and on a tiger skin, forsooth (very sexy).

It spawned the popular rhyme of the time:
'Would you like to sin
With Elinor Glyn
On a tiger skin?
Or would you prefer
To err
With her
On some other fur?'

Lucy coined the word 'chic'; her sister coined the word 'It' to mean sex appeal, which itself spawned the name of a fashionable and popular cocktail,'Gin and It' (Gin and Italian Vermouth).

Both sisters, one feels, were born in advance of their time.

Elinor did not travel on the *Titanic*, and neither sister had strong 'Channel Island connections' …. except, in one important respect: for both of them, Jersey was their childhood home.

FROM A JERSEY CHILDHOOD TO A LONDON MODISTE

Lucy Christiana (her friends always called her by her second name) was born in 1862 in St John's Wood, London, of Canadian parents. Her father, Douglas Sutherland, was an engineer, married to an Anglo-French-Canadian wife Elinor Saunders.

A few months after her birth, her mother took her to Jersey to live with an aunt while her father travelled in connection with his work. Her younger sister, Elinor, was born in Jersey, but very shortly afterwards her mother heard that her husband had contracted typhoid fever while on a trip to Turin.

She travelled to Italy, and brought him home to London, where he died very shortly afterwards. His widow then left with the two little girls for her own family home in Canada.

Life back in her parental home was grim for both mother and daughters, mainly on account of her own stern and puritanical mother – 'a terrifying old lady in stiff, black silk dresses,' she was to remember later. From her early experiences with her harsh grandmother, originated the streak of tomboy rebelliousness that would only grow stronger as she grew older.

She also began to dress her dolls in material, creating clothes for them to wear, and showing signs of her future talent as a dress designer.

Her mother was desperate to get away and to return to England. When, a few years later, she met a Scotsman named David Kennedy, many years her senior, who showed interest in her, she accepted his marriage proposal. They wed, and a year later Elinor and her two daughters left with him for Britain.

It was only after his marriage to Elinor that he showed his true character: mean, domineering and cruel, a tyrant to his wife, and determined to crush the spirits of his unwanted step-daughters.

On their arrival in Britain they first of all paid a visit to the Scottish estate of Kennedy's elder brother, and then travelled on to stay with relatives in Yorkshire. There Kennedy developed bronchitis, and he was advised to spend the rest of the winter in a milder climate. So they travelled to Jersey. They spent the rest of the winter of 1871 in the Island, and afterwards Kennedy found it congenial to stay on.

He had little money of his own – so the comparatively cheap cost of living in Jersey made the Island an attractive residence. His Scottish family's landed connections also made him acceptable to the Island's strata of expatriate British residents, many of them retired military officers or colonial officials; Government House and its social activities played a large part in the family's life.

A few years after their arrival, in March 1874, the daughter of the St Saviour Rector, Emily (Lillie) Le Breton, married the wealthy Edward Langtry. Lucy remembered the harbour being decorated with flags, and garlands of flowers festooned from the windows.

Both Lucy, Christiana and Elinor (her sister) would become, in their later lives, friends of Lillie Langtry.

The Kennedy's settled into Island life, and rented an attractive and well-furnished house, 'Richelieu', in Bagot – then a country area in St Saviour outside the town. This is now the private hotel, Richelieu Lodge, located in the very urban setting of the Bagot Road.

As the girls grew, they became more and more ungovernable, partly in reaction to their step-father, and also because their mother was submissive and so dominated by her abysmal husband that she provided no corrective balance in the family.

Both girls hated learning – or at least in the form it was presented to them by a succession of governesses. Elinor made no secret of the fact that she thought them stupid – and as her step-father was too mean to pay for first-class tuition, she was probably right.

Lucy Christiana was much more interested in painting and drawing and making dresses for her dolls.

Their friends were limited to the 'Government House circle', principally Ada Norcott, the youngest daughter of the Lieutenant-Governor, Lieutenant General Sir William Norcott. When the Kennedys left Jersey for a visit to England, their daughters stayed at Government House, and spent much of their time playing charades and performing little musical pieces.

During their stay there, the young Mrs Langtry paid a visit to Jersey with her husband. In her memoirs, she wrote: 'After our first experience of London life, we paid a visit to the Island in the yacht *'Hildegarde'* and incidentally dined at Government House. As I deposited my cloak and took a last survey of myself in the glass, I observed two pretty red-haired girls peeping from under the muslin-covered dressing table. How they got there, I don't know, but somehow contrived this ambush to satisfy their curiosity.'

Back at Richelieu with their parents, life for the girls was a sad contrast to the cheerfulness of life at Government House. The step-father's health declined with age; circumstances became more straightened. He spent much of the time in bed, with their mother in constant attendance. He became, if anything, even more morose and parsimonious.

Lucy Christiana and her step-father were by

now on such bad terms that she insisted, aged just 16, that she leave the Island and spend time living with relations in England and Scotland.

The Lieutenant-Governor had by now come to the end of his posting, and had returned to England, together with his daughter, Lucy Christiana's friend Ada Norcott – another reason for wanting to leave Jersey.

At the time that she left Jersey, her step-parents and younger sister left Richelieu – its lease had now expired – and settled at 55 Colomberie, an address long since disappeared and replaced by the modern 'Colomberie Parade'.

Two years later, Lucy, having finished her extended visits, was back in Jersey and living again with her parents at their new address. She had very little money, and had by now graduated from designing and making clothes for her dolls to designing and making clothes for herself, her sister and her mother.

It was during this time that she developed her expertise with the needle, and also in making dresses that reflected the personality of the wearer. By now aged 18, she had come to the conclusion that clothes must not follow the dictates of contemporary style, just as one's personal character need not necessarily follow contemporary standards.

In her autobiography, *Discretions and Indiscretions* (1932), she wrote: 'I studied my own type with as much care as I used to study, many years later, the types of women who came to consult me from all over the world. I found out exactly what suited me, and I decided to adopt an original style of dress, taking my inspiration from the old masters.

'I had one dress of which I was particularly fond. It was in black velvet which fell in soft folds to the feet. And there was a little tight bodice, finished with a deep belt.'

And then she fell in love – for the first time.

'Before that I had only been loved, and it was a new and wonderful experience. He was a young Captain, not one of the usual group of officers who used to be in and out of our house

every day, but a newcomer to Jersey, and I met him for the first time at a dance where I wore this black frock.'

It was hardly surprising, considering her tempestuous character, that the path of true love did not run smooth – despite the best efforts of her mother in encouraging the match.

They quarrelled, she was too proud to be reconciled, and in a huff she packed her bags and left Jersey to stay with a friend in Hertfordshire.

'I used to suffer agonies of grief in silence, for I was very proud and would hide my wounds at all costs. I decided that there was only one thing to be done. I must let him see that I did not care. So to this end I married the next man who asked me.'

The tale does not end happily; the Captain did not come chasing after her from Jersey; he did not arrive at the church in time to whisk her away before she could say her vows. The marriage with 'the next man' went ahead, and it was, of course, a tragic mistake.

This was James Stuart Wallace, a wine merchant who suffered from the occupational risk of wine merchants: an over-fondness for their own stock in trade. He was also over-fond of pretty women. He was more than 20 years older than her; they were unsuited to each other in every way, and she had only married him out of stubbornness and pique.

The night before the wedding she cried herself to sleep.

They lived near London at first, and then moved to Drayton Gardens in Chelsea. Her sister, Elinor, would also make a disastrous marriage – in her case to a philanderer, Clayton Glynn. For both girls, Jersey was now past history.

They both went on have eventful lives, but as we need to fast forward, in the case of Lucy Christiana, to 1912 and the *Titanic*, the subsequent years can be quickly summarised. The year following her marriage she had a daughter, Esmé, to whom she was devoted and for her was the only compensation for her appalling husband, who became ever more wayward as time went on. But appearances were preserved, at least, and the family lived in apparent felicity in their London home with Roy, their collie dog, and two servants from Jersey.

Then her husband ran off with a music hall danseuse – and it was assumed that 'danseuse' was a charitable description of her. Typically, Lucy decided on what was then a bold if not shocking course of action: she sued him for divorce.

She could not afford to do so – it was a hugely expensive step - but her step-father had recently died, and her mother, now herself released from an unhappy marriage, paid for her daughter to be released from her own marriage with money she had inherited from her husband's estate.

There was little money left over; Mrs Kennedy had moved from Jersey to London, and she, her daughter and grand-daughter lived together in a little house in Davies Street, Mayfair – perhaps not a money-saving proposition today, but rather more so, apparently, in the 1890s.

In order to make some money, she converted her dressmaking skills from hobby to business, adopting the trade name 'Lucile'. The business thrived. By 1894 she had opened Maison Lucile in Old Burlington Street. A larger shop was opened in Hanover Square three years later. There were further moves as the business became ever larger and more successful.

Despite her flair for dress-making, she was not so proficient as a businesswoman. This side of the business was managed by her second husband, Sir Cosmo Duff-Gordon, a prominent Scottish landowner and sportsman, who became a director of her business, and whom she married in 1900.

He was a noted fencer, and he represented Great Britain at the 1906 Olympics. His family was connected to the Duff Gordon sherry bodega in Jerez.

Branches of Maison Lucile were opened in New York in 1910 and Paris in 1911. Chicago would follow in 1915.

THE ORDEAL ON THE TITANIC

It was from Paris that Lucy Christiana (then aged 48), her husband, and her secretary, Laura Mabel Francatelli ('Miss Franks') travelled to visit the New York branch. They boarded the *Titanic* at Cherbourg, and for some reason signed on to the ship as 'Mr and Mrs Morgan' – possibly to avoid the attentions of the press upon landing in New York. However, the disguise was not adequate after all: the press, sifting through the passenger list while waiting for the arrival of the *Carpathia,* assumed it was the American financier, J Pierpoint Morgan, and were just as anxious to discover whether or not he had survived the sinking.

The tickets (first class) for the three passengers cost £39 12s.

Before boarding, she had a premonition of disaster – or so she said afterwards (her word need not be invariably taken as gospel truth): 'The first days of the crossing were uneventful. Like everyone else I was entranced by the beauty of the liner. I had never dreamed of sailing in such luxury ... my pretty little cabin, with its electric heater and pink curtains, delighted me, so that it was a pleasure to go to bed. Everything about this lovely ship reassured me.

'I remember that last meal on the *Titanic* very well. We had a big vase of beautiful daffodils on the table, which were as fresh as if they had just been picked. Everyone was very gay, and at a neighbouring table people were making bets on the probable time of this record-breaking run. Various opinions were put forward, but none dreamed that *Titanic* would make her harbour that night.'

Recounting her experiences of the sinking for an article in the *Daily Sketch*, she wrote: 'I had been in bed for about an hour when I was awakened by a funny rumbling noise. Then the boat stopped and immediately there was the frightful noise of escaping steam and I heard people running along the deck outside the cabin. But they were laughing and gay. "We must have hit an iceberg," I heard one of them say.

'Boat after boat was being lowered in pandemonium of rushing figures. Over the confusion the voices of the ship's officers roared: "Women and children first!" And once I heard the sharp bark of the revolver.'

Another account appeared in American newspapers, including the *Denver Post* and the *Sunday American,* shortly after the disaster, and was afterwards reprinted in the *London Evening News.* Her signature appeared below the article, although at the Board of Trade Inquiry, in which she was later to give evidence, she disclaimed responsibility for it. She maintained that she had recounted the story at dinner in the New York hotel to which they moved on arriving in the city in the *Carpathia.* One of the guests then wrote this column, which began 'Lady Duff-Gordon dictated the following…' and she told the Inquiry that this account of what she had actually said had been very - creative.

There is no way of knowing now whether she wrote this account or not. Statements that she would later explicitly deny having made are printed in the account below in italics. One can at least assume that its content was at least inspired by her, even if later supplemented by some journalistic embellishment:

'I was asleep. The night was perfectly clear. We had watched for some time the fields of ice. There was one just before I went below to retire. I noticed among the fields of ice a number of large bergs.

'There was one which one of the officers pointed out to me. He said that it must have been 100 feet high and seemed to be miles long. It was away off in the distance. I went to my bedroom and retired.

'I was awakened by a long grinding sort of shock. It was not a tremendous crash, but more as though someone had drawn a giant finger all along the side of the boat.

'I awakened my husband' [they had separate cabins] 'and told him that I thought we had struck something. There was no excitement that I could hear. My husband went on deck and told me we had hit some ice, apparently a big iceberg, but there seemed to be no danger. We were not assured of this, however, and Sir Cosmo went upstairs again. We went on deck. He came back to me and said: "You had better put your clothes on, because I heard them give orders to strip the boats."

'We each put on a life preserver and over mine I threw some heavy furs. I took a few trinkets and we went up to the decks. There was no excitement at that time. The ship had listed slightly to port and was down a little at the head.'

'As we stood there, one of the officers came rushing and said: "The women and children are to go in the boats." No one apparently thought there was any danger. We watched a number of women and children and some men going into the lifeboats. At last one of the officers came to me and said: *"Lady Gordon, you had better go in one of the boats." I said to my husband: "Well, we might as well take the boat, although I think it will be only a little pleasure excursion until morning."'*

Lucy expanded on this during the Board of Trade Inquiry a few weeks later. In her words: 'After the three boats had gone down, my husband, Miss Franks and myself were left standing on the deck. There were no other people on the deck at all visible and I had quite made up my mind that I was going to be drowned, and then suddenly we saw this little boat in front of us and we saw some sailors, and an Officer apparently giving them orders and I said to my husband "Ought we not to be doing something?" He said, "Oh, we must wait for orders" and we stood there for quite some time while these men were fixing up things, and then my husband went forward and said, "Might we get into this boat?" and the Officer' [First Officer Murdoch] 'said in a very polite way indeed "Oh certainly, do. I will be very pleased."

'Then somebody hitched me up from the

deck and pitched me into the boat and then I think Miss Franks [Miss Laura Francatelli] was pitched in. It was not a case of getting in at all. We could not have got in, it was quite high. They pitched us up into the boat and after we had been in a little while, the boat was started to be lowered and one American gentleman got pitched in while the boat was being lowered down.'

Returning to the text of her supposed article:

'The boat was the twelfth or thirteenth to be launched. *It was the captain's special boat. There was still no excitement. Five stokers got in and two Americans, A. L. Salomon of New York City, and C. W. Stengel of Newark.* Besides these there were two of the crew, Sir Cosmo, myself and a Miss Frank, an English girl. *There were a number of other passengers, mostly men, standing nearby and they joked with us because we were going out on the ocean. "The ship can't sink," said one of them. "You will get your death of cold out there in the ice."*

'We were slung off and the stokers began to row us away. *For two hours we cruised around. It did not seem to be very cold.* There was no excitement aboard the *Titanic.* We were probably a mile away.

'Suddenly, I clutched the sides of the lifeboat. I had seen the Titanic give a curious shiver. Almost immediately we heard several pistol shots and a great screaming arise from the decks. Then the boat's stern lifted in the air and there was a tremendous explosion. After this the *Titanic* dropped back again. The awful screaming continued. Two minutes after this there was another great explosion. The whole forward part of the great liner dropped down under the waves. The stern rose a hundred feet almost perpendicularly.

'The screaming was agonising. I never heard such a continued chorus of utter despair and agony. The great power of the *Titanic* slowly sank as though a great hand was pushing it gently down under the waves. As it went the screaming of the poor souls left on board seemed to grow louder. It took the *Titanic*

perhaps two minutes to sink after the last explosion. *It went down slowly without a ripple.*

'We had heard of the danger of suction when one of these great liners sinks. There was no such thing about the sinking of the *Titanic.* The amazing part of it all to me as I sat there in the boat looking at this monster being destroyed was that it all could be accomplished so gently. Then began the real agonies of the night.

'Up to that time no one in our boat, and I imagine no one on any of the other boats, had really thought that the *Titanic* was going to sink. For a moment an awful silence seemed to hang over all, and then from the water all about where the Titanic had been there arose a bedlam of shrieks and cries. There were men and women clinging to the bits of wreckage in the icy water. It was at least an hour before the last shrieks died out. I remember the very last cry was that a man had been calling loudly: "My God! My God!" He cried monotonously in a dull, hopeless way. For an entire hour there had been an awful chorus of shrieks, gradually dying into a hopeless moan until this last cry that I speak of. Then all was silent.'

The boat in which they escaped from the *Titanic* had room for 40 people; it was lowered with just 12, most of them crew.

They pulled away some distance from the stricken ship, and were too far away, according to the Duff-Gordon's own testimony in the ensuing inquiry, to return to pick up people swimming in the water.

However, this is not exactly the version of events that suddenly appeared all over press reports on both sides of the Atlantic. It was alleged that one of the occupants of the boat, Leading Fireman Charles Hendrickson, asked whether they ought to go back to help the people swimming in the water, but Lady Duff-Gordon warned they might be swamped by people trying to get on board. Several of the men agreed that it would be dangerous to go back. Eventually Hendrickson was persuaded by Charles Henry Stengel's suggestion that they should head for a light that could be seen in the distance. So the twelve survivors set off while hundreds more were left dying in the water.

As they rowed and the cries of swimmers began to die down, it was said that tempers began to fray. They were still rowing towards a light but it got no nearer and hailing other boats brought no result. Stengel continually shouted directions until Duff-Gordon eventually told him to keep quiet.

Meanwhile, Fireman Robert Pusey overheard Lucy say to her secretary: 'There is your beautiful nightdress gone.'

Annoyed by her comment, Pusey replied that while the couple could replace their property, he and the other crew members had lost everything in the sinking. Cosmo then offered each of the men £5 to assist them until

they received new assignments. This was a pledge he would honour on board the *Carpathia,* presenting the men with cheques drawn on his bank, Coutts.

Later Sir Cosmo would appear before a packed Inquiry in London to defend himself against the accusation that he had bribed the men to secure his escape from the *Titanic* and that they were thus encouraged not to return to the scene of the sinking to rescue swimmers.

He continued always to deny this, and at the Board of Trade Inquiry held in London the following month, he was exonerated of having tried to bribe the crew in this way. But the rumours persisted, fuelled by the yellow press on both sides of the Atlantic.

Another passenger in the same boat,

Richelieu, Bagot Road, childhood home of Lucy Christiana,

Charles Stengel from Newark, gave an interview in the *Newark Star*, published on 24 April, in which he said the rumours were 'absolutely untrue'.

Quoting from the interview: 'The report was circulated by an able seaman, Robert Hopkins, when he asked for assistance at the City Hall, New York. Hopkins declared that had he been in what he described as the "money boat" he would not have to apply for assistance. Questioned, he said that all of the sailors in the dinghy in which Mr. Stengel and Sir and Lady Duff-Gordon escaped, were paid for putting off as quickly as possible. "I don't know the fellow," Mr. Stengel said. "He must be looking for sympathy or money. I know Sir Cosmo Duff-Gordon did give the crew something after we were taken on board the *Carpathia,* but it was merely a reward for the work they had done."

'Besides the passengers in the boat there were three stokers, two seamen - ten in all. The crew wouldn't stick to the oars. They lighted cigarettes, laid down in the bottom of the boat and yelled jokes at each other'.

This is what really happened. The men weren't working the way they ought to have done. Sir Cosmo Duff-Gordon said, 'You take care of us safely and I'll make you all a present.' 'Lady Gordon, who wasn't feeling well, added, "I've quite some money myself." Sir Cosmo then gave each one of the sailors a cigar and afterwards, on the *Carpathia,* an order on Coutts Bank, London. 'It was pointed out to Mr. Stengel that Lord Gordon was quoted as saying: 'We sang hymns to keep our spirits up and drown out the cries of the dying'

"No, we didn't sing anything," Mr. Stengel replied. "The men were joking and laughing. 'Is that you, Boxy?' one of the men yelled to a man in another boat. 'What have you got there? 'I've got a bunch of dagoes,' the fellow called back". Mr. Solomon was equally emphatic in discrediting and denying the story of the "money boat."

ORDEAL BY INQUIRY

A little while later, the Duff-Gordons returned from New York to London on board the *Lusitania.* Many years later, she wrote: 'I shall never forget Cosmo's stricken face when we landed from the *Lusitania* and caught the boat train for London. All over the station were newspaper placards - "Duff Gordon Scandal"..."Baronet and Wife Row Away from the Drowning"..."Sir Cosmo Duff-Gordon Safe and Sound While Women Go Down on *Titanic*." Newsboys ran by us shouting, "Read about the *Titanic* coward!"

'My son-in-law, Lord Tiverton, met us and his loyalty was a great comfort to us both, but he looked rather grave as he spoke of the Court of Inquiry, already in session. "You will have to give evidence," he told us. "It is only fair that you should. You must have a chance of showing how false these abominable stories are. Of course Esmé and I know there is not a shade of foundation in them but they have given rise to a lot of nasty gossip."

'So we made the journey back to London feeling wretchedly dispirited. At our home in Lennox Gardens we found a stack of letters and telegrams waiting for us. Most of them were from old friends who were furiously indignant at the stories that had been circulated and wanted to assure us of their sympathy. Others were from complete strangers who had read of the case in the papers. 'These were generally written in the most abusive strain. Some contained offers of advice, more or less practical. Margot Asquith wrote to tell me that she would be at the hearings every day and that she was sure I would come out of the ordeal with flying colours. She advised me to take a stiff dose of brandy "to buck me up," hardly a wise suggestion as preparation for the witness box, but fortunately I did not act on it.

'I never realised until the day I attended the Court how absolutely alone we all are in

Lady Duff-Gordon

our moments of sorrow. The Scottish Hall in Buckingham Gate, where it was held, was so crowded there was scarcely a vacant place anywhere. Looking at them all as I went in I recognised many who regarded themselves as my intimate friends, yet it came to me that they were rather enjoying the novelty of seeing two people standing in a moral pillory, watching for us to make some slip in our evidence.

'Looking back on it after all these years I think the real cause of the storm which raged round us was that public opinion had to be offered some sacrifice. In the squabble as to whether the Duff Gordons had or had not acted in a cowardly manner the real issue of the Inquiry was very much obscured, at least from the point of view of the man in the street.

'Nobody can doubt that the wreck of the *Titanic* was, as the verdict of the court described it, "an act of God." But equally nobody can deny that had the ship been better equipped in the way of lifeboats, and better organised in the manning of them, far more lives would have been saved. 'I think the tragic reticence of the officers, which kept the majority of passengers in ignorance of the fate of the *Titanic* and so lost valuable time in which every boat could have been filled to its utmost capacity, was responsible for unnecessary loss of life.

'I do not for a moment suggest that anyone was to blame for this. It is very easy to be wise after an emergency and say what ought, or ought not, to have been done. What actually happened at the time was that nobody believed this magnificent boat, the "unsinkable" *Titanic*, as she had been proclaimed far and wide, could possibly go down. They trusted in her wonderful construction, her powerful pumps and watertight compartments.

'There had to be some outlet for the public's emotion and so the same thing happened in England as in America. The Duff-Gordons were known to have escaped in a lifeboat that contained their secretary, two American gentlemen, and seven sailors. Therefore everybody assumed our escape was one of flagrant selfishness and with one accord mud was heaped upon us. Lord Mersey, President of the Court, repeatedly emphasized that the "Duff Gordon incident" had only a small bearing on the inquiry, but this fact was lost from the sight of the general public, who were apparently disposed to regard us as criminals on trial. The spectacle of two people who had just come through the frightful ordeal of the wreck facing an infinitely worse ordeal was one that appealed to the popular imagination and they flocked to the Court to appreciate it to the full.

'The charge we had to face was a moral one. We could have incurred no legal penalties, nothing would have been demanded of us had it been proved, but the real issue at stake was to both of us infinitely more serious. As one of the papers put it: "The audience was not to be cheated out of the smallest particle of what has become the scandal of the day in England. It was a terrible spectacle, this man of old family, battling pale-faced, almost pleading, for something still dearer than life, fighting for honour and repute."

'The accusation actually brought against us was one of incredible cowardice. It was based entirely on the statement of one man among our boat's crew, Charles Hendrickson. He stated that after the *Titanic* went down he had been the only one in the boat who wanted to return to try to pick up survivors, but that all others had overruled him with their

objections. I had been the one to offer the most resistance, he said, for I had protested that there was too great a danger of our being swamped and that Cosmo had upheld my objections.

'This story, coupled with the one Hopkins had spread in America of a five pound bribe, was as terrible as it was untrue. 'Hendrickson admitted, as did all the men of the boat's crew, that there had been no foundation whatever to the story of the bribe. The explanation he gave was the correct one: the cheques had been offered as a voluntary contribution towards a new kit for each man, and the offer had been made long after the sinking of the *Titanic*. Even so, the story had persisted and it was only after we had both been through a very searching cross-examination on the question of the cheques, and the other witnesses had given their evidence, that we were completely cleared on that point.

'It was a lovely spring day, I remember, as we drove to the Court, and it was difficult to believe we were not going to some pleasant social function for there were such rows of elegant cars outside. Inside, too, there was little of the atmosphere of a court, in spite of the imposing array of counsel. All the women there seemed to have put on their prettiest spring frocks. I caught sight of the Duchess of Wellington, Lady Eileen Wellesley, and Margot Asquith, whose bright eyes followed every posture of the witnesses, Prince Maurice of Battenberg, Prince Albert of Schleswig-Holstein, the Russian Ambassador, and many other people who had been guests in our home, eager all of them to see what would happen.

'Our only defence was a complete denial of Hendrickson's story. There had of course been no such conversation in the boat, certainly none in which we took part. Nobody had suggested going back to rescue possible survivors because we were at far too great a distance from the ship when she went down to have been able to do so. When the *Titanic* disappeared we were left in our frail boat without a light of any sort, without a compass or any other means of knowing where to search for people in the water.

'Miss Francatelli and I had been the only women in the boat because we had been the only women left on the forward starboard boat deck when it was launched. My husband and the two American men had only got into the boat because there was no one else there to do so and the officer superintending the loading of the boat had given them permission to get in. The crew of seven had been appointed to man the boat by this officer and they had acted on his instructions in pulling well away from the ship.

'When the *Titanic* sank I was too seasick to have taken part in a discussion as to which direction we ought to follow even if I had wanted to. And Cosmo, who had only been a passenger in the boat, had left the entire navigation to Symons, the seaman placed in charge. Symons in the course of his evidence stated under oath that he considered that to have returned to the place where the *Titanic* had sunk would have endangered the safety of all on board, as we should have more than probably been swamped. He also affirmed there had been no discussion whatever as to the advisability of returning and that neither Cosmo nor I had made any suggestions on the subject whatever. The story that we had deliberately rowed away and left the drowning to their fate was monstrous.

'It was surely never intended that the inquiry should resolve itself into a species of Star Chamber by torturing witnesses who were fortunate enough to survive and to cast the gravest reflections on their characters and conduct. Still less was the Court constituted that efforts might be made to stir up class against class in order to prove that undue preference was shown to the aristocrat and the wealthy.

'Even the order of seating in the embattled lifeboat was dissected in the press.

'Hendrickson's evidence is not supported by a single other person in the boat. Seaman Symons, who was in charge of the lifeboat, assumed full responsibility for all that occurred and declared that in his considered opinion it would have been most dangerous to have ventured into the drowning multitude and that he refrained from doing so in order to preserve the lives of those on board.

'All efforts of counsel failed to prove that either of us ever said a single word against going back or that they attempted to induce the crew to row away from the scene of the disaster by offering them a monetary reward.

'The scene in court on Friday will never be forgotten by those who witnessed it. There did not seem to be a single, commonsense man of the world with any idea of fair play in the room. It was not an inspiring spectacle to watch the row of lawyers increasing the sufferings of those who have passed through the most awful ordeal which a man or woman could be called upon to face.

'But despite our complete vindication before the Inquiry a great deal of the mud that was flung stuck to us both.

'For years afterwards, I was quite used to hearing people who did not know me whisper: "That is Lady Duff-Gordon, the woman who rowed away from the drowning."

'For myself I did not mind, for none of the people whose opinion I cared about believed such an outrageous story, but I minded very much for Cosmo's sake. To the end of his life he grieved at the slur which had been cast on his honour.'

On 17 May, Cosmo Duff-Gordon testified and on 20 May Lucy Christiana took the stand. Their testimony attracted the largest crowds during the inquiry.

According to a contemporary newspaper report: 'It was Ladies' Day at the *Titanic* inquiry yesterday. Expectations of hearing more about the strange tales of "the Money Boat" had excited keen interest in the day's proceedings, and the prospect of seeing Sir Cosmo and Lady Duff-Gordon in Court relating their version of the incidents of that tragic vigil in mid-ocean was a compelling attraction to the fair and always curious sex.

'From floor to topmost gallery the Scottish Hall was thronged. Mrs Asquith was an early comer, Miss Ismay, sister of the much-talked of chairman of the White Star Line, was an interested auditor. The Duff-Gordons were in court at 10.30 a.m., and took their seats at the outer end of the first row of advocates. Sir Cosmo was wearing a black frock coat and light striped trousers, and Lady Duff-Gordon, who is, of course, familiar to the West End as Mme Lucille, the Court costumier, was in black with a cloak faced with purple.'

The Times reported the session in which Lucy Christiana gave evidence: 'The President had previously expressed the hope that her evidence might not be necessary but her counsel, Mr. Duke, M.P., urged that the insinuations made against her were of such a character that she thought it essential that she should be called.

'Lady Duff-Gordon was accordingly sworn and denied that she heard any of the cries of the drowning, or that she said it would be dangerous to go back to them. The only new feature brought out by her examination was her repudiation of a vivid account of the wreck which first appeared over her name in a New York newspaper. The article contained many things which were inconsistent with Lady Duff-Gordon's evidence yesterday, and which she affirmed that she had never said.'

Lucy Christiana noted that for the rest of her husband's life he was broken-hearted over the negative coverage by the 'yellow press' during his cross-examination at the inquiry. The final report by the inquiry determined that the Duff-Gordons had not deterred the crew from any attempt at rescue.

Cosmo and Lucy Christiana Duff-Gordon

are portrayed in both major *Titanic* films, *A Night to Remember* (1958) and *Titanic* (1997), although not with any great accuracy.

Lucy Christiana had another close call three years after surviving the *Titanic* when she booked passage aboard the *Lusitania* on its last voyage. It was reported in the press that she cancelled her trip due to illness. The *Lusitania* was destroyed by a German torpedo on 7 May 1915.

Her connection with Maison Lucile diminished following a restructuring of Lucile Ltd in 1918–19. By 1922 she had ceased designing for the company, which gradually lost its prominent place in the market after her departure. She continued to work from private premises designing personally for individual customers. She maintained a ready-to-wear shop of her own and lent her name to a wholesale operation in America.

She also continued as a fashion columnist and critic after her design career ended, and she penned her best-selling autobiography in 1932. However, in her last years during the slump of the 1930s her income diminished, and she was living in reduced circumstances in Hampstead.

At the time of her death in April 1935, aged 71, she was living in a nursing home in Putney, London. She died of breast cancer, complicated by pneumonia, on the fourth anniversary of her husband's death.

They are both buried at Brookwood Cemetery, near Woking in Surrey.

Lucy Christiana Duff-Gordon had a fascinating life, and as she said, enjoyed some happiness and much sorrow. Through her imagination and eye for clothing, she helped lay the foundations for today's couture and ready-to-wear markets, and was instrumental in creating the impact that fashion now plays on our contemporary world.

She was a true pioneer of fashion, and, in her way, a pioneer who guided the way to the modern era.

Leaving Southampton

(II)

THE LADY'S MAID

'Because most mistresses preferred their personal maids young (and this was reflected by the lady's maid's salary growing smaller each year as she grew older), unless the position of "Housekeeper" became available and she could step into it, the future of the middle-aged lady's maid was indeed grim'

Website on the employment conditions of Victorian servants

The story of Rosalie Bidois, personal maid to Madeleine Astor

The only person born in the Channel Islands who was travelling first class on the *Titanic* was Rosalie Bidois. And she was only doing so as she was attending on her employer, Madeleine Astor.

Mrs Astor was the newly-married wife of Colonel John Jacob Astor IV, reputedly the richest man in the US, certainly the wealthiest passenger on the *Titanic*.

Rosalie Bidois, born in Jersey, was her personal maid.

Rosalie's parents, her father's brother and his wife had all come from Normandy some time before her birth. They were just two of thousands of families who came to Jersey – very often to work on Island farms. Many of them returned to France after greater or shorter periods of residence. Some of them 'made good' in the Island, bought their own land, farmed it, and over the generations assimilated seamlessly into Jersey life; their descendants are an integral – even traditional – element of the Island's population today.

Rosalie Bidois (the daughter), however, and her sister, Augustine, neither returned to settle in France nor continued to live in Jersey, preferring instead to seek employment and experience in the wider and more cosmopolitan world outside Jersey.

She was born in St Helier on 10 May 1865, the oldest of five children of Pierre Bidois, and his wife, Rosalie Martillet. After Rosalie came three sons and then their youngest daughter, Augustine Marie.

Although claimed wrongly to have been born in Guernsey (as a result of a misleading statement in an American newspaper report of the time), her connection to the Channel Islands is through Jersey, where she spent her early years.

After the 1871 census, in which the family is detailed as living in Jersey, the family disappears from sight. They feature in neither the Jersey nor the Guernsey census of 1891, and it is reasonable to suggest that by then they had returned to their native Normandy – Rosalie always called herself French, never 'Jersey'.

However there remained a close connection with Jersey: her uncle and his family remained in the Island and some of their descendants live in Jersey today. For a while Rosalie's youngest brother, Jules, lived in Jersey, staying with one of his cousins. Both Rosalie and Augustine were always close; the former was pretty; the younger sister was said to be plain, although this is not borne out by a surviving photograph of her.

It would have required at that time a great deal of perseverance and initiative for a young girl, born in humble circumstances, to make an independent career for herself. Rosalie and Augustine achieved this, once they had grown into mature young women, by travelling to London and seeking work as domestic servants.

Evidently they were good at their work, and achieved the relatively genteel and privileged status of upper servants. So when they decided, in the autumn of 1900 (Rosalie was then aged 35), to travel to New York to work there, they had no trouble in bringing with them influential references from reputable employers.

They travelled to New York on board the SS *Cedric*, and on their arrival there on 23 October were quickly able to gain employment. Over the next decade they were employed by some very wealthy and prominent New York families.

In 1910 Rosalie was recommended to the Astors by an exclusive Fifth Avenue domestic service agency, which catered for the needs of the very rich. Thus she became the personal maid to the new Mrs John Jacob Astor.

The Astors were one of the super-rich families of the United States plutocracy. The founder of the dynasty was the German-American John Jacob Astor, a fur trader, who had achieved colossal wealth by shrewdly realising how fast the city of New York was growing: he bought up as-yet undeveloped land and was able to profit hugely from its subsequent development.

Colonel John Jacob Astor IV ('Jack Astor') was his great-grandson. Born in Rhinebeck, New York, in 1864, he was Harvard-educated and lived at the family mansion on 840 Fifth Avenue and at Ferncliff in Rhinebeck, a building he had commissioned to be built and based on the Grand Trianon Palace.

He was an author and inventor, helping, among other things, to develop the turbine engine and the pneumatic road drill. In 1897 he built the Astoria Hotel, New York, adjoining the Waldorf Hotel which had been built by William Waldorf Astor, his cousin. The new complex became known as the Waldorf-Astoria.

At the time of the Spanish-American War in 1898, he was commissioned as a lieutenant colonel in the US volunteers. He placed his yacht *Nourmahal* at the disposal of the U.S. government and equipped a mountain battery of artillery for use against the Spanish.

In 1891 he had married Ava Willing of Philadelphia, with whom he had one son and one daughter. But in 1909 Astor divorced Ava and, two years later, married Madeleine Force, who was only in her late teens. She had what would nowadays be called a pushy mother, who wanted her to 'marry well'. She had been sent to expensive private schools, and, having just finished school at the age of 18, she met Astor at the fashionable and very expensive resort of Bar Harbor, Maine. He took a liking to her; she was introduced to New York society, and the next year their engagement was announced.

Public opinion was shocked – or at least divided – by this marriage with a woman who was a year younger than his own son. But the age difference was not the only problem: according to the terms of his divorce, they could not marry in New York and the couple had difficulty locating a minister who would officiate. One was only found after Astor offered $1,000 as a fee.

They wed on 9 September, 1911; to get away from the gossip, they decided to winter abroad, travelling first to Egypt and later to Paris.

But, in the spring of 1912, on account of her pregnancy, they decided to cut short their European stay and return home. And so, in April they boarded the *Titanic* when she docked at Cherbourg.

Travelling with them were Colonel Astor's manservant, Victor Robbins, Madeleine Astor's maid, Rosalie Bidois, and her private nurse, Caroline ('Carrie') Endres – as well as their pet Airedale dog, Kitty.

Their ticket for the party cost £224 10s 6d.

The chivalrous conduct of John Jacob Astor during the *Titanic* disaster is an integral part of the legend. He was the author of the famous (and apocryphal) comment after the collision: 'I asked for ice in my drink, but this is ridiculous'.

While the lifeboats were being made ready, he and his wife sat on mechanical horses in the gymnasium, apparently not really believing that there was any real danger.

But by 1.45 am he seems to have become concerned about their safety. They climbed through the window of the enclosed promenade, towards where Second Officer Charles Lightoller was finishing the loading of Lifeboat 4. Astor installed his wife, her maid, Rosalie, and nurse, Carrie, into the lifeboat, and then asked Lightoller if he could join his wife, because of her 'delicate condition'. Permission was refused – only women and children were allowed in the boat. He bade farewell to his wife and then stood back.

His wife had a last sight of him from the boat – they waved to each other one last time as the lifeboat was lowered.

In the words of a Toronto newspaper report of the time: 'Faithful unto death was Kitty, Colonel Astor's Airedale terrier and constant companion on land or sea. Kitty was never far from her master's heels, and the two were familiar figures on Fifth Avenue.

'When the crash came, Robbins [Astor's manservant] went below and brought Kitty up on deck. There, the most faithful of friends, she stood beside her master, while the sea embraced them, and now she shares his grave.'

Astor's body was later recovered by the cable ship *McKay-Bennett,* and he is buried in New York. Robbins' body was never recovered.

Rosalie Bidois

osalie was 42 when she accompanied the Astor family to Europe, and boarded the *Titanic* with them at Cherbourg.

On the night of the disaster she accompanied her mistress into Lifeboat Number 4; the seaman in charge was Walter Perkis, the brother-in-law of Jerseyman Alfred Olliver. The boat had a capacity of 65 people; there were only 30 on board.

Quoting from an article that appeared in the *New York Times* on 22 April 1912:

'As the boat was slowly being lowered from the ship's side a man in a state of great excitement fought his way through the throng of

Augustine Bidois

men gathered on the deck, and before the officers of the ship could stop him jumped into the boat with the women.

'As the lifeboat pulled slowly away from the *Titanic* it began to ship water rapidly. The *Titanic* was then sinking rapidly, and the boat was almost swamped in the suction created by the big steamer.

'After he found himself in the lifeboat the man seized the few available blankets which had hastily been thrown into the boat for the women, many of whom were thinly clad, and, wrapping them about himself, grovelled in the bottom of the boat.

'As the lifeboat found the water Mrs. Astor seized an oar, as did several other women. The women, with the exception of Mrs. Astor, handled the oars clumsily, having had little experience in rowing, and it was with difficulty that they were able to pull away from the fast-sinking steamer.

'About the big steamship the ocean was swelling and sinking, and the women found themselves in a sort of whirlpool. It looked for a time as if the small boat would surely be swamped. The women pleaded with the man grovelling at their feet to take an oar, but the trembling creature paid no heed to their entreaties, wrapping himself more securely in the blankets he had taken from them.

'When the lifeboat began to fill rapidly with water Mrs. Astor with undiminished strength helped the other women to bail it out. Several of the women, badly frightened, were unable to give Mrs. Astor and the other women in the boat any assistance.

'After the *Titanic* disappeared the women rowed back to the spot where the ship had gone down, to see if there were any lives they could save. They could see several men in the water, and they rowed towards them.

'In the work of rescue Mrs. Astor's maid played a conspicuous part. Six men believed to be seamen were dragged by the women into the boat. One of the men was dead when they found him, and another died shortly after he was pulled into the boat.

'On reaching the water near where the *Titanic* disappeared they found only wreckage floating about them. The lifeboat circled several times about the spot which marked the grave of the *Titanic*, but found no signs of human life.

'Mrs. Astor, from the time she entered the lifeboat until the long interval which followed before she and her companions were picked up by the *Carpathia*, displayed the greatest courage and fortitude. After being taken aboard the rescue ship she experienced a nervous collapse.'

There is, as might be expected, no independent testimony from her of the sinking and her subsequent rescue. But newspapers in the days following the sinking speculated feverishly on whether or not Madeleine Astor had escaped the sinking. According to news agency reports printed in Jersey's *Evening Post* newspaper, Madeleine Astor was taken to a private cabin in the *Carpathia,* as soon as she was rescued from the lifeboat, and was not seen again until she emerged from her cabin at New York. She was collected by Vincent Astor, her husband's son, and driven quickly away.

However, in an article in the *Guernsey Evening Press,* the director of the employment agency who introduced Rosalie to the Astors, Mrs A. J. Dickinson, is quoted as saying: 'Just as soon as I heard that Rosalie had been saved with Mrs Astor, I knew that the Colonel's bride was in safe hands. I would rather have that little Frenchwoman beside me in an emergency than many a man.'

At the time the New York newspaper, *Evening World,* stated that it was 'a striking commentary on the democratic rule that puts the salaried maid above the millionaire master, and the millionaire mistress above the wage-earning valet'.

Other newspapers said that the Astor family had the greatest respect for Rosalie, and what a good thing it was that she was on the *Carpathia* to be able to look after her pregnant young mistress.

We lose track of Rosalie for the next ten years or so; she seems, apparently, to have been employed as a domestic and continued to live in New York. Together with her sister, Augustine, she was a strong member of the French community in Manhattan. In 1924, then aged 59, she applied to become an American citizen. In her form she described herself as 'a ladie's maid' (sic). She was naturalised in 1929.

Her sister and great friend, Augustine, died aged 52, as a result of breast cancer. Rosalie arranged for her burial in St Raymond's Cemetery in the Bronx.

Rosalie sadly did not enjoy a graceful or happy old age: in 1932, now aged 66, she married a Frenchman called François Courtinade who was working in the Bronx; he was nine years her junior. Seven months later she came home to their flat early one day and caught her husband in bed with a woman she had never seen before. Four days later, she filed for divorce.

As her age advanced her health deteriorated; she developed arteriosclerosis and diabetes. She died in the welfare ward of a Manhattan hospital on 24 September 1938. By then she was all alone, and had no relatives or money. If it had not been for the recollection that she owned her sister's grave plot in the Bronx cemetery, she would have been put in a pauper's grave. She was put to rest in the same grave as her younger sister.

Her former employer, Madeleine Astor, gave birth to a son, ('John Jacob Astor VI') in August 1912. She re-married twice; both marriages ended in divorce. She died of a heart condition at Palm Beach, Florida, in 1940, aged 46.

A wealthy woman, it would be charitable to suppose that she had lost touch with her former loyal servant, who, two years before her wealthy mistress, had died – ill, alone and in destitution.

Cabin B-57

Verandah Cafe

(III)

GIRL ON HER OWN

'With the exception of two very harrowing leave-takings, we saw nothing but perfect order and quiet on board the Titanic

– Elizabeth Walton Allen (29) first class passenger

Bertha Ilett was travelling to the USA to see her father, who had moved to New York. She was aged 17 when she sailed on the *Titanic* as a second class passenger from Southampton.

She was born in Millbrook, Jersey, on 12 October 1894, and was living with her mother there. She was the daughter of Edward and Elizabeth Ilett, and she had three sisters: Lily, Florence and Elsie –possibly a fourth, Dora.

Her father had been born in the village of Hounsdown, near Eling in Hampshire in 1858 and had later moved to Jersey, where he became head gardener at the home of Jessie Boot, owner of Boots the Chemist.

By 1912 Edward Ilett had moved to New York –

Sister ships the Olympic and Titanic side by side

history draws a veil as to why, but it is reasonable to speculate that he had separated from his wife, Elizabeth (née Hamling), who came from Alderney.

Bertha found her original sailing on the *Olympic* cancelled on account of the national coal strike then taking place, but she would doubtless have been pleased to be transferred, as were so many other passengers, to the *Titanic* – the new liner, so much in the news, that was making its maiden voyage.

It is believed that she booked to go steerage, but decided to 'upgrade' – to use the modern term, and travel second class.

On board, she sat at the same table in the salon as Edwina Troutt, who left a detailed record and was in later life a notable member of *Titanic* passenger reunions, dying in 1984 at the age of 100. She could remember little of Bertha.

On the night of Sunday 14th April Bertha was woken by another woman passenger, who told her that there was no danger. She had just dozed off again when she was woken, for a second time, by a steward, who advised her to get dressed, pack a few things and go on deck. She was frightened, and the steward reassured her, helping her to put on two coats and a lifebelt, and taking her up to the boats.

On deck, she realised how bitterly cold the weather was. 'My hands are like ice,' she told the steward, who took off his own gloves and gave them to Bertha. He then saw her safely into lifeboat number 14.

'Poor fellow,' she later wrote in a letter to her mother, 'he must have been drowned because I never saw him again. Perhaps he could have been saved but for his attention to me.'

From the lifeboat, she listened to the sound of the orchestra playing. She was sure that near the end they played 'Nearer, My God, to Thee.'

The boat, she noticed, was leaking.

Lifeboat 14 tied up with several other boats, and Officer Harold Lowe, in charge of number 14, transferred his passengers, including Bertha, in to other lifeboats, so that he might return to the wreck to rescue people from the water. So Bertha Ilett found herself in lifeboat 12.

At dawn she was rescued by the *Carpathia,* which brought her to New York, where she was met by her father. She was one of the first to be listed drowned, and her father mourned her until a message from the *Carpathia* announced she was alive and well.

In Jersey, her mother was woken up at two o'clock in the morning by a *Morning News* reporter and told that her daughter was safe.

Bertha received help from the Women's Relief Committee, who gave her clothing and $25. The Red Cross, noting that she was a housemaid, gave her a further $50.

Bertha settled with her father, and later married Chris Kristen Christensen. They made a home in Geneva, Ontario County, New York, where she lived for 45 years. They had two sons and a daughter: Edward, Richard and Phyllis.

She died on 20 September 1976, aged 82, and is buried in Brookside Cemetery, Geneva.

Taking a stroll on deck

Bertha Ilett (Morning News)

THE JERSEY CONNECTIONS THE CREW

(I)

THE ST OUENNAIS ON THE BRIDGE

'The sound was like she touched something; a long grinding sound, like'

Alfred Olliver, giving evidence to the Senatorial Inquiry
Quartermaster on the Titanic,

THE STORY OF ALFRED OLLIVER

THERE were few survivors who actually saw the iceberg that holed the *Titanic* with such devastating consequences. One of those who did was Jerseyman Alfred Olliver, who was a member of the crew and actually on duty on the bridge at the moment that the iceberg struck.

In his testimony to the American Senatorial Court of Inquiry on 28 April, he stated: 'The iceberg was about the height of the boat deck; if anything, just a little higher.' [It was level with the bridge]. 'It was almost alongside of the boat - the top did not touch the side, but was almost alongside... it was not white, as I expected to see an iceberg. It was a kind of a dark-blue.'

This strongly suggests that the iceberg had recently 'turned turtle', as sometimes happens, before the impact, so that it was still full of water, giving it a blue

Alfred Olliver

appearance. This could explain why the look-outs (Fred Fleet and Reg Lee) did not see it until it was too late to take avoiding action.

Alfred Olliver was a Quartermaster on the *Titanic* - a rank that in the merchant navy refers to the experienced seamen assigned to bridge watches. The main task of a Quartermaster is to steer the ship under the command of the Captain or watch-keeping officers.

His last ship before the *Titanic* was its sister ship, the *Olympic,* where he had also worked as a quartermaster, and experienced a collision between the Olympic and the naval cruiser, *HMS Hawke,* in the Solent.

Alfred was born at Vine Villa, Rue Ville au Bas, St Ouen (a building that is now either re-named or disappeared), on 2 June 1884 and gave his age as 27 when he signed on the *Titanic's* articles on 6 April 1912.

He was the third child (second son) of Pierre and Eliza Olliver out of a family of eleven. His father, born about 1859, was a native of St Brieuc in Brittany, who had travelled to Jersey as a young man to work on the land; he spelt the name 'Ollivier'. His mother's family name was Le Cornu - her own family had lived at Les Landes for centuries. She was born there in the same year as her husband. When he was a boy the family moved from St Ouen to St Brelade, probably because of his father's work for different farmers.

Alfred went to sea at the age of 16, joining the Royal Marines at Alverstoke Barracks, Hampshire, and then, after seven years, left to join the Merchant Navy, in which he served for a further five years.

He married Amelia Collins in December 1910 and they shared a house with his wife's sister, Phoebe, who was married to another merchant seaman, Walter Perkis. Their shared house, in Victoria Road, Bitterne, Hampshire, was called '*Olympic*' – named after the White Star Line ship on which both husbands were then employed.

When his first child (Alfred) was born in 1911, he soon decided that that as he was now a family man, he wanted to leave the sea, and settle down with a land-based job, but his brother-in-law persuaded him to have 'just one last voyage' on this wonderful new liner that had just been built - the *Titanic.*

In April 1912 both he and his brother-in-law were employed as Quartermasters aboard this ship. He joined the *Titanic* in Belfast in late March and was on board for her final trials and voyage to Southampton. As a quartermaster, he could expect to earn a monthly wage of £5. He shared a cabin with the four other quartermasters, on the port side of E deck.

At the time of the collision he was stand-by Quartermaster, running messages for the officer on watch, William Murdoch. Earlier, he had been at the helm, but at 10 pm – just under two hours before the collision with the iceberg - he was relieved by Robert Hichens, who was still on duty at the time of the collision.

From 10 pm onwards he was running errands and doing various duties, and at 11.40 pm he was re-entering the bridge after running an errand to check the ship's standing compass, and trim the lights, when the ship struck the iceberg.

He heard the three warning bells from the crow's nest that indicated that the lookouts had spotted something. He looked, but could see nothing initially. Straight away he heard First Officer William Murdoch give the orders for the watertight doors to be closed in an attempt to 'port around' (i.e. to keep to starboard of) the iceberg, and later he recalled recording the closing of the doors in the ship's log.

But the last-minute attempts to avoid the iceberg failed, and moments later he felt the shudder of an impact. He knew they had hit something and in a few moments he saw the iceberg go past on the starboard side, level with the bridge.

In his own words from the Senatorial inquiry in New York, in answer to questions put to him by Senator Theodore Burton:

'I happened to be looking at the lights on the standing compass and was trimming them so that they would burn properly - then I heard the report and was just entering the bridge when the collision occurred.

'…The sound was like she touched something, a long grinding sound. It did not last many seconds. The sound was before I saw the iceberg – it was just abaft [sternwards from] the bridge when I saw it. It was impossible to see the length of the iceberg from where I was standing; I only saw the tip-top, which had a star-pointed shape.

'It went aft the afterpart of the ship. I did not see it afterwards – I did not have the time to know where it was going.'

He remembered First Officer Murdoch giving an order to 'hard a-port' as he entered the wheelhouse and Sixth Officer Moody standing next to Hichens to make sure the order was carried out. Questioned at the US Senate Hearings regarding this, one Senator asked if he meant "hard a-starboard" to which he replied, 'No, hard a-port was the only order he heard given.'

The point of this question and answer was that commands had not changed since the days of tillers, so the command 'hard-a-port' meant 'turn the ship in the starboard direction', and 'hard-a-starboard' meant the opposite – turn it port-wise. The ship needed to be turned towards the starboard to turn away from the iceberg.

Right after this, the order was given to stop the engines. At this moment, Captain Smith, who had been taking a break and having a short nap on the sofa in the chart room, arrived on the bridge. He ordered Olliver to locate the carpenter, John Maxwell, and to tell him to 'sound' the ship. When he found the carpenter, on E deck, he was already at work doing this.

After that Smith ordered him to take a folded message for the Chief Engineer, Joseph Bell. Bell, who did not survive, told Olliver to inform the Captain that his order would be carried out. Olliver did not open the folded note and never found out what the order was, as all the engineers died.

He returned to the Bridge to give Captain Smith the news that Bell would do the job asked of him as soon as possible. By this time, the stokers were coming out of the stoke rooms into the alleyway.

It was just after this that the Chief Officer sent him to the Boatswain to tell him to uncover the lifeboats and make them ready for lowering. After carrying out these orders, Olliver went down to lifeboat 5 on the starboard side, where Third Officer Herbert Pitman was in charge, and he assisted passengers into the boat.

He noticed that the deck was not crowded and 45 people got into the lifeboat. Pitman and Alfred Olliver manned the boat, and crew members were two firemen, two stewards and a sailor – perhaps six to eight men. The rest were women and children.

There was no rush to get into the boat, he reported afterwards.

By this time the water line of the *Titanic* was, by his account, about 15 to 20 feet at the bow.

As the boat was lowered, Olliver realised that the bung was not in and that there was a danger it would be swamped. He crawled under the legs of the women and pushed some of them out of the way when they would not move, in order to get the bung in and save them and the boat.

After the lifeboat was in the water, Olliver took an oar and helped row. It pulled clear of the ship by a distance of some 300 yards.

When the ship sank, Pitman suggested that the lifeboat return to the scene and rescue people from the water – the boat was not full, and there was space for at least another 20 people in the lifeboat. All but one of the First class women passengers objected strongly to the idea and threatened to seize the oars. So Pitman reversed his order – it was a decision that would haunt him for the rest of his life.

In the US Hearing, Olliver backed up Pitman's story that the Third Officer wanted to go back for survivors but 'the women passengers implored him not to go because they reckoned it was not safe.'

There were two equal dangers, first, that the boat would be caught up in the suction as the *Titanic* sank, and that the struggling people in the sea would capsize the boat as they attempted to clamber in.

As the ship went under, Olliver told the inquiry, the *Titanic* 'was well down at the head first...and to my idea she broke forward, and the afterpart righted itself and made another plunge.'

He then heard several small explosions, which he reckoned were the bulkheads giving away. By this time, he estimated they were about 500 yards off when they began to hear cries and screams of people in the water - this lasted for about ten minutes. Later, he recounted that their lifeboat was the fourth or fifth to be picked up by the *Carpathia*. Perkis was helping

to man another lifeboat, so both brothers-in-law survived.

While in the lifeboat, he gave the socks he was wearing to a first class passenger, Ruth Dodge, who was in the lifeboat with her baby son. She had dressed hurriedly to go on deck, and was freezing. At first she turned up her nose at the offer, until he assured her that the socks were clean on that morning!

Ruth's husband had escaped in another lifeboat and they were reunited on the *Carpathia* some five hours later. Creditably, she had argued against the other women in the lifeboat who had refused to allow it to be rowed back to pick up people struggling in the water. Later, tired of listening to the 'hysteria' of the other women, she transferred to another lifeboat.

In family history notes written by Alfred's granddaughter, Mary Jordan, she wrote: 'Amelia and her sister, Phoebe, joined many others at the dockside in Southampton every day, desperately reading the list of survivors posted on the gates as the news slowly came in. It was quite some time before they learned that Alfred and Walter had survived, and even longer before their husbands returned home to Southampton.'

Alfred Olliver and Walter Perkis were brought by the *Carpathia* to New York, where Alfred was detained by the authorities to appear at their inquiry into the disaster. He did so, and on return to England, he signed off the ship's articles on 13 May 1912. He received wages of £1. 1s. 0d.

Walter Perkis made a full recovery and later returned to the sea, but Alfred Olliver's nervous system had been badly affected by the traumatic experience he had suffered. He had a nervous breakdown, as a result of which he never worked regularly again, only working intermittently, on land, for the White Star Line. His health declined and he became nervous and depressed.

Their second son, William, was born in 1914, and their daughter Hilda was born in 1916. There was no benefit of social services or social

Unmarked grave of Alfred and Amelia Olliver, St Saviour's Churchyard

Another boat leaves Jersey for Southampton

security, and there was no financial help available, apart from a little help from The Oddfellows, of which he was a member.

Quoting again from Mary Jordan: 'The Oddfellows' money was the only thing that supported Amelia over the years in her struggle to feed and clothe his family.

'Fred (Alfred's eldest son) was very clever at school and won a scholarship to college, but when he was old enough he had to cease his studies and seek employment in order to help the family financially. During this stressful and worrying time, Alfred became very depressed that he was unable to work to feed and clothe his family, and one day [in 1928], in desperation, he took himself off to the outside privy with a knife, intending to end it all.

'He was discovered before it was too late, and a doctor was called, but in those days it was an offence against the law to try to take your own life, and so a court case ensued.'

At his trial the judge ordered that he return to his native birthplace (Jersey) under the care and protection of his son, Fred - who was only 16 at the time.

They lived in Poplar Avenue, Maufant. Apparently he never talked, or wanted to talk, about his experience on the *Titanic*. Six years after his return to the Island he died, on 18 June 1934 aged 50. His wife, Amelia, died in 1975 aged 91 at Sandybrook Hospital in St Lawrence.

They are both buried in St Saviour's Churchyard. At the time of writing his daughter, Hilda, is an elderly lady living in a Jersey nursing home; Alfred 'junior' ('Fred') was an accountant with Alex Picot and Company, and a director of St Helier Garages. He died in the 1980s.

Hilda's son, Michael Talibard and Fred's children, Bob and Pat and their families, live in the Island.

Alfred and Amelia's grave is unmarked, a small oblong of grass between two graves on either side, with a small vase in the centre. Jersey *Titanic* researcher Mandy Le Boutillier, with her knowledge of the drawing power that visible grave stones and memorials have for members of what she calls 'the *Titanic* community', believes that that there should be a headstone in place to mark his last resting place:

'It is my hope that a headstone for Alfred Olliver can be erected in recognition of his brave actions on 14 April 1912, and in appreciation of a Jerseyman whose life was forever afterwards blighted by the *Titanic*.'

THE JERSEY CONNECTIONS THE CREW

(II)

THE MUCH SHIPWRECKED JACK POINGDESTRE

Captain Smith: 'Mr Murdoch, what was that?'
First Officer Murdoch: 'An iceberg, sir'

Overheard on the bridge of the Titanic

John Thomas ('Jack') Poingdestre was born at 28 Old St John's Road, St Helier. He gave his age as 32 years old on joining the *Titanic.* His father was Philippe George Poingdestre, a carpenter, and his wife, Eliza Jane Warr. He was one of twelve children and left Jersey at an early age in order to go to sea.

He settled at 4 Elm Road, Shirley, Southampton, with his wife Florence Maud Gallagher, and had five surviving children of his own by the time he signed up for the *Titanic's* maiden voyage.

The *Titanic* was the second shipwreck in his life, and it occurred only one month after his first one. On 12 March 1912 he had been serving on the P&O liner *Oceana* when, shortly after its departure en route to Bombay, it collided with a sailing ship, the German four-masted barque *Pisagua,* and sank off Newhaven.

The *Pisagua* hit the *Oceana* amidships, creating a 40 feet long gash in her side. Nine of the *Oceana's* crew lost their lives when one of its lifeboats capsized, but the other 241 passengers and crew were rescued. The *Oceana* sank but *Pisagua* survived with severe damage to the bow and foremast.

After a few weeks back in Southampton, Jack joined the *Titanic* at 6 a.m. on 10 April 1912 as an able bodied seaman, at a monthly wage of £5.

On the night of the disaster, he was on duty, but because it was a Sunday he was only on standby, and had actually been told to stand down.

When the ship struck the iceberg, he was standing outside the seaman's mess on C Deck, in the forecastle. When he felt the impact, he went straight away to the forward well deck, where he picked up a piece of ice, and took it back to the crew's messroom.

Like so many people on board he did not believe at first that there had been a serious incident, so when he met the ship's carpenter, and was told by him that the ship was making water, and that perhaps he should go to the boats – he did nothing, until the boatswain called the seamen together and ordered them all to go to the boat deck.

There he helped to uncover and to swing out the lifeboats on both the port and starboard sides. Afterwards he would state that he remembered seeing one lifeboat with a 65-passenger capacity being lowered with fewer than 40 people on board.

After helping with the lifeboats he decided to return to his quarters on E Deck to retrieve his rubber boots. He picked them up and was on the point of making his way back outside when a wooden wall separating the crews' quarters from the third class rooms collapsed, releasing a torrent of water, and he was forced to wade back through water waist-deep.

He got back on deck, and made his way to where lifeboat 12 was being loaded under the supervision of Second Officer Lightoller. He helped to fill lifeboat 14, and then returned to lifeboat 12, entering the boat as part of the crew.

This was also nowhere near to capacity, and contained only about 20 women. He was asked by Lightoller how many crew members were in the boat, and when he answered 'one', another seaman was ordered to join.

The lifeboat was lowered, and once in the water it pulled away about 100 yards from the *Titanic.* It was joined by other lifeboats, and transfers were made to fill Lifeboat 12, so that Lifeboat 14 could return to pick up some survivors in the water. There were almost 70 people aboard no 12 when it was picked up by the *Carpathia.*

The *Carpathia* brought him to New York, and on the Saturday, 20 April, he returned to Britain on the *Lapland* with the other surviving crew members.

On arrival at Plymouth, he and the other crew members were detained by the British authorities, and then released after giving a statement of his experience. He signed off the ship's articles on 30 April, and received wages of £1. He returned home to his family in Southampton, after a two week absence.

Subsequently he appeared as a witness in the Board of Trade inquiry into the disaster, appearing as witness Number 8 on the fourth day of hearings

On the outbreak of the First World War he went back to sea – where another ship sank under him after being torpedoed.

He always refused to talk about the *Titanic* disaster. He was not close to his children, who at one stage were placed in a home as their mother could not manage them.

It is not known if he ever returned to Jersey. The date and place of his death are unknown, but there was a family story that he had collapsed in a street in Manchester. His second surviving son, Percy James Philip, who was aged 87 in December 1998 and was then living in Edinburgh with his wife, is reported to have said that his father had 'lost it' after the *Titanic.*

Descendants still run Poingdestre's Angling Centre in Shirley, Southampton.

THE JERSEY CONNECTIONS THE CREW

(III)
OTHER JERSEY CREW MEMBERS

"What are we waiting for, Mummy? Why are we waiting such a long time? "We are waiting for news of father, dear."

Overheard in Canute Road, Southampton
- reported in Daily Mail, 18 April 1912)

Percy Ahier
Steward, first class.

He was born in 1892, the second and youngest son of John William Ahier and his wife, Clara. The family then lived at William Cottage, 32 Columbus Street, St Helier. The 1901 Census show them still living there, but some time between then and 1911 the whole family had moved from Jersey to Southampton. His father worked as a carpenter and his mother as a dressmaker. Their address was 136 Northumberland Road, Southampton.

Percy was at sea, and served as a steward on the *Oceanic*; in April 1912 he was transferred to the *Titanic*.

For the voyage, his duties were to wait on passengers during mealtimes, and to reset the saloon in preparation for meals. His wages for this work were £3. 15. 0d.

He died in the sinking of the *Titanic* and his body was not recovered from the wreck scene afterwards.

Birthplace of Percy Ahier, 32 Columbus Street

His elder brother, Clarence, joined the Hampshire Regiment in the First World War, and was killed on 7 May 1918 while serving in the Middle East, in what is now called Iraq.

Their widowed mother, Clara, received financial assistance from the *Titanic* Relief Fund.

William Henry Rattenbury
Aged 36, he was the brother of E.J. Rattenbury, the secretary of the Jersey Football Association.

William Rattenbury

He trained as a cabinet maker, and in the 1901 census is listed as a furniture dealer, living with his wife, Louisa, and new-born son, Henry William, in Chevalier Road.

He was separated from his wife, Louisa, at the time of the *Titanic* disaster, so his sign-on address is listed as Southampton. His wife and ten-year-old son were living with her brother, Thomas Price, a photographer in Peter Street, St Helier, and then at 95 Bath Street in the flat above the old Tanner's bakery opposite the site later occupied by the Odeon Cinema.

At some time before 1912 he had moved to

William Rattenbury's family home in Bath Street

Southampton and started to work on liners as a steward. His last ship before the *Titanic* had been the *Olympic*.

When he signed on to the *Titanic* on 4 April 1912 he gave his name as "W. Henry" and his address as 27 Romsey Road, Southampton. As an 'assistant boots steward' in First Class (one of seven in First Class with that title) he received monthly wages of £3 15s. His job title might infer that he was employed to clean shoes, but in First Class in particular that would have meant he didn't have much to do: passengers would have had their own valets to do that job for them.

In fact 'Boots' is an obsolete Edwardian job title. 'Boots' were allocated a deck each and it was their responsibility to keep the stairs and passageways clean and tidy. They were, in effect, indoor cleaners. The external cleaning was handled by the Able Seamen.

His wife was able to claim from the Relief Fund for herself and their son, Henry William, who in later years is believed to have been a member of Jersey's first paid Fire Service, and played football for the Island.

Thomas Ryan
Steward, third class.

Born in St Helier, his father was employed by the Gas Company. There were two sisters, Rita and Mary, and a brother, Charles.

Thomas is listed in the 1901 census as an errand boy; he later worked as 'boots' at the Halkett Hotel – a job title of the period that signified an indoor cleaner.

It is believed he moved to Southampton in or approximately around 1907, by which date he had married 'Beatrice' and had two daughters, Mabel and Florence. An elder daughter, Georgina, had died as a young child.

He gave his age as 27 when he signed on the *Titanic's* articles on 6 April 1912. By then the family lived at 87 Albert Road, Southampton.

Before working on the *Titanic*, he had been working on the American liner, the *St Louis*.

He joined the *Titanic* at 6 am on 10 April as a third class (steerage) steward. For the voyage

he could expect to earn monthly wages of £3. 15s.

He died when the ship sank. It has been speculated that his body was one of those recovered later that week by the cable ship *Mackay Bennett*, but if so, it was never positively identified, and the body was returned to the sea during the course of a religious service.

His sister, Rita, was married to Frederick Charles Farmer who lived at La Chasse, St Helier, and they had three daughters. The unfortunate Rita received another sad blow less than three years later, in February 1915, when her husband, who had joined the Army, died as a result of wounds he had received on the Western Front. His youngest daughter, Violet, was only five weeks old. Rita died two years later – it was said from a broken heart, as a result of her double tragedy.

Thomas Ryan

Thomas Ryan's widow, Beatrice, and her children were awarded a weekly allowance from the British *Titanic* Relief Fund as a result of his death and the loss of his income.

Philip Vigot

Born in St Mary on 6 October 1879, Philip Vigot was 32 when he signed on the *Titanic*'s articles on 6 April 1912.

He was the son of Philip Vigot, a St Mary farmer, and his wife, Eliza. There were three other children, Eliza, Sidney and Susan.

In 1881 the family lived at Auckland House, St Lawrence.

He was 5ft 4in tall, with fair hair and blue eyes. He had tattoos on both arms, a crest on the right arm, and 'True Love' on the left.

Before sailing on the *Titanic*, he had been working on board the *Kinfauns Castle*.

He joined the *Titanic* at 6 am on 10 April 1912 as an able bodied seaman, at a monthly wage of £5. He gave his address as 2 Windsor Terrace, Southampton, and signed-on spelling his surname 'Vigott' – presumably as everybody with whom he came into contact pronounced his name in an English fashion, to rhyme with 'spigot'. He is also referred to as 'Pigott'.

He survived the sinking, leaving the ship as part of the crew of lifeboat number 13, from the starboard side. He was rescued by the *Carpathia*, brought to New York, and then returned to England on 20 April with other surviving crew members on the *Lapland*.

On arrival at Plymouth, the crew members were detained by the authorities, and he gave a statement of his experiences and was then released, signing off the ship's articles on 30 April, when he received wages of £1.

In mid May 1912 he made a brief visit to his sister, Susan, in Jersey, and then in London was called to the British *Titanic* Inquiry. However although attending the Inquiry, he was never called. He was able to charge attendance expenses of £8 12s and 6d – considerably more than the £1 he had received

Philip Vigot

for the few days he worked on the *Titanic*. Afterwards he resumed his work at sea.

In September 2010, the Société Jersiaise received a note from a 'Mrs Collins' in the UK enclosing what purported to be a form that he had completed when embarking on the *Titanic*, listing his personal belongings.

It is unclear why he would have had to fill in such a chit, which is dated 5 April. Included in his possessions are a can opener, pocket knife, lighter, gold ring, three-piece cutlery set and a silver pocket watch.

The letter read:

22.9.10
I have this Titanic document from P. F. Vigott Seaman on the ship Titanic. It was given to my cousin who died in May 2010, I would love the Société Jersiaise to have it.
Mr Philip Francis Vigott was born in St Mary's Jersey on the 6th October 1879 the son of Philip

(farmer) and wife Eliza.
He signed-on as "Vigott" and was rescued in Lifeboat 13. I hope this is of some help.

Yours sincerely
Mrs Collins
PS Sorry about the writing but I'm old.

'Mrs Collins' did not supply any contact details, so there was no way the Société could contact her for any more details. Suspicions arose that this document might have been some sort of fake, even if it did look suitably old, and even if it had been sent to the Société in good faith.

Commenting on this find to the Société, Jersey *Titanic* expert Mandy Le Boutillier wrote: 'Why is this [list of belongings] anything to do with the [White Star] line, anyway? The men had their dunnage bags, which were liable to inspection in case they didn't have just personal effects? Who would want to list these? Why would he have a can opener when he gets all his meals provided hot and free aboard? Why is it dated April 5th? Recruitment of general crew for all departments began in the Union hiring halls in Southampton on Saturday 6th April?'

It was also suspicious that the envelope that contained Mrs Collins' note and the chit did not have a discernable postmark. Furthermore, the font used on the printed form was not in use until

Wedding group: Tom Ryan (left); front, his sister, Rita and the groom, Fred Farmer. John Joseph Farmer VC, a relative of the groom, is pictured back row, 3rd from left.

the 1920s.

In short. although it appeared to be, at first sight, as Société librarian Anna Baghiani said, one of the most interesting pieces of information she had received in the decade she had worked at the Société, the likelihood is that the document is not genuine.

Walter Williams

Lived in Southampton, and was a steward on the *Titanic* working in second class.

He was born in 1884 in Southampton, the second of three children of Elizabeth Williams. There is no mention of a father living with the family in the 1891 or 1901 censuses; in the 1901 census his occupation is given as 'plumber'.

There is a definite Jersey connection by virtue of his marriage to Emily Eva Landick in 1907. Eva was the daughter of 'Mr L Landick' of Phillips Street, St Helier. She was a lady's maid, and they may have met and married in Southampton. By 1911 he and his wife were living there, with an 18-month-old son, Walter. They had three children in total; only Walter survived beyond infancy.

By now he was a seaman, and signed on the *Titanic* on 3 April 1912, having transferred from the *Olympic.* He gave his address as 52 North Bid Road, Southampton.

While on the *Olympic* in 1911, he had expressed concerns that there were insufficient lifeboats. He was on board that liner when it had a collision with *HMS Hawke*, which necessitated a trip to Belfast for repairs.

As a second class steward on the *Titanic* he received monthly wages of £3 15s.

Afterwards he recalled that the ship was in an unfinished state, and that paint on one of the lockers was still wet. He was surprised that no lifeboat drills had been held at any point during the voyage.

On the night of 14 April, a colleague joked to him: 'We've only hit an iceberg. It's another job for Belfast.'

As the ship went down, he made a jump for Lifeboat 13, which, like many others, appeared to be far from full. However, he was struggling in the sea and calling out for help, when he was heard by Guernseyman Joseph Duquemin in Collapsible Lifeboat D, who had himself just been hauled on board, much to the ire of the survivors who were already in the boat.

Duquemin in turn hauled Williams aboard, despite the anger of the other survivors, who threatened to throw Duquemin back into the sea.

He recalled later: 'During the night we were passed by what looked like a sailing ship. As we got closer we realised it was a small iceberg.'

At first, his family heard nothing from him, then, on Sunday 21 April, they received a cable from New York telling them he was returning to England immediately.

He lived the rest of his life in Southampton, and died there in February 1972 aged 87.

His niece, Elvina Pearce, was still living in Jersey in the 1990s.

Rita Farmer and her Daughter and Nieces

139

HOW THE NEWS WAS REPORTED IN JERSEY

'It is believed that not a single life has been lost'

The Morning News, Jersey, 15 April 1912

Monday 15 April

It was late in the afternoon that Islanders could read the first alarming reports in the Evening Post – and on the front page, no less, that was usually reserved for advertisements other than for exceptionally important or serious stories, the latest sports results or the most up-to-date reports on parliamentary debates.

The 'full story' could be found inside; as the front page carried only the latest stop press news, it gives the impression of starting in the middle of the story:

THE DAMAGED LINER SLOWLY MAKING FOR HALIFAX.

TWO STEAMERS STANDING BY.

VESSEL MAY BE SAVED.

PASSENGERS SAFE.

The Central News says: -

The majority of the 900 men forming the crew of the Titanic are either natives or resident at Southampton, and the first rumour of the disaster, which spread like wildfire, caused much consternation in the port. Captain E. J. Smith, the commander of the Titanic, has always been a conscientious worker, and his abilities fitted him for the command of the world's greatest ship. The connection with the White Star Line is a long one.

New York, Monday.

Mr. Franklin, Vice President of the International Mercantile Marine, has issued the following statement: -

"We have heard nothing direct from the Titanic, but are perfectly satisfied that the vessel is unsinkable. The fact that the Marconi messages ceased means nothing. It may be due to atmospheric conditions, or the coming up of the ships or something of that sort. We are not worried over the possible loss of the ship, as she will not go down, but we are sorry for the inconvenience caused to the traveling public. We are absolutely certain that the Titanic is able to withstand any damage. She may be down by the head, but would float indefinitely in that condition. We figure that the Virginian will be alongside the Titanic at 10 o'clock this morning, the Olympic by 3 this afternoon, and the Baltic by 4 o'clock."

The Olympic, which sent a wireless message to the Titanic direct at 4.24, was informed in a reply that great damage had been done. The captain reported that he would tranship the passengers to the first steamer which came alongside.

JUVENILE CONTRIBUTORS TO THE TITANIC FUND

A little girl in the front of the picture has a bottle in which a slit has been made for the reception of contributions to the above fund. Another juvenile is placing her offering in the box (Jersey Weekly Post).

The Virginian, which will in all probability be the vessel, will, it is believed, go back to Halifax (Nova Scotia). – Central News.

New York, Monday.

A dispatch from Halifax states that all the passengers on the Titanic had left the ship by 3.30 this morning. – Reuter.

New York, Monday, 10.40.

A wireless message has just come through from the Virginian stating that the Titanic is sinking. – Central News.

New York, Monday.

The "Montreal Star" reports from Halifax that the Titanic is still afloat and is pushing her way slowly to Halifax. – Reuter.

Halifax (Nova Scotia), Monday.

A message just received here states that the Titanic is still afloat at 8.30, and her engines were working. She was crawling slowly in the direction of Halifax and towards the Virginian. It is further reported that the women and children are in the lifeboats, which are ready to be lowered at a moment's notice, but this will not be done until it is certain that the vessel is actually sinking. The weather continues to be clear and calm. The

Titanic 's pumps are working at their utmost power.

The forward holds are full, but the watertight compartments are holding. There is good hope of the vessel making port. – Central News.

New York, Monday.

Mr Franklin, Vice President of the International Mercantile Marine, has issued an official message in which it is stated that the Titanic is heading for Halifax under her own steam.

A wireless message received at St. John's (New Brunswick), states that all the Titanic's passengers are safe. – Central News.

New York, Monday.

A message from Montreal timed 8.30 a.m. says that the Titanic is still afloat, and heading towards Halifax with her own engines.

The women and children have not been taken off, though the lifeboats are ready in case of emergency. It is thought the bulkheads will prevent her sinking.

A later message says that wireless telegraphy brings word that two vessels are standing by the Titanic and all the passengers have been taken off. – Central News.

The following are the Guernsey passengers on board: - Mr. Peter Renouf and wife, L.

Gavey, H. Williams, E. Jeffrey, C. Jeffrey, A. Denbuoy and Miss Emily Rugg, all of St. Samson's; Mr. C. R. Parker, St. Andrew's, Messrs. E. H Wheadon, H.H. Mitchell and C.R. Bainbrigge, St. Peter Port.

There was further amplification inside the newspaper on page 2:

THE LEVIATHAN TITANIC STRIKES AN ICEBERG.

CALL FOR ASSISTANCE.
Ships answering the Call for Help.

Hope for Passengers and Crew.

The Titanic Unsinkable.
MONTREAL, Monday.

A wireless message was received late last night from the Allan Liner Virginian, which sailed from Halifax yesterday morning, which reports that the huge White Star liner Titanic has struck an iceberg off Cape Race.

It is understood that the Virginian is now on the way to answer the call for assistance which was given by the liner, and is prepared, if necessary, to take off the Titanic's passengers.

The Allen Line officials have received no further news, but are expecting a message at any moment. – Central News.

NEW YORK, Monday.

A Cape Race telegram,

received at 10.35 on Sunday evening, says that the Titanic reports that she has struck an iceberg. Immediate assistance was required.

Another message, half-an-hour later, stated that the Titanic was sinking by the head, and the women and children were being taken off in lifeboats.

The liners Virginian, Olympic and Baltic are hastening to the assistance of the Titanic. The Virginian is 170 miles away, and the Baltic is 200.

The Virginian's operator says that the last signals from the Titanic were blurred and ended abruptly. – Reuter.

NEW YORK, Monday.

A telegram from Cap Race, Newfoundland, states that it is calculated that the Titanic struck the iceberg at about 10.30 last night. She carries 1,300 passengers, and was making her maiden voyage.

Later.

The messages, which are arriving here from Newfoundland with regard to the Titanic disaster, are reassuring in so far as they show that a number of vessels are within call of the Virginian and the disabled leviathan.

The Mauretania and Cincinnati are responding to the signal, as well as the German liners Prinz Adalbert, Amerika, Prinz Friedrich Wilhelm and other smaller ships.

Mr A.S Franklin, Vice-President of the International Mercantile Marine, in a statement this morning, says:- "No message has been received reporting the accident and if the collision occurred, the vessel is in no danger, since she is absolutely unsinkable. There is no cause for serious anxiety."

A wireless message which was sent to the Virginian and other vessels has failed up to the present to bring any responses. No news is expected for several hours.

Advices from Cape Cod state that the position of the Titanic when she struck the iceberg was 41.46 N, 30.14 W.

At midnight the Allen Line liner Virginian was 170 miles distant, and she was expected to reach the Titanic early this morning.

The White Star Liners Olympic and Baltic were also hastening with all possible speed to the Leviathan's assistance. – Central News.

The Central News was informed at the head offices of the White Star Line in London this morning that no official information has been received there regarding the disaster which had overtaken the Titanic. On learning of the accident from the papers the manager immediately telephoned to the firm's offices at Liverpool, but no information was to hand there.

The Central News says: - A rate of 80 guineas per cent is being quoted by undertakers this morning for business in reference to the Titanic.

In an interview, a prominent underwriter in the City said: "Even if the vessel gets into port the owners will have to calculate on a loss of at least a hundred and fifty thousand pounds; but if she becomes a total loss it will be a very serious matter for the company.

"The ship cost £2,000,000 to build, and her hull is valued for insurance purpose at a million sterling. Then there are all sorts of miscellaneous matters to be taken into account: Disbursements of passage money, freight (mostly paid in advance), stores, baggage, and other things. I do not suppose that the owners are covered to the extent of more than one million and a quarter, or at the utmost a million and a half."

So far as can be ascertained, there is no specie on board the Titanic, but the Central News learns that the vessel was carrying a large number of valuable postal packets.

The White Star liner Titanic and her sister ship Olympic are far and away the largest vessels ever built. The dimensions of each are:- length 682ft 6in, beam 92ft 6in, depth from keel to boat deck 97ft and tonnage 45,000.*i Their huge hulls divided into 16 watertight compartments contain nine steel decks and provide accommodation for 2,500 passengers besides a crew of 860. They are triple screw boats and their engines are 50,000 horsepower which propels them at a speed of 21 knots. Each vessel cost over £2,000,000.

JERSEY PERSONS ON BOARD THE TITANIC

With regard to the mishap to the liner Titanic, particulars of which appear in our telegraphic news, we learn that Mr Walter Williams, son-in-law of Mr. W. Landick, is serving as a 2nd class steward on the steamer.

Miss Ilett, of Millbrook, is amongst the passengers, and was bound for America.

Tuesday 16 April

The following morning, the next reports became available to the Jersey public via 'The Morning News.' It is remarkable rapportage, in so far that any connection with what actually happened is by and largely coincidental. As with so much of the initial press reports, there was little hard news, so gaps in information were filled creatively.

DISASTER TO THE TITANIC.

WORLD'S GREATEST LINER STRIKES AN ICEBERG.

Assistance Called by Wireless.

C Q D : C Q D : C Q D : Ships Respond and Hasten to the Rescue.

Late on Sunday night the White Star liner "Titanic" on her maiden voyage from Southampton to New York

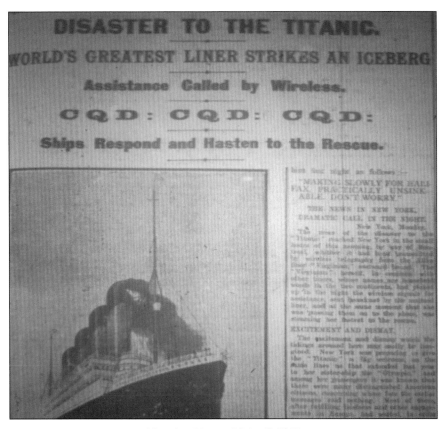

Morning News, 16 April 1912

collided with an iceberg in latitude 41.46 North, longitude 50.14 West. This is the season of the year at which the southward drift of the bergs calls for incessant watchfulness on the part of mariners traversing the North Atlantic, and the vessel's position shows that she was following the Southerly route.

The circumstances under which the disaster happened have yet to be narrated. The space-annihilating powers of wireless telegraphy alone made it possible for news of what had occurred to be known ashore within an hour or so, and since then, as may be readily understood, such messages as have come through have been brief and confined to statements as to the actual state of affairs at the time of despatch.

Up to last evening even these have been vague and occasionally contradictory. The latest advices, however, give grounds for the belief that while the great liner is in a perilous condition, there is no danger.

NO LOSS OF LIFE.

The "Titanic" carried altogether 2,359 souls, of whom over 1,400 were passengers. Her wireless signals picked up along the busy Atlantic shipping lines brought several big liners to the rescue, and all the passengers appear to have been safely removed. When they reach land at Halifax, or elsewhere, the world will hear the full story of the misfortune which has overtaken its largest and finest ship. Meanwhile an effort is being made to get the "Titanic" into Halifax, and given fair weather, she may yet be docked there.

LINER'S DANGEROUS CONDITION.
Halifax, N.S., Monday.

Wireless messages received here early this afternoon state that the condition of the "Titanic" is dangerous and that the lives of those that still remain aboard are in some peril. Great excitement prevails in the vicinity of the disaster, and in a mire of wireless messages from various steamers, it is difficult to get any connected story. The Government tug "Lady Laurier" is going from here to render assistance.

WIRELESS STORY OF THE DISASTER

The story of the disaster is briefly, and yet graphically told, in a wireless message received this afternoon from the Cunard liner "Carpathia," which runs in the Company's Mediterranean Service, and as will presently be seen, picked up the "Titanic's" signals when four days out on her voyage from New York to Gibraltar.

The "Titanic" struck the iceberg at 10.25 last night (American time). She was then running at reduced speed,

presumably from the knowledge of the proximity of the ice. The "Carmania," which came in yesterday, reported an abnormal amount of ice in the track of Trans-Atlantic shipping and some minor mishaps have been chronicled.

A THUNDEROUS IMPACT.

Most of the passengers had retired to bed, and were awakened and terrified by a thunderous impact which crushed and twisted the towering bows of the liner, and broke them in like an eggshell. It was clear that the promptest action was necessary. The behaviour of the crew is stated to have been exemplary, and they were assisted by many of the male passengers, who also succeeded in calming the women and children.

The wireless was immediately set going and, as a precaution, the majority of the passengers were placed in the liner's boats, which were swung out ready to be lowered.

The sea was calm, and although the sea was pouring into the vessel forward, her machinery had not been disabled, and when it was found that, with the pumps working, and the watertight bulkheads holding well, there was a good chance of the liner making port, the Captain set about proceeding slowly and cautiously in the direction of Halifax, notifying his intention to the vessels already speeding towards his aid.

A TRYING VIGIL.

It would have been a long and very trying wait until the hour at which the "Virginian," in her fastest stride, could have come up with the "Titanic," and happily most of the suspense was avoided, for just before daylight, the Cunard liner "Carpathia" which left New York last Thursday, arrived, and after an exchange of messages with the "Titanic," began preparations for the transference of passengers.

As soon as there was sufficient light, the boats were lowered away, and 1,300 of the 1,400 odd passengers which the "Titanic" carried were carried over to the "Carpathia" without accident of any kind.

THRILLING MOMENTS

Whilst the transhipment was in progress, the wind began to rise, and for a while, the work had to be suspended, but fortunately the calm was renewed.

Altogether twenty boatloads of people, according to an account which Capt. Haddock of the "Olympic" sent to New York by wireless, were thus taken from the "Titanic" to the "Carpathia".

The "Olympic", when this message was sent, was still 260 miles away from her luckless sister, but was in close wireless touch with her, and was able to assure New York this afternoon that the fears, which the temporary cessation of communication had aroused were groundless. Capt. Haddock added that the Allen liner

"Parisian" was standing by, and that the White Star "Baltic" was approaching.

Presently the "Virginian" also arrived and while the remainder of the passengers were being transferred to the "Parisian", the "Virginian" got ready to attempt the difficult task of towing the "Titanic" into Halifax.

The "Titanic" by this time was low in the water, and her foreholds were full, but her captain and crew were sanguine that the task would be accomplished, and that she would be safely docked. The rescued passengers are also being taken to Halifax, and I understand that the White Star Company is making special arrangements for their conveyance to New York. One special train to carry 600 people has already been ordered.

According to newspaper reports the "Titanic" was carrying something like five million dollars' worth of bonds, and jewels, etc. All these valuables, it is believed have been saved.

The latest messages state that the "Titanic" towed by the "Virginian" and under her own steam, is making slow progress towards Halifax.

PASSENGERS DUE AT HALIFAX WEDNESDAY.
Halifax, N.S., Monday.
Later.

A message was received here at 2 this afternoon stating that the "Titanic" is being towed to Halifax by the Allen liner "Virginian".

Her passengers have been transferred to the "Parisian" and the "Carpathia" and are expected to arrive here on Wednesday. Arrangements for their conveyance to New York are proceeding rapidly.

No direct news has yet been received from the "Titanic's" captain.

It is stated that there was some tendency towards panic among the passengers during the first few moments after the collision, but that the majority of them behaved admirably. Salvage tugs are preparing to go out and assist the "Virginian" in bringing the "Titanic" into port.

It is believed that not a single life has been lost.

TITANIC TO BE BEACHED.
New York, Monday.
Later.

A wireless message from the Anglo-American Coy's cable steamer "Minia," to the Government Marine Bureau, received late this afternoon states that the "Titanic" is slowly sinking. An effort will be made to beach her near Cape Race.

The Central News says the wireless operator on board the "Titanic" is Mr. Jack Phillips, son of Mr. and Mrs. G. A. Phillips. of Farncombe, Godalming, Surrey.

His parents received a message from him last night as follows:-

"MAKING SLOWLY FOR HALIFAX. PRACTICALLY UNSINKABLE. DON'T WORRY."*2

THE NEWS IN NEW YORK. DRAMATIC CALL IN THE NIGHT.
New York, Monday.

The news of the disaster to the "Titanic" reached New York in the small hours of the morning, by way of Montreal, whither it had been transmitted by wireless telegraphy from the Allen liner "Virginian," eastward bound. The "Virginian" itself, in company with other liners whose names are household words in the two continents, had picked up in the night the wireless signals for assistance, and broadcast by the maimed liner, and at the moment that she was passing them on to the shore, was steaming her fastest to the rescue.

EXCITEMENT AND DISMAY
The excitement and dismay which the tidings aroused here may easily be imagined. New York was preparing to give the "Titanic" a big welcome, on the same lines as that extended last year to her sister-ship the "Olympic," and among her passengers it was known that there were many distinguished American citizens, concerning whose fate the earlier messages said nothing. Most of these, after

fulfilling business and other engagements in Europe, had waited in order to enjoy the thrill of making the homeward journey in the world's greatest liner – the "millionaire's ship", - on board which they might almost be pardoned for considering themselves as safe as in their hotels on shore.

GREYHOUNDS RACING TO THE RESCUE.

The publication of the Montreal message, sent scores of anxious folk to the White Star offices here in quest of further information but there was nothing to tell them. For several long hours the officials were emphatic that the huge hull of the "Titanic," divided into watertight sections, each as big as a goodsized ship, was in no danger of sinking, and even, when the wireless at Cape Race announced that the liner was down by the head, and that preparations were being made to take the passengers off, they repeated their assurances, which in the light of later news seem to have been well founded. The cheering announcement was forthcoming that besides the "Virginian," which at midnight was 170 miles from the scene of the disaster, the White Star liners' "Olympic" and "Baltic," the Cunard liner "Mauretania," and three or four German and French liners were all hurrying in the same direction.

MESSAGES CEASE ABRUPTLY.

Some alarm was caused by newspaper statements that wireless messages from the "Titanic" had ceased abruptly, but Mr. A.S. Franklin, vice-President of the International Mercantile Marine, promptly discounted the rumours to which this statement gave rise, explaining that the cessation of communication might be accounted for in many ways. All that remained, therefore, was to await, with all possible patience and optimism, the results of the race which the vessels already named were putting up.

It was thought that the "Virginian" would be the first to come up with the "Titanic" and that the latter's Captain had already intimated by wireless to the "Olympic" that he should tranship his passengers at the first opportunity, in view of the extensive damage that had been done.

At the conclusion of the "Morning News' coverage there is a further section of 'STOP PRESS NEWS', added after the other articles had been laid out on the page, This 'news just in' is in a much more serious vein than the cautiously optimistic articles that precede it:

TITANIC REPORTED SUNK

Feared Great Loss of Life.

New York, Monday

A wireless message received at the New York Office of the White Star Company from Captain Haddock, of the "Olympic" states that the "Titanic" went down at 2.20 a.m.

The "Carpathia" is proceeding to New York with passengers.

Further news is anxiously awaited, dismay reigns at the White Star offices and fears are entertained that a number of the passengers and crew of the "Titanic" are lost.

Later.

Six hundred and fifty five of the "Titanic's" passengers and crew are known to have been saved. It is feared that the others have been lost.

NO MESSAGES FROM THE "TITANIC".

New York, Monday night.

Up to six o'clock this evening not a single message had been received here direct from the "Titanic," and it is assumed that the wireless telegraphic installation is out of commission owing to the stoppage of the engines.

Most of the news obtainable has been sent via the "Olympic".

WHITE STAR OFFICIAL'S OPINION
New York, Monday.

Mr. Franklin, Vice-President of the White Star Company in New York, at nine o'clock issued the following:

'The situation looks very alarming. There have been rumours from Halifax that there were three steamers with "Titanic" passengers aboard, namely the "Virginian," "Parisian," and the "Carpathia." We have heard from Capt. Haddock that the "Titanic" sank at 2.20 and also that the "Carpathia" has 675 passengers aboard. It is very difficult to say whether the "Parisian" and the "Virginian" have survivors aboard until we get a report from them. We have asked for that report from Haddock, and also from our agents at Halifax. We very much fear that there has been a severe loss of life, but it is impossible to give further particulars until we have assured ourselves that the other steamers have survivors.'

That same evening (Tuesday 16 April) the front page headlines in the Evening Post were:

THE TITANIC DISASTER - THE LINER'S FATE -

DETAILS OF WIRELESS MESSAGE FROM THE CARPATHIA.
New York, Tuesday 11.15 a.m.

The following wireless message from Captain Rostron of the Carpathia, timed 7.55 a.m., (New York time) and sent from latitude 41.45 north long. 50.14 west, has been received at the offices of the Cunard Co., New York :-

"Am proceeding to New York unless otherwise ordered with about 800 survivors. After consulting Ismay, and considering the circumstances, with so much ice about, considered New York best."

The message goes on to state that large numbers of icebergs are adrift in the vicinity of the disaster, the Carpathia, having traversed 20 miles of ice fields with large bergs imbedded in them.

After receipt of the foregoing message the following delayed wireless telegram came to hand from the Carpathia via Cape Race:-

"The Titanic struck an iceberg, and sank Monday, 3 a.m., at 41.46 north 50.14 west. The Carpathia picked up many passengers from boats. Will wire further particulars later. Proceeding New York. "

SCENES IN NEW YORK
Indescribable scenes are being enacted this morning outside the offices of the White Star Company, New York, and it has been found necessary to employ a guard of police to keep back the mob of hysterical people seeking news

of their friends and relatives. Men and women alike may be seen to break down as each successive bulletin is posted.
– Central News.

FEARED NO SURVIVORS ON THE PARISIAN AND VIRGINIAN.
New York, Tuesday, 11.30.
A telegram from Halifax, N.S., states that the Marconi wireless station is not yet in communication with the Virginian, but it is feared no Titanic passengers are aboard her. The Marconi wireless station at Sable Island is now in communication with the liner Parisian which states she has no survivors aboard her. A private message from Montreal announces that Mr. Charles M. Haye, President, Grand Trunk Railway, has been saved.

– Central News. New York, Tuesday, 12 o'clock.

A TELEGRAM FROM MONTREAL STATES: -
Capt Gamball of the Virginian has sent a wireless telegram to his agents at Montreal saying he arrived too late to rescue anybody and is proceeding to Liverpool.
– Central News.

THE SURVIVORS ON THE CARPATHIA.
New York, Tuesday.

A delayed wireless message received to-day by the Cunard Line from Captain Rostron, of the Carpathia, states: "We have about 800 survivors. We expect to proceed to New York. The ship at present is in the ice fields."

– Central News.

St John's, Tuesday.

The latest Cape Race advices indicate that only 675 people aboard the Carpathia were saved from the Titanic.

All the boats launched are accounted for, and they are mostly filled with women and children.

Most of the men aboard the Titanic went down with her.
– Reuter.

There was still a shortage of exact information, as can be judged by some of the contents of the inside page:

New York,
Monday 12.30 a.m..

A wireless message says twenty boatloads of passengers have already been taken aboard the Carpathia from the Titanic.

The Olympic is also nearing the Titanic, as also is the Baltic, while the Parisian and Carpathia are in attendance.
– Reuter.

New York, Monday.

The transfer of the Titanic's passengers was made safely in calm weather to the Carpathian and the Parisian. They should reach Halifax to-morrow.

Most of the Titanic's crew remain on board.

It was reported at 8 o'clock that all the passengers had been transferred from the Titanic.

Steamers are towing the Titanic and endeavouring to get her into shoal water near Cape Race for the purpose of beaching her.
- Reuter.

THE ACTUAL IMPACT
The Leviathan's Bows Stove in.
New York, Monday.

The Titanic was proceeding at reduced speed when she struck the iceberg, but the impact was sufficiently severe to crush in her bows like an eggshell.

The Cunard liner Carpathia, bound for the Mediterranean, arrived on the scene shortly before daybreak, and most of the Titanic's passengers were transferred to her; the remainder were taken on board the Allen liner Tunisian.
– Central News.

It was becoming clearer that there might be no survivors on other ships apart from the Carpathia:

Casualties Admitted.

New York,
Monday 8.40 p.m.

The White Star officials now admit that many lives have been lost – Reuter.

The "Daily Mail" New York correspondent telegraphed at 9.30 p.m. - The White Star Line now admit that probably only 675 persons out of the 2,300 persons on board the Titanic have been saved.

Mr Franklin, Vice-President of the White Star Co, admits that there has been a "horrible loss of life".

Mr Franklin adds that the monetary loss cannot be estimated tonight, but the loss is in the millions. "We can replace the money," he said, "but not the lives." The public is assembling in huge crowds outside the newspaper offices.

Anxious Relatives at New York.
Sufficient Lifeboats for all.
New York, Monday night.
The latest reports indicate that an unprecedented catastrophe has occurred in the sinking of the Titanic.

Six hundred and seventy-five of the passengers and crew of the vessel are known to have been saved, but 1,500 are not accounted for, although it is hoped that other survivors may be aboard the Virginian and the Parisian, but no reports have been received from these steamers.

When the news of the probable extent of the disaster became known many friends and relatives of passengers by the Titanic motored in evening dress from the Opera and from the theatres to the offices of the White Star Company.

Some of the ladies were sobbing hysterically and one frantically inquired for news of her sister who was returning from her honeymoon.

It is reported that Colonel J.J. Astor was drowned, but that Mrs. Astor was saved.

Mr. W.T. Stead, Mr. Bruce Ismay, and Major Butt (Mr Taft's Aide-de-Camp) are believed to be among the lost.

Mr Vincent Astor, accompanied by his cousin, and by Mr Dobbins, his secretary, called to see Mr Franklin at the White Star offices at 10 o'clock, and left the building ten minutes later. He was weeping.

General surprise is expressed at the inaccuracy of the news given out during the day.

ANOTHER JERSEYMAN ON THE TITANIC

Mr J. Ahier, a son of Mr J. Ahier, who formerly carried on a carpenter's business in the Island, but who had been residing in Southampton for some years, is a first-class-steward on board the Titanic, and the news of his safety will be welcome alike to his parents and his many relatives in the Island.

A rumour was current that Mr W.G Le Brun and family sailed by the Titanic, but we are officially informed that at the last moment they transferred from the Titanic to the Olympic.

Amongst the names of the second class passengers appear those of Mr A. Mallet, Mrs Mallet, Master A. Mallet, and Mr H.J Beauchamp, but at present, we are unable to state whether these are local.

Wednesday 17 April

The 'Morning News headlines read:

THE TITANIC TRAGEDY
– APPALLING LOSS OF LIFE – HELP THAT CAME TOO LATE

– LITTLE HOPE OF ANY FURTHER RESCUES

– Death toll approximately 1,200
– Terrible scenes when the Liner went down
– Survivors see the doomed boat disappear with hundreds on board.

And so, with every day that followed, the details were amplified and came a little nearer to what we now know to have been the facts of the disaster.

The general reporting of the disaster is fascinating to follow, especially on the Friday, once the Carpathia had docked at New York and reporters swarmed over the emerging survivors in order to obtain their 'stories'.

Each survivor interviewed could only have seen the disaster from his or her own necessarily limited or incomplete standpoint, and so some of the stories that were then reported became the origin of the 'Titanic myth' that subsequently developed.

As fascinating as it would be to reproduce all the articles, the space that would be needed to do so would entail a book in itself. Thus the only articles that follow are those that refer to Jersey survivors and local stories:

Morning News:

CHANNEL ISLANDERS ON THE "TITANIC."

Quite a large number of Channel Islanders were passengers on board the liner "Titanic," while three Jerseymen at least – Williams, Rattenbury and J. Ahier – were members of the ill-fated vessel's crew.

The following local names appear in the official list of passengers:-

Miss Bertha Ilett, Mr. A. Mallet, Mrs. A. Mallet, Master A. Mallet, and Mr. H. J. Beauchamp, (all believed to be of this Island).

Brother of the J.F.A. Secretary on Board

Much sympathy will be felt for Mr. E.J. Rattenbury, the Secretary of the Jersey Football Association, whose brother is one of the crew of the "Titanic". Up to a late hour last night no tidings had been received regarding his brother's fate.

From the Evening Post:

ANOTHER JERSEYMAN WHO WAS ON THE TITANIC.

Another Jerseyman was also on board and formed part of the staff, viz.: Mr W.H Rattenbury, son of Mr W Rattenbury, of Waterloo-street, and a brother of Mr. E.F Rattenbury, Secretary of the J.F.A. He was formerly in the furnishing business with his father in St Helier, and was second-class steward on the ill-fated vessel.

Amongst those saved from the Titanic, the name of Master Andre Mallet appears on the list published by the London "Globe".

Thursday 18th April

From the Evening Post:

THE TITANIC DISASTER

The following telegram was received by Mr G. Francis this morning: (Copy of telegram)

"Francis West's Pictures, Royal Hall, Jersey. Select early convenient date and commence advertising, under best obtainable patronage, benefit exhibition on behalf of bereaved Southampton widows and orphans through Titanic disaster, donating entire gross receipts of evening performance."

(Leading article)

THE TITANIC DISASTER THE RELIEF FUND

As the details of the disaster on the Titanic come to hand, and are pieced together, the more appalling it appears to be, and to the full justifies the Lord Mayor of London in opening a Mansion House Relief Fund and appealing to the Press of the United Kingdom to support his effort. We have every confidence that the Jersey public will add their mite to the list which we have opened in connection with this fund. There seems to be hardly a place in Europe or town in America, and even Jersey has not escaped, but can count some who have a relative or friend among the missing.

The harrowing scenes at the White Star offices in London. Liverpool, Southampton and New York tell of the agony of suspense endured by those on board the ill-fated vessel.

It is little use for us to be wise after the event by speculating why the vessel had not sufficient boats to accommodate all on board in case of disaster, or how so terrible a loss of life can be avoided in the future; this will receive the attention of those in authority. It rather behoves us to look facts in the face as they are, and realise that widespread distress which has been caused

	£.	s.	d.
H.E. Maj.-Gen., Mrs. A.N. Rochfort (Lieut.-Governor)	2	2	0
W. E. Guiton ("Evening Post")	1	0	0
W. G. Bellingham	1	0	0
W. Perrier	0	10	0
C. Metivier, jun,	1	0	0
R.	0	2	6
Col and Mrs. Stoddart	1	0	0
C. S. H.	0	5	0
M. F. H.	0	5	0
C. V. W.	0	2	6
G. M	0	2	0
J. F. T	0	2	0
	£7	**12**	**0**

to orphans and other dependants for their daily bread upon the efforts of father, brother or relatives who have gone down with the Titanic, and to do our share to alleviate their sufferings.

To this end we ask our readers to give as liberally as their circumstances will allow.

We have much pleasure in acknowledging the following sums, already received at our offices:

Still Another Jerseyman who was on the Titanic

We learn that another Jerseyman was on the Titanic. Yesterday Mr Fred Farmer, of La Chasse, telegraphed to his sister-in-law, who resides at 67, Albert Road, Southampton, asking if her husband, Mr Tom Ryan, was on board the Titanic, and last evening he received a reply from her stating that Mr Ryan was on board, and that she was worried as she had had no news as to his safety.

Mr Tom Ryan, who had been "boots" at the Halkett Hotel, left Jersey for Southampton some five years ago, and had since been sailing from that port on one or another of the Trans-Atlantic Vessels.

Titanic. It concludes: 'It is for the Board of Trade to see that whatever else besides, no passenger or seaman shall be left to drown because the boats carried are already full.'

From the Evening Post:
THE TITANIC DISASTER.
TWO MORE JERSEYMEN MEMBERS OF THE CREW.

A telegram was received this morning that Mr Olliver, one of the crew of the ill-fated Titanic, and a brother of Mr Olliver, third lighthouse-keeper at Corbière, is amongst the survivors.

Still another Jerseyman is reported as forming part of the crew of the ill-fated Titanic, the name of the seaman being Mr John Poingdestre, a son of Mr P.G. Poingdestre of No. 28, Old St John's Road.

Mr Poingdestre served in the Royal Navy, and after taking his discharge joined the White Star Company. His wife, whose maiden name was Gallichan, and who formerly lived with her parents in Albert-street, is now living with her four children at Southampton.

ill-fated Titanic at New York we are the better able to realise the heroic conduct of those who have perished, and the truly Christian fortitude with which they went to their watery grave. It is an example to which future generations can proudly point as the world's greatest example as to how a Christian should die – doing his duty and putting his trust in God, his Creator.

Here we have husband and wife parting, a wife leaving her husband to die a hero's death. Again, we read of those who have preferred to enter into the mysteries beyond the veil together. What more characteristic of the true Briton than the conduct of the Captain and his Officers who did their duty to the last.

Even the military fortitude of those British soldiers who, drawn in line on the deck of the ill-fated transport Birkenhead pales beyond the fortitude of the Band of the Titanic encouraging their fellows to bravely meet death to the strains of that best of hymns, "Nearer, my God to Thee." Surely such heroism deserves recognition at our hands, and how better can we do this than by giving our mite to succour the widowed and the fatherless.

A long leading article in the Morning News addresses the question of there being insufficient lifeboats for the number of people on board the

[Leading article]

THE TITANIC DISASTER

Now that the SS Carpathia has landed the survivors of the

From: The Morning News

Mrs Ilett's Thanks
Mrs Ilett, of Millbrook, whose daughter, happily, is a survivor

from the "Titanic", Miss Bertha Ilett, one of the survivors from the "Titanic" desires to express her deep gratitude to the many friends who expressed such sympathy and solicitude while her daughter's fate was still uncertain. As may well be imagined, Mrs Ilett was in a terrible state of anxiety and suspense, and the welcome news which we were able to communicate to her during the small hours of yesterday morning, afforded her inexpressible joy and relief.

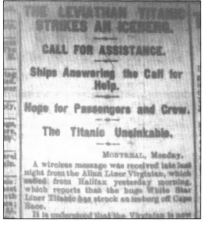

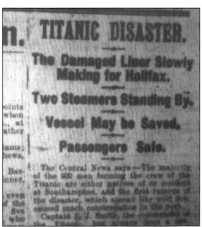

Jerseymen on the "Titanic"

Yesterday morning Mr E. F Rattenbury learnt by wire from the Company that his brother sailed on the "Titanic" and in reply to a subsequent wire sent from Jersey, received an answer to the effect that the Company much regretted his name was not among the list of the crew saved. Mr I. Poingdestre, of 28, Old St John's Road, reported to be on the "Titanic" left Southampton on the ill-fated steamer, but apparently did not go beyond Queenstown. We learnt that the family has received news of his safety.

From: The Jerseyman

The "Titanic"
– a *Titanic* Catastrophe

"Oh, hear us when we cry to Thee
For those on peril on the sea!"

The whole world stands appalled. Rarely in its history has there been such a ghastly calamity as that enacted in the blue but all-devouring Atlantic last Sunday night, the full significance of which no one will realise for months to come. The greatest ocean leviathan, but a few days ago the pride of her owners, who had witnessed hopefully the toil through long and anxious days, and the pride of the British nation, now lies irrecoverably buried in fathomless depths. The colossal amount of work expended on her becomes a mass of useless scrap-iron, a mere crumbled hulk. But worst of all, hundreds of human lives have been hurled into Eternity at a moment's notice. Oh, the tragedy of it all!

Words fail us – indeed they would fail the most brilliant word-painter of human tragedy – to depict the harrowing scenes when the Titanic took her final plunge; when her thousands of expectant passengers, full of buoyant hope and enthusiasm, contemplating their new surroundings in the New World, realised the awful fact of going "down to the sea in ships" and doing "business in great waters". All of it baffles realisation.

When we try to contemplate anxious relatives at home – aye, in our own sea-girt isle – scanning down with quick-pulsating hearts the lists of survivors and drowned, and when we think of that great port of Southampton, but a few miles from here, to which we ply daily and where scores of houses are wrapped in bitter sorrow, overwhelmed through the loss of the breadwinner, our heart bleeds. God! Is it a reality or is it only a dream?

One lesson does this terrible holocaust teach us. The Great Architect of the universe, who rules land and sea, is no respecter of persons. Millionaire and artisan – the occupant of the £850 staterooms and the £7 10s steerage passenger – have perished together and may at this very moment be locked in each other's arms "in the caverns deep of the ocean cold". Wealth does not mean immunity at the moment of peril; the two are by no means synonymous. Wealth, after all, is a multiplier of cares, the æs triplex of the heart, a barrier to the sincerest friendship.

The papers are full of regret of the wholesale destruction of these moneyed men. We are sorry for those they have left behind, but these are provided for. The world is worse off for the passing of that veteran journalist, W.T Stead, who (though he had passed the meridian of years, and though the views he held were not in agreement with many folk) must rank as one of the greatest men of modern times, but we are principally concerned with the hundreds of women and children, in a moment rendered widows and orphans by this appalling catastrophe. Words are but poor consolation, but if anything we can do or say will prompt one reader to give, however little, to the relief funds which will be opened, we shall feel that our appeal has not been in vain. If, looking back over life's little day, we shall be able to truthfully say that we have assisted, in however so small a measure, towards the alleviation of some misery, we shall realise that we have not been a failure, no matter how meagre our purse may be.

From: The Evening Post

SAFETY OF MR J POINGDESTRE.

We are pleased to learn that the relations of Mr John Poingdestre, who informed us yesterday that he was a seaman on the Titanic, have received a telegram informing them that he is safe.

Tom Ryan

ANOTHER VICTIM OF THE TITANIC.

On Thursday last we stated that Mr Fred Farmer, of La Chasse, had received a telegram from his sister-in-law in Southampton, stating that her husband, Mr Tom Ryan (who was previously the 'boots' at the Halkett Hotel) was on board the Titanic in the stewards' department. This morning another telegram was received by Mr. Farmer from Mrs. Ryan stating that her husband is among the lost. The deceased was only 27 years of age and leaves a widow and two children, aged 4 and 2 years respectively.

From the Deaths column

RATTENBURY – Drowned on the ss. Titanic. William Henry Rattenbury, oldest son of Mr and Mrs W Rattenbury, in his 29th year. Deeply mourned.

Monday 20 April
From: The Morning News

ANOTHER JERSEY SURVIVOR.

Anxiety concerning Mr. Walter Williams' safety was allayed yesterday, when a cable message was received from New York reporting him to be safe and on his return journey to England.

Mr. Williams, who is a son-in-law of Mr. W. Landick of Philip Street, was a steward on board the "Titanic". His wife resides in Southampton.

"TITANIC" BENEFIT PERFORMANCE AT THE OPERA HOUSE.

Another benefit performance in aid of the "Titanic" Relief Fund is announced for next Friday evening, when a grand benefit performance of Albany Ward's picture and variety entertainment will be given at the Opera House. Simultaneous "benefits" in aid of the same cause will be given that night at no fewer than twelve of the Albany Ward theatres, while it may be noted that Mr. Ward has already forwarded to the Lord Mayor's Fund a cheque for 100gs.

From The Evening Post

THE LOSS OF THE TITANIC
MEMORIAL SERVICES

Practically in every place of worship in the Island yesterday reference was made to the terrible disaster that had befallen civilisation in the loss of the Titanic, and in many instances, though not holding a special memorial service, the preachers made direct reference to the disaster in their sermons and prayers.

At a very large number of both churches and chapels the beautiful and touching hymn, "Nearer, my God, to Thee", was sung, and there is no doubt that the words went home to the hearts of many with greater force than ever before.

At several of the places of worship the "Dead March" was played at the conclusion of the service as a tribute to those who went down with the vessel.

Collections on behalf of the fund for the relief of sufferers were made at some of the churches and chapels and a large proportion of the others are devoting next Sunday's offertories to the object.

ROYAL CRESCENT CHURCH

The preachers yesterday at the above Church were the Rev Herbert Jones in the morning and the Rev J Penry Davey in the evening; the latter preached a most impressive memorial sermon on the loss of the Titanic. Special hymns were sung, and "Nearer, my God, to Thee" was sung by the congregation, whilst the Dead March in "Saul" was played at the close of the service. A collection was devoted to the fund.

PRIMITIVE METHODIST CHURCH

At the Primitive Methodist Church in Aquila-road, the Pastor, the Rev F.S Clulow preached on the Titanic disaster and the lessons to be learnt therefrom at the morning service, and took for his subject "The sympathetic Christ" in the evening. Both services, which were largely attended, were of a most impressive character. During the evening Mrs W.P Nicolle gave a most sympathetic rendering of the beautiful solo "Some day we'll understand". "Nearer, my God, to Thee" was sung at both services.

VICTORIA-ST. CONGREGATIONAL CHURCH

At the Victoria-street Congregational Church last night Miss K.N Forbes' sweet soprano voice was heard to great advantage in the sacred solos "O, Rest in the Lord" and "Nearer, my God, to Thee". Mr Ph. Syvret, jun., church-organist, played Chopin's funeral march before the sermon, and the Dead March in "Saul" at the close, the congregation standing. The Rev. Carey Walters preached a most impressive sermon on the lessons to be learnt by the Titanic disaster. Good congregations attended throughout the day.

SALVATION ARMY, NO. 1 CORPS

The band of the Salvation Army, No. 1 (St Helier) Corps, played the Dead March in "Saul" last evening in the Parade, in the presence of a large gathering, proceeding later through the streets of the town. A memorial service in connection with the Titanic disaster was held later in the Oddfellows' Hall.

Next Friday night has been set apart at the Alhambra for the benefit of the Titanic Disaster Fund. Mr Munro has secured the services of a number of local artistes, who will appear on this occasion. The proceeds of this entertainment will be handed over to the Lord Mayor's Fund. The performance will commence at 9pm. Carriages at 11.45pm.

THE LOSS OF THE TITANIC

Proudly sailed the finest vessel
That the world had ever seen,
In the glorious April sunshine,
With her human freight serene;
Stately gliding, grand majestic,
Like a Queen!

Though it was her maiden voyage,
Not a qualm was there, for sure
Were the great Titanic's water-
Tight compartments, vast, secure,
Scorning dangers, were these
not a Cynosure?

But when South of Bable Island,
Crept a stealthy, unseen fate,
For which no man's skill and
wisdom,
Iron and steel were adequate,
Where the Ice-floes and the
Icebergs
Lay in wait!

They made sport of man's
invention,
Split the vessel's hull like glass,
And the Ice-fiends tossed their
fragments,
Killing some on board, alas!
There were thirty miles of shifting
Ice to pass!
For two hours none dreamed of
danger,
With the snow some played and
laughed,
But at length the boats were
lowered;
She was sinking! This safe craft!
In the ice cold sea some plunged to
Seek a raft!

In these days of waning manners,
The Titanic's heroes shine;
They cried: "Women first and
children!"
For their selflessness sublime,
Glory in their glory! Sound their
Praise condign!

Who can tell the tales heroic
Of the Captain's nobleness?
Of the Officers' the Seamen's
And the Passengers' address?
When they realised their utter
Hopelessness?

Who can tell the deeds of courtesy
When to give place meant sure
doom?
When the scarceness of life-saving
Apparatus cast its gloom,
And self-sacrifice bore humbly
Glory's plume?

There were Captain Smith and
Astor,
There were simple gentlemen,
Aye! And rough uncultured
sailors,
Everyone was ready, when
Sounded forth the call for them to
"Die like men!"

Every heart is rent with anguish
At our noble heroes; fate;
At their lofty, high-souled courage,
At their deeds, compassionate,
At their noble self-repression
Passionate!
Let us bow our heads, imploring
God to comfort all who weep,
Who have left their loved ones
waiting
Their dread summons to the
deep!
They have yet another sacred
Tryst to keep!

"Nearer, my God, to Thee," they
played
On Titanic's sinking deck,
As they saw their last hope
vanish,
Sixteen hundred, neck by neck!
Sixteen hundred! Desolated
On the wreck!

The Titanic pitched prow forward
Two explosions! – rearing high
In the air her stern, she slowly
Settled – Darkness ! – To the sky
There arose the mingled shrieks of
Agony!

Thou who gav'st Thy life for
others,
Thou alone canst tell the price
That it cost those noble heroes,
And how great their sacrifice!
They are "Nearer, now, to
Thee," in
Paradise.

SARAH BENSON
Holly Lodge.

Thursday 25th April

From: The Evening Post

A SURVIVOR OF THE TITANIC DISASTER.

Amongst the survivors of the ill-fated Titanic disaster is Lady Duff-Gordon, the sister of the well-known authoress, Mrs. Carr-Glynn, both being in their youth, as the Misses Sutherland, very well-known members of island society, when these two lovely sisters were the belles of every social function! Lady Duff-Gordon was going with her husband on a trip to New York, and we offer our heartfelt congratulations on their fortunate escape from the fate which befell so many of their fellow passengers.

BENEFIT PERFORMANCES OF THE TITANIC FUND.

To-morrow evening three benefit entertainments are being given in aid of the Titanic Disaster Fund : - At the Opera

House at 8 o'clock when in addition to the magnificent pictorial and variety programme being given this week, there will be extra attractions. Price as usual.

At the Alhambra, Phillips-street, at 9 o'clock, there will be a big programme. The usual fine entertainment will be augmented by items by well-known local artistes. Prices as usual.

At the Oddfellows' Hall at 8 o'clock, by request and in presence of Mr. J. B. Pinel (Mayor) and the Municipality of St Helier, and under the patronage of H.E. the Lieutenant-Governor, "The Tyranny of Tears" recently performed with much great success will be repeated. Admission 3s. 1s. 6d., and 1s.

Saturday 27th April

From: The Evening Post

THE TITANIC FUND FOOTBALL MATCH ARRANGED

We are informed that the local Football Association are endeavouring, at the request of the English F. A., to organise a match in aid of the Titanic Fund. The game will probably be between a representative Island XI, and the 1st Devon Regiment, and efforts are being made to bring it off on Thursday next, the F. A. having extended the playing season to May 4th for the purpose of these benefit matches.

West's Picture Palace should be well patronised on Monday next, when every penny received at the three performances (3, 7 and 9) will be forwarded intact to the Titanic Disaster Fund. A special train will leave the Terminus Station for St. Aubin's at 11 p.m.

The Brigade Band, under the direction of Mr. A. McKee, will play in the Triangle Park on Sunday, May 5th, when a collection will be made in aid of the widows and orphans of the Titanic disaster.

From: The Jerseyman

LESSONS FROM THE TITANIC.

The news which reached Jersey (as we were printing last week's issue on Friday) of how the Titanic went down, was such as to stir the hearts of the most stolid. The reading of the latest and most graphic details, though heartrending enough, had one redeeming feature, for it showed to all the world that heroism is not yet extinct. That gallant orchestra playing as the great ship dived on and into the grey Atlantic; that hero of heroes, Captain Smith, on the bridge with his last megaphonic message, "Be British"; the sacrifice made by noble men for the weaker sex – all these things will live till the end of all time. We read stories of heroism of the

olden days; they appear like fairy tales to us, and we treat them of very little significance, but here today, in our own lifetime, are displayed acts of self-sacrifice and bravery such as the world has never known. Men and women have hearts after all, and there is something good in the most vile. It is not always necessary to go about with a sanctimonious face. What counts is to know what to do and how to act at the critical moment. Those souls on the Titanic met death like brave men; and after all, perhaps dissolution ion this form, though terrible and tragic, is to be preferred rather than in a long, lingering and painful illness. "Greater love hath no man but this, that a man lay down his life for his friends."

Tuesday 30 April

From: The Morning News

THE "Titanic" RELIEF FUND WEST'S SUCCESSFUL EFFORT

The management of West's Picture Palace have scored a splendid success over their generous and unsparing effort on behalf of the Mayor of Southampton's "Titanic" Relief Fund. Each of the three entertainments given at the Royal Hall yesterday on behalf of that deserving fund was well attended, it being strikingly noticeable that at the 7 and 9 o'clock entertainments the audience that filled practically every seat in the comfortable hall was representative of every class of local society.

Among those present at the 9 o'clock house were His Excellency Maj.-General A. N. Rochfort, K.G.B., C.M.G., Lieut-Governor, Brigadier General J. W. Godfray, Mr. and Mrs. Whitaker Maitland, Col. and Mrs J R. Yourdi, Col. Bishop and party, Dr, Mrs., and Miss Bentlif, Mrs. and Miss Le Cronier, and Lieut T.L. de Faye. The members of the St. Helier's Fire Brigade were also present in uniform.

During an interval in the evening performance, Mr. Geo. Francis, to whose indefatigable efforts much, if not all, the success is due, announced, amid considerable applause, that although it was not then known exactly how much the fund would benefit as a result of that day's special performances, the sum raised would at any rate exceed £32 out of which £6 12s. 0d. had been raised by little Miss Marie Francis. Mr. Francis also expressed his own and the Management's thanks for the prompt and ready support which His Excellency the Lieut.-Governor had accorded the effort.

It is not necessary for us to add that the programmes presented by the Management gave very considerable pleasure to the audience, and that tis fact was borne out fully by the hearty outbursts of applause which resounded at intervals through the hall.

It but remains for us to warmly congratulate Mr. Francis and the Management of this hall for the very gratifying success achieved. The efforts made to ensure the day's performances being successful have been, in our opinion, amply rewarded.

From the Evening Post

THE TITANIC FUND THURSDAY'S FOOTBALL MATCH

The Island selection committee last evening selected the following team to represent the Island in Thursday's football match against the Garrison: - Garnier; *Whitworth, Boones; Beasley, Reed, Millow; Bonnen, Moyse, Turner, Wheway, Fox.*

Wednesday 1 May

From the Evening Post

The Salvation Army in St. Helier's No. 1 Brass Band will play in the Triangle Park to-morrow evening from 8 to 10, in aid of the Titanic Fund.

A Grand Whist Drive and Dance in aid of the Titanic Fund will be held at the West Park Pavilion to-morrow evening. Also, in aid of the Titanic Fund a grand football match – Island v. Garrison – will be played at Westmount to-morrow evening kick-off at 5.15.

Friday 3 May

From the Morning News

When anything happens, Mr. Albany Ward is one of the first to secure cinematograph records of such occurrences, therefore at great expense a film, dealing with the greatest maritime disaster of recent years, has been obtained, and shown at the Opera House last evening before a crowded audience.

The pictures are brim full of interest from start to finish, as well as being especially steady and clear. Capt. Smith is first shown standing on the bridge of his vessel, and an exceedingly fine view of icebergs in the vicinity of the catastrophe is also obtained. Society ladies are next seen bringing clothing and other necessaries for the survivors, prior to the "Carpathia's" arrival in dock, this vessel also being shown on her way to New York with the rescued. The other scenes include the crowd anxiously awaiting news at the White Star offices, New York; the Cunard Docks; the "Mackay Bennett" leaving Halifax, and numerous survivors, ending with a magnificent coloured effect of the last resting place of the "Titanic's" victims.

These pictures will be again on view this and to-morrow

Another " Titanic " Survivor.

On Two Wrecks in a Month.

John Thomas ('Jack') Poingdestre

evenings and we would recommend those who have not already seen this remarkable film to certainly do so.

Saturday 4 May
From the Evening Post

THE OPERA HOUSE
In consequence of the great success of the Titanic disaster film, it will be retained for three nights longer, Monday, Tuesday and Wednesday : - also next week's magnificent coloured drama film (over three thousand feet in length) "Tragedy at the Court of Milan," will be shown, in addition to a big programme.

COLLECTIONS FOR TITANIC FUND
At St Ouen's and St George's Churches, to-morrow, collections will be taken on behalf of the Titanic Disaster Fund.

The Brigade Band of the R.M.I.J. (under the direction of Mr. A McKee, bandmaster) will play in the Triangle Park from 8.15 to 9.45 to-morrow evening, when a collection will be taken on behalf of the Titanic Relief Fund.

Tuesday 7 May

From The Evening Post

By this time the Relief Fund had reached a total of £373- 7s- 3d

ACKNOWLEDGMENT FROM THE LORD MAYOR

We have received the following to-day from the Lord Mayor of London, in acknowledgment of the £300 which we forwarded last week, as a first instalment to the Fund which he so promptly opened for the relied of the sufferers by the Titanic disaster:-

Mansion House
London, E.C,
May 6th, 1912

DEAR SIR, -

I sincerely and gratefully thank the kind-hearted residents in the Island of Jersey, who touched by the pathetic narratives in the columns of "The Evening Post" and the "Jersey Weekly Post" of the Titanic disaster, have remitted to you, already, a sum of £300 for the relief of the sufferers. Their help in this respect will be greatly appreciated. If you will express my appreciation to the donors I shall be deeply obliged.

Yours truly,
Thom. Boor Crosby

Lord Mayor.

W. E. Guiton Esq.,
"The Evening Post."
St Helier, Jersey.

Friday 17 May

From the Evening Post

We have now closed this Fund, which, for Jersey, we may say without fear of contradiction, forms a record for any newspaper list, not only in the amount raised, but in the prompt and generous spirit in which the public responded to our appeal, on behalf of the Titanic sufferers.

In the name of those bereaved ones we tender the warmest thanks to those who according to their means contributed to such happy results. Especially are thanks due to those Anglican and Free Church clergymen who joined hands in pleading the cause of the widows and orphans with such marked success.

Those who have given will have the satisfaction of knowing that the Fund will be administered under the advice of the Lord Mayor of London, whose grateful acknowledgment of the first of instalment of £300 we have already published, and to whom we have forwarded a sum of £107 6s. 9d. making in all £407 6s. 9d. for which we know that we may expect a similar expression of gratitude and congratulations to the people of Jersey for the practical manner in which they have shown their sympathy for the sufferers by the Titanic disaster.

Saturday May 18th
From: The Jerseyman,

THE TITANIC DISASTER

The night was calm; the stars shone bright
O'er North Atlantic seas
As the mammoth liner ploughed her way
Before the gentle breeze.
Her passengers, both rich and poor,

Revelled in spirits bright;
No thoughts of danger crossed their minds
On that clear starlight night

Suddenly a cry rings out
From crow's nest up aloft:
"Icebergs ahead, Sir!" shouts the man
In accents loud and short.
Then comes a crash! The vessel shakes
As she receives the blow;
The keel is torn from bow to stern
By ice, the mariner's foe.

She staggers like a wounded thing
This grand, palatial ship,
As the cruel water rushes in
(This was her maiden trip).
"All hands on desk," the cry goes round,
"The boats now, lower away":
"Women and children first to leave"
Is the order of the day.

Husbands and wives must parted be,
There are not boats for all;
And O! the agonizing scenes.

How they our hearts appal!
Meanwhile, by wireless telegraph,
For succour they've appealed,
But other ships are too far off;
The steamer's fate is sealed.

The lifeboats now have got away,
But many souls remain
Aboard the slowly-sinking ship –
All honour to their name;
For each man stands unto his post
Prepared to meet his death.
The Captain shouts, "Be Britishers!"
With his last dying breath.

The liner slowly settles down,
The waters reach her decks;
The lifeboats, in the distance dim,
Appear as tiny specks.
But stay! What is that sound we hear?
Oh, look! The sight is grand!
There, grouped together on the deck.
Is the liner's little band.

"Nearer, my God, to Thee! – the strains
Come floating o'er the seas –
O God! If ever heroes lived
Of noblest breed, 'tis these.
At last she takes her final plunge
In that cold, icy sea,
And fifteen hundred souls are hurled,
Into Eternity!

Once more the sea its toll hath ta'en
O Lord! We raise this prayer
For wives and children: Give them strength
Their awful griefs to bear.
Comfort them now, and give them grace
To look for that bright dawn
When the sea again gives up its dead,
On the Resurrection morn.
R.J.W.

Footnotes

1) The gross register tonnage of the *Titanic* was 46,329. The year after it sank, the German liner Imperator eclipsed it with a gross tonnage of 52,117. The tonnage of these gigantic vessels of the time is compared to the *Queen Elizabeth* (1940) 83,673 and the *Queen Mary 2* (2004) 151,400. In Channel Island waters, the *Condor Express, Vitesse* and *Rapide* weigh in at 5,005; the *Condor Clipper* conventional ferry has a gross tonnage of 14,000.

2) This was a misunderstanding. The telegram was sent by Jack Phillips' uncle (also called John Phillips) from London, but his parents assumed incorrectly that it was from their son. They informed the press of their mistake the following day.

Birthplace of Jack Poingdestre, 28 Old St John's Road

OTHER CHANNEL ISLAND CONNECTIONS

(I)

TWO LIVES TO REMEMBER

'There were 2,200 people on board that ship - that means 2,200 different stories '

Jersey Titanic researcher Mandy Le Boutillier

The stories of actor Kenneth More, and of Commander Charles Lightoller, whose character he portrayed in the film, 'A Night to Remember'

Of all the films that recount, interpret or embellish the story of the *Titanic,* a good candidate for winning an award to be the best and most true to life of them is the 1958 film, *'A Night To Remember'*. It is a factual account of the sinking, based on the first-hand information available at the time from survivors.

It starred the well-known actor, Kenneth More, then at the height of his fame – and the connection with the Channel Islands is that as a boy he lived in Jersey and attended Victoria College from 1926 to 1931.

In 1957, the year before *'A Night to Remember'* was released, he presented his old school with an oil painting of King Charles I, which still hangs prominently in College Hall.

This great *Titanic* film was based on the book of the same title by Walter Lord, published in 1955. Both book and film had the benefit of using as consultants a number of people who had been on the *Titanic*, and there appears to be a degree of authenticity in the film lacking in other productions.

It is certainly more authentic than the 1997 film, *'Titanic'*. This latter film is undeniably entertaining and certainly a good film - which it should be: at $200 million, it cost more than it did to build the *Titanic* itself: to construct the ship in 1910-1912 cost only £1.5 million or $7.5 million.

But however entertaining the Cameron film might be, whatever the quality of the acting and the power of the special effects, it seems a shame that, in telling a story of a ship that contained so many people with interesting lives and such real-life drama, the film focused on an imaginary romantic sub-plot, and on some fanciful incidents that subsequently caused great offence and distress to the descendants of those portrayed, such as the relatives of First Officer William Murdoch.

The most authentic parts of the *'Titanic'* film were 'borrowed', more or less intact, from the earlier *'A Night to Remember'* film. Kenneth More had earlier starred in a number of other famous films of the 1950s, such as *Genevieve* (1953) *Doctor in the House* (1954) and *Reach for the Sky* (1956), in the latter film portraying Douglas Bader, the famous RAF fighter ace.

In each of these films he played, affable, bright and breezy characters that, to quote a review: 'epitomised the traditional English virtues of fortitude and fun.' At the height of his fame in the 1950s he was Britain's most popular film star. Later in his career he played Jolyon Forsyte in BBC Television's "*The Forsyte Saga*" (1967) and the title role in "*Father Brown*" (1974).

Born in 1914, his father had independent means, but unfortunately had a habit of spending more money than came in.

One of the many posters for the film.

Things improved when he was offered the job of general manager of 'Jersey Eastern Railways'.

For the young Kenneth More, coming to Jersey meant release from a boarding school in Sussex that he hated. His family arrived in Jersey during the summer holidays, so he had a month or so swimming, wind-surfing on a 'sand-yacht' he rigged up himself, and lazing by the Havre des Pas swimming pool, 'eating sweets and drinking pop'. They lived at Ellangowan, a house near Fauvic that was supposed to be haunted.

He started school at Victoria College Prep, and moved up to the senior school at the age of 12. He did well at soccer and 'not too badly' at athletics, and, to quote from his autobiography, *'Happy Go Lucky'*: 'My favourite trick at that time was pedalling my cycle down a hill near the school' [College Hill?] 'and swerving round a sharp corner at the bottom, seeing how close I could get my head to the ground.'

Aged 15 he took part in his first school play, *"The Sport of Kings"* playing the part of a red-haired girl.

'The applause was gratifying. I was such a dud at lessons that praise made a welcome change. But girls' parts seemed a horribly unnatural piece of type-casting. The other boys ragged me, passing me bits of paper with "Kiss me, sweetheart" written on them in class, and wolf-whistled at me in the corridors. From now on, I thought indignantly, I'm going to play my own sex.'

His first male part at the school was in J.M. Barrie's *'The Admirable Crichton.'* Years later he would play the lead in both the screen adaptation and the stage musical.

'"Watch Mr More," wrote the critic in the school magazine, "he should go places." I carried that review in my pocket for days, forcing the conversation round to it and thrusting it at people whether they wanted to read it or not. On the whole though, I didn't give much thought to theatricals, I was far more keen on sport.'

He continued his narrative: 'Father settled down well in Jersey. The line he controlled was exactly nine miles in length, running along the southern coast of the Island from St Aubin through St Helier to Gorey Castle. It was thought by some of the Islanders to be an inefficient railway. Father breezed in and changed all that. The trains were again running on time.'

'Father did a lot to improve relations between the railway management and employees. I have a clear memory of him setting off every Christmas morning to give a turkey, a box of cigars and a bottle of whisky to every stationmaster on the line.'

However, the end of his time in Jersey was not too happy: his father was once again spending more than he earned, but a financial crisis was staved off when he was offered another job. It kept him travelling a good deal and his wife often accompanied him, but Kenneth stayed on in Jersey, staying at a friend's house. When his father developed a kidney infection his fees at College were paid by his mother.

It was 1931; he was aged 17, had failed School Certificate in nearly every subject, and had to earn a living. He was summoned to the study of the headmaster, A H Worrall, who asked him: 'What are we going to do with you? Your scholastic record is appalling.'

His father obtained for him an apprenticeship at Sentinel Rail Waggon Works at Shrewsbury, and although it didn't seem too exciting, at least it seemed a secure job at an uncertain time. So he packed his suitcase, kissed his family goodbye, and bought a train ticket to Shrewsbury.

From there, after many adventures, he drifted on to the stage, and his acting career began.

In 1962, he presented to his old school the annual Kenneth More Prize for Drama. He died in 1982 from the effects of Parkinson's Disease.

The *Titanic's* Second Officer, Charles Lightoller, whom he portrayed in *'A Night to Remember'*, had led an adventurous life, both in his previous and subsequent careers.

At the age of 13 in 1888, he had left his native Chorley in Lancashire to begin a sea-going apprenticeship. By the time he was 21 he was already a veteran of one shipwreck, a fire at sea and a cyclone. He obtained his Mate's ticket, and left sailing ships for steamships. After a further three years, in which he almost died of malaria on the West African coast, he left the sea and went to the Yukon to prospect for gold in the Klondike Gold Rush. That proved unsuccessful, and afterwards he had a stint as a cowboy in Alberta, Canada before working his passage home to Britain as a cattle wrangler on a cattle boat. He arrived back in Britain penniless, obtained his Master's Certificate in 1899 and re-joined the Merchant Navy, working again in a cattle boat, this time as a Third Mate.

In January 1900 he joined the White Star Line, serving on the *Majestic* under Captain Smith, then on the *Oceanic,* and was then promoted to First Officer on the *Majestic,* before moving back once more to the *Oceanic* as its First Officer.

Lightoller boarded the *Titanic* just two weeks before her maiden voyage, and sailed as First Officer for the sea trials, but was dropped to Second Officer as sailing day approached.

On the night of the disaster – well, the story can best be told by watching the film. However, in brief: he had been on duty, but his watch finished at 10 pm. Before going off duty he instructed the crow's nest to keep a sharp lookout for ice. After being relieved by First Officer Murdoch, he did his rounds and then returned to his cabin at 11.40 pm.

He was just nodding off when he felt a grinding vibration. He went on deck and concluded that the vessel had hit something, but there was nothing to be seen, and no sign of undue alarm on the bridge. He returned to his cabin, where ten minutes later, Fourth Officer Boxhall told him that the water was already flooding the Mail Room. So he pulled on some clothes over his pyjamas and went out on deck.

As soon as he received the orders, he started loading women and children into the lifeboats, at one point threatening a group of men with an (empty) gun and driving them out of the boat, which enabled him to load 36 women and children into it.

A collapsible life boat was loaded and sent away, and he was working on freeing the second collapsible lifeboat when the ship took a great plunge forward. He dived in to the sea, and although he was sucked against the grating of one of the large ventilator shafts,

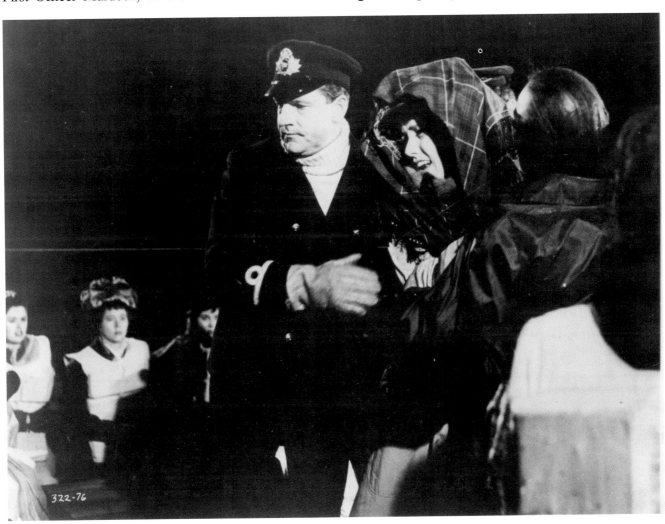

A picture from the film showing Kenneth More as Second Officer Charles Lightoller

167

and was taken down with the ship, a blast from the still hot boilers blew him back to the surface again. He found himself near the collapsible Lifeboat B, and clambered on to it.

When they were picked up by the *Carpathia,* he helped all the survivors out before climbing on board himself – the last *Titanic* survivor to be taken on board. After it arrived in New York, he testified at the American Inquiry and then at the British Inquiry.

In 1913, he returned to sea as First Officer of the *Oceanic.* On the outbreak of war, the liner became HMS *Oceanic,* an armed merchant cruiser, and he was commissioned as a Lieutenant in the Royal Navy.

In the course of his war-time service he suffered two further sinkings, including that of the *Oceanic.* In late 1915 he got his first command: a torpedo boat, with which he attacked a Zeppelin with the ship's guns, and was awarded the Distinguished Service Cross and was also promoted to commander.

He achieved a bar to his DSC and left the Royal Navy at the end of 1918.

He returned to the White Star Line, but found that, in common with the other surviving *Titanic* officers, he was always being passed over for promotion and seemed destined to remain a chief officer. After 20 years of company service, Lightoller resigned.

He tried various civilian occupations before purchasing a former Admiralty steam launch, which he had refitted and converted into a diesel motor yacht, the *Sundowner,* for trips around England and Europe.

In July 1939, Lightoller was approached by the Royal Navy and asked to perform a survey of the German coastline. This he and his wife did under the guise of an elderly couple on holiday in their yacht.

A poster advertising the film

When World War II started in September 1939, the Lightollers were raising chickens in Hertfordshire.

On 31 May 1940, Lightoller got a phone call from the Admiralty asking him to take his yacht to Ramsgate, where a Navy crew would take over and sail her to Dunkirk. Lightoller informed them that nobody would take the *Sundowner* to Dunkirk but him.

On 1 June 1940, the 66-year-old Lightoller, accompanied by his eldest son, Roger, and an 18 year old Sea-Scout named Gerald, took the *Sundowner* and sailed for Dunkirk. Although the boat had never carried more than 21 persons before, they succeeded in carrying a total of 130 men safely from the beaches of Dunkirk.

It is said that when one of the soldiers who clambered into the rescuing yacht heard that the skipper had been on the *Titanic,* he wanted to jump overboard again – he preferred the idea of waiting on the beaches for the next boat. It was pointed out to him that if Lightoller could survive the *Titanic,* he could survive anything and that was all the more reason for staying.

Following Dunkirk, Commander Lightoller joined the Home Guard, but the Royal Navy engaged him to work with the Small Vessel Pool until the end of the war.

His youngest son, Brian, was in the RAF as a pilot and was killed on 4 September 1939 in a bombing raid on Wilhelmshaven.

Their eldest son, Roger, went on to join the Royal Navy where he commanded Motor Gun Boats. In March 1945 he was killed during the German Commando raid on Granville that was launched from Jersey.

Charles Lightoller was 'demobbed' in 1946 at the age of 72. He died in 1952.

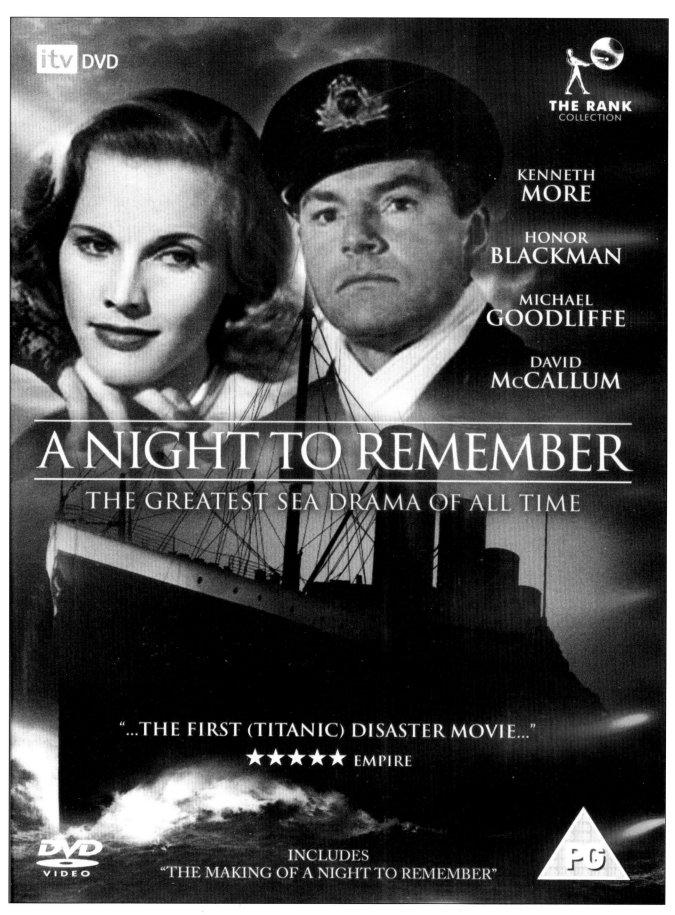

The latest DVD version of the Classic film

OTHER CHANNEL ISLAND CONNECTIONS

(II)
THE COLLECTOR

'Turn out, you haven't half an hour to live'

- Boatswain Alfred Nichols' rousing the crew after the collision

A collection of bits and pieces that, like their owners, survived the *Titanic* – and, unlike their owners, are still with us today… to handle them seems to make that tragic night quite real and close to hand.

The items are part of a much wider collection owned by David Gainsborough Roberts, a collector and resident of Jersey.

Mr Roberts has some 50,000 antique pieces in his ownership, of which 5,000 have got a personal association with the rich or famous – or infamous. It is these items with 'personal association' that particularly fascinate him.

Examples include the robes worn by T.E. Lawrence (Lawrence of Arabia), the largest collection of Bonnie and Clyde memorabilia, including the bullet-proof vest worn by Clyde Barrow, and a selection of Wyatt Earp memorabilia. He is perhaps best known for his collection of dresses worn by Marilyn Munro in a number of famous films. These were the subject of an exhibition in the Jersey Museum in 2009 and 2010, and at the time of writing in late 2011, are on display at the American Museum in Bath.

His first 'collectible' was a piece of wood from HMS Victory, given to him as a birthday present at the age of 10.

'I remember looking at this piece of wood, and was amazed that I was handling something that perhaps Lord Nelson had touched, or perhaps he had died close to it. At a later date I acquired one eighth of the flag in which his body had been wrapped; again, I like to imagine that my piece of material was once in contact with his body.'

A second theme of his collection is articles that are associated with violence or calamity. In 1997, he acquired a watch owned by Dr. Hawley Crippen, who famously murdered and dismembered his wife in 1910, and the death mask of the 1930s American gangster, John Dillinger ('Public Enemy Number One'). He has been a frequent visitor to Tombstone, Arizona, and is an authority on the career of Wyatt Earp.

Among much else in his collection he owns a deckchair and lifejacket from the passenger liner *Lusitania,* which was torpedoed in 1915, and also several pieces of *Titanic* memorabilia, all of which he has acquired at public auction.

His pieces relating to the *Titanic* are:

- a set of keys to the lamp locker on the *Titanic,* which crew member **Samuel Hemming** put in his pocket before swimming away from the sinking ship;

- a silver napkin ring, the property of first class passenger **Edith Rosenbaum**;

- a '**Carpathia Medal**' – the survivors from the *Titanic* presented every member of the *Carpathia's* crew with a medal as a token of gratitude and appreciation;

- a medallion given to a volunteer, for fund raising work for the *Titanic* Relief Fund in London;

- a fur coat belonging to **Mabel Bennett,** a stewardess, in which she wrapped herself to keep warm before climbing into a lifeboat;

- the certificate of discharge for **Mabel Martin,** who worked in the ship's Ritz Restaurant.

Samuel Hemming, a native of Southampton, was the lamp trimmer on the *Titanic*; he was married with several children. Aged 43 at the time of the *Titanic* disaster, he had been at sea since the age of 15, and had been with the White Star Line for the previous five years, serving as a lamp trimmer, Boatswain's mate, and Boatswain. His

The set of keys

duties on the *Titanic*, in his own words (from the evidence he gave to the US Senatorial *Titanic* Inquiry, were: 'to mix the paint, and all that kind of thing for the ship, and to look after all the decks, trim all the lamps, and get them in proper order, and to put the lights in at night-time and take them off at daybreak.'

He was in his bunk at the time of the impact, was woken by it, and on looking out of a porthole to find out what had happened, he saw that the ship had scraped an iceberg. He heard the noise of escaping steam coming from the forecastle at the bow of the ship, went to investigate, and discovered it was air escaping from the locker where the anchor chains were stowed. The water was rushing in very fast, and was displacing the air under pressure – hence the hissing sound. Hemmings reported what he had found to the Chief Officer, and then returned to his bunk, presumably to get some more sleep.

Unfortunately for him, he was only just getting himself comfortable a few minutes later, when the ship's joiner appeared to advise everyone in the cabin: 'If I were you, I'd turn out. She's making water one-two-three, and the racquet court is getting filled up. Then the Boatswain, Alfred Nichols appeared: 'Turn out, you haven't half an hour to live' - a remark that could well define that popular phrase 'a wake-up call'. He continued: 'That is from Mr Andrews' [the shipbuilder]. 'Keep it to yourselves and let no-one know.'

Wisely, he got out of bed once again, and left the cabin so quickly that he left his lifebelt behind. He helped prepare the lifeboats, and then went to collect lamps for the lifeboats, which were in a locked compartment in the Lamp Room. He unlocked the compartment, collected the lamps, and returned with them to the lifeboats, where he distributed them. He then resumed working to clear lifeboats and the collapsible boats. Finally, he swam away from the sinking ship (without his life belt but with the keys to the lamp closet still in his pocket) and was picked from the water by the occupants of lifeboat 4. He died in Southampton in 1928 aged 59.

Mr Roberts said: 'He was known as 'Plenty-of-Time-Sir Hemming' because that is what he said as the officers tried to make him hurry to the boats.

Perhaps he thought that despite everything, this was to be only a precautionary evacuation. In the end, he heard the call "Every man for himself" – shouted three times – and it was at that point that he slipped into the water.'

A silver napkin ring might seem an odd priority to choose to take into a lifeboat. But it was in the pocket of the coat of **Edith Rosenbaum,** a fashion buyer and consultant, and correspondent of 'Women's Wear Daily' newspaper. She had been reporting on the latest French fashions at the Easter Races at Longchamps, Paris, and then decided to return on the *Titanic* (first class), which she boarded at Cherbourg. She was aged 33 at the time and was a member of a wealthy Jewish family in Cincinnati, Ohio.

The napkin ring

As the *Titanic* lay off Queenstown, she posted a letter to her secretary in Paris, mentioning the fact that she had a premonition of something going badly wrong on the voyage.

In the time of confusion before entering the lifeboats, she ordered a steward to retrieve from her cabin a 'lucky mascot': - a small toy pig covered with white fur. Winding its tail caused it to play a piece called 'Maxixe'. The incident is portrayed in the film 'A Night to Remember'.

Perhaps the silver napkin ring – it is marked with her pet name, 'Edille' – was another such lucky or sentimental keepsake.

David Gainsborough Roberts with Mabel Bennett's fur coat

She eventually left the *Titanic* on lifeboat 11; while arguing with sailors about whether to climb into a lifeboat or not, a sailor grabbed her 'lucky pig' and said: 'You can do as you want, but I'm going to save your baby', and grabbing the pig, he threw it into the lifeboat.

She recollected later: 'I said "That settles it. Here I go. I'm going to follow that pig." He threw me head foremost and I fell on to the bottom of the boat… In the lifeboat I sat on the gunwhale , and the children were crying and whimpering and it suddenly struck me, "I believe I'll play music, and the little children will be diverted and amused." And there I sat and all night long I played them my pig and the poor little children were so interested in the music box that they stopped crying.'

During the First World War she became what was possibly the first female war correspondent and spent time in the trenches with the troops. The rest of her life continued to be adventurous – she even escaped a second shipwreck. It is easy to imagine her as a celebrity television news reporter, born before her time. She lived for many years in London hotels, and died in London in 1975 at the age of 98. She never married.

The **Carpathia Medal** was presented to the crew of the *Carpathia* by the grateful survivors of the *Titanic*. The captain, Arthur Rostron, received a silver and gold medal and a silver cup; officers received a silver medal; other crew members received a bronze medal.

The back of the Carpathia Medal

The medal now in the possession of Mr Roberts is one of the bronze medals presented to crew members.

All the medals were presented to the ship's company by that famous and heroic *Titanic* survivor, Margaret Brown – who was called afterwards 'the Unsinkable Molly Brown'. The nickname was something of a media invention, since her friends always called her 'Maggie'. However it is as 'Molly Brown' that she has gone down in history.

She was a strong-spirited woman; she and her husband were both the children of Irish immigrants and together had realised the American dream; her husband had become very wealthy in a career involved with engineering and mine ownership. She was a philanthropist, a socialite and an activist in various causes such as campaigning for women's suffrage, and alleviating poverty among miners' families.

On the night of the *Titanic* disaster, she was on her way from Cherbourg to New York, travelling first class (she had separated from her husband a few years before). She helped others board the lifeboats, and was persuaded finally to leave the ship in Lifeboat Number 6. Afterwards, she was regarded as a heroine for her efforts to force the boat to go back to search for survivors. She took an oar and helped row the lifeboat, and vigorously urged that the lifeboat should return to the immediate area of the sinking to try to save more people.

In charge of the lifeboat was Quartermaster Robert Hichens, who believed that not only would anybody more be saved by going back, but that the boat would be capsized by the mass of people struggling to get into it from the water. It is unclear who won the argument – acording to some reports she seized the tiller of the lifeboat from Hichens to turn it around in order to pluck survivors from the freezing ocean. It is believed that at least some extra people were taken on board and saved, thanks to her efforts.

In later life she continued with her philanthropic work, and during the First World War helped wounded French and American soldiers, as well as restoring localities in northern France devastated by the warfare. She received the

Légion d'Honneur from the French government for her work.

'The Unsinkable Molly Brown' died in 1932 at the age of 65.

Captain Arthur Rostron of the Carpathia was acclaimed as a hero for his major part in saving the *Titanic* survivors. He was a guest of President William Taft at the White House, and was presented with a Congressional Gold Medal, the highest honour the United States Congress could confer upon him.

The medal of the **'Balham and Tooting** *Titanic* **Relief Fund'** refers to one of the very many fund-raising initiatives that sprung up around the country after the tragedy: a generous response by the public to the unexpected tragedy that devastated the families of passengers and crew, and left families of crew members bereft of their financial support from the breadwinner of the family.

The sinking of the *Titanic* was the largest maritime disaster ever to hit one city. A total of 724 of the crew members lived within the Southampton area; only 175 of these returned home.

The RMS *Titanic* Relief Fund was started within days of the tragedy, and raised by public subscription upon the invitation of the Lord Mayor of London. Funds poured from countless sources, and from all parts of the English-speaking world.

The medal in the possession of Mr Roberts was struck by the Heaver Estate in South London, and presented to local fund raisers.

A fur coat that saved a *Titanic* survivor is a real link to the night of the disaster. It is an imitation beaver coat, worn by *Titanic* stewardess **Mabel Bennett.** She was aged 30, married, and lived in Southampton. She had two close relatives working as stewards on the *Titanic*: her brother, Alfred Crawford (survived), and her nephew (son of her elder sister), Leonard Hoare.

She was in bed at the time of the collision; startled by the noise of the impact, she jumped out of bed, and flung her fur coat over her night dress before rushing on deck.

According to her great-niece, who inherited the

coat in due course, she was in a nervous state, and did not think to make contact with her relations, and the fact that her nephew died in the disaster meant that she was ostracised by the rest of her family for ever afterwards.

She got away from the stricken ship in Lifeboat 5, and the warm coat undoubtedly helped to keep her alive until rescue by the Carpathia.

In the early 1960s she gave the coat to her great-niece, Renée Wedge, as the weight of the coat had become too much for her. Mrs Wedge did not realise that the coat had any particular significance, and even had it shortened as it was much too big for her, and shorter-length furs had by then become more fashionable.

Mabel Bennett, who had married a second time to a Mr Walker, died in about 1975, in her late eighties.

In the mid 1990s, her great-niece attempted to donate it as part of an aid appeal for war victims in Bosnia, but the coat was rejected because it was too heavy.

By this time she was a pensioner, and on moving out of her home, sent many of the contents for auction. The house clearers almost rejected the coat as well: they did not see any market for such an 'un PC' item and did not want something like that to be auctioned by them.

According to Mr Roberts: 'The men from the auction rooms were much more interested in an antique silver photo frame. Inside was a picture of an old lady wearing a fur coat. They suggested to their customer, the pensioner, that she might like to keep the photo if it had sentimental associations for her. She replied "That's my great-aunt, wearing the coat I showed you just now. She was wearing it when she left the *Titanic*...."

'The auction house changed their minds about that coat very quickly! Their customer got a very nice windfall sum of money for it!'

There was some doubt about the details of the provenance of the coat at the time of the auction, and some experts on the *Titanic* challenged its authenticity. The details of Mrs Wedge's signed statement at the time of the auction seem to confirm the authenticity of the coat as a *Titanic* 'relic'.

The final artefact in his collection belonged to **Margaret ('Mabel') Martin,** who worked as a cashier in the ship's Ritz Restaurant. It is her certificate of discharge.

She was 20, single, and came from Acton in west London. The *Titanic* was her first ship. She was rescued in lifeboat 6.

The Ritz Restaurant where she worked was a superlative restaurant, and was for the exclusive use of first class passengers. It was in addition to the sumptuous first class dining saloon. The Ritz had the advantage of being open from 8 am till 11 pm daily. The manager was Luigi Gatti, who had been poached by the White Star Line from what was at that time one of the best West End Restaurants: Oddenino's, in Regent Street.

Most of the staff were Italian (26) or French (17). There were only six English nationals employed. In all 68 men and women were employed in the restaurant; of these, three survived the disaster.

Two of them were women employees; the two cashiers Ruth Bowker and Mabel Martin were

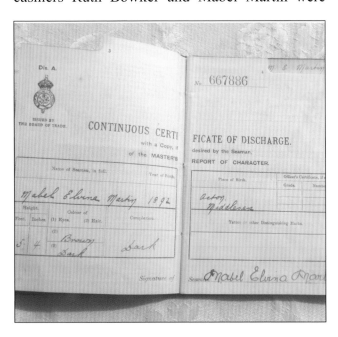

Certificate of discharge

All of the artefacts together

found places in a lifeboat on the principle of 'women and children first'. Of the rest of the staff, only the head waiter, Paul Maugé, survived by jumping from the deck into a lifeboat that had just been launched. In doing so, he broke the legs of

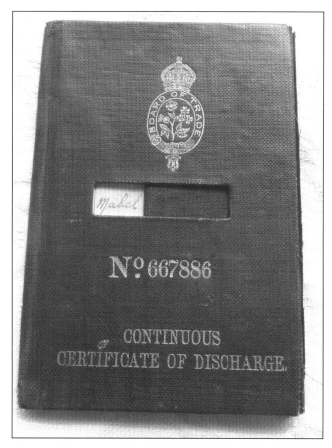

Front of the certificate of discharge

The front of the Medal

the woman passenger on whom he had landed.

In St. Joseph's Church, Bugle Street, Southampton, is a small memorial to the men of the Ritz restaurant. It is a small brass plaque attached to a table leg, under the table top, and is inscribed: *In memory of the Restaurant Staff, subscribed by Colleagues and friends.*

Mr Roberts said: 'I met her daughter and she told me that her mother never spoke about the ordeal. She said that she never went on a boat again, except for a trip they made on the Serpentine, and when she was splashed by her children, she said: 'If you had heard those screams you would never do such a thing.' It made her children feel as if they had done something truly terrible.

'Tragically, after surviving the *Titanic* when she was just 20, she was killed in 1960 on a zebra crossing by a motorcycle that failed to stop.'

He added that when entering into the employment of the White Star Line, she must have had it drummed it in to her: 'Never lose your certificate of discharge.'

There is, of course, only one entry in her book, which was completed by the White Star Line after her return to England. In the box for 'conduct' is written the word 'good'. Under the ship's name, is written, unintentionally as laconic as any famous epitaph, the two simple words: 'Vessel lost'.

OTHER CHANNEL ISLAND CONNECTIONS

(III)

THE MARITIME HISTORIAN AND COLLECTOR

'There was too much brag and not enough seaworthy construction.'

Sir James Bisset, future Commodore of the Cunard-White Star Line, in 1912
second officer on the Carpathia, discussing the construction of the Olympic and Titanic.

John Ovenden was born in Jersey. He began diving in 1989 and has extensive knowledge of the wrecks around the Channel Islands. A specialist in underwater videography he has formed his own company devoted to search and recovery and underwater film production.

In 1995 he produced a television documentary *"The Wreck of the Stella , Titanic of the Channel Islands"* which was broadcast on BBC as well as German and Discovery television channels around the world. In 1999 he collaborated with David Shayer on the hardback book *"The Wreck of the Stella, Titanic of the Channel Islands"*

This was followed in 2001 by a 60 minute documentary *"PT 509 - The Last Patrol"* The PT 509 was a motor torpedo boat which sunk off Jersey in 1944 by the Germans. This film was broadcast on the History channel around the globe.

This led to their publication of their second book *"Shipwrecks of the Channel Islands"* in 2002. This book describes twenty-two sea disasters from Roman to modern times, covering passenger, cargo vessels and warships.

The book provides a wealth of new information and brings together a large collection of previously unpublished photographs.

John has always been a keen collector of Maritime history. The largest piece in John's collection is the wreck of the *MV Heron* which sank in 1961 after hitting the Paternosters. John has accumulated a large collection of local memorabilia as well as White Star and Cunard Line items. He has a passion for *Titanic* and *Olympic* artefacts.

John Ovenden

Memorial service, St Luke's, April 1912

White Star Line logo on the plates

Plate and sugar sifter, knife and fork from White Star Line First Class, These used on Titanic's sister ship, Olympic.

White Star Line serving dish and cover from the Olympic

Titanic's sister ship Olympic arrives in New York on her maiden voyage, 21 June 1911.

RMS Olympic was the lead ship of the Olympic-class ocean liners built for the White Star Line, which also included Titanic and Britannic. Unlike her sisters, Olympic served a long and illustrious career (1911 to 1935), including service as a troopship during World War I, earning the nickname "Old Reliable." For a short time she was the largest ocean liner in the world.

OTHER CHANNEL ISLAND CONNECTIONS

(IV)
THE RESEARCHER

It was a terrible sight all around (the upturned lifeboat) — men swimming and sinking. Others came near. Nobody gave them a hand. The bottom-up boat already had more men than it would hold and was sinking. At first, the large waves splashed over my clothing; then they began to splash over my head and I had to breathe when I could'

- Harold Bride, radio operator on the Titanic, interviewed by the New York Times.

A Jersey crew member of the *Titanic* is buried in St Saviour's Churchyard in an unmarked grave.

There should be a headstone or visible marker above it, believes researcher Mandy Le Boutillier, to mark the resting place of Alfred Olliver, quartermaster, and one of the few *Titanic* survivors to have actually seen the iceberg at the time of impact.

Mandy is the person who in Jersey, at least, is probably best qualified to be called an authority on the *Titanic*.

A member of the British *Titanic* Society, the *Titanic* Historical Society, and the *Titanic* Verein Schweiz (there were a number of Swiss nationals on the *Titanic*), she has a particular interest in the *Titanic's* senior radio operator, Jack Phillips. She was instrumental, in 1997, in assisting his home town of Godalming to organise the 85th anniversary commemoration of his death, with the curator of the local museum at the time, Adela Goodall. In 2012, she is helping to organise a similar commemoration to mark the centenary.

She said: 'Everybody remembers about Captain Smith, Mrs Astor, and Ben Guggenheim, but how many people know about William Rattenbury, the assistant "boots" steward, who lived in Bath Street, St Helier, in a flat above a baker's shop? His story, and that of so many other people aboard the *Titanic*, is equally interesting and important.'

Any visitor to her home would quite soon realise that here lived someone for whom the *Titanic* was, at the very least, a serious hobby. A framed photo of the doomed liner leaving Southampton takes up a significant space on the wall of her sitting room. The books in the capacious bookcase are, solely, about the *Titanic*.

Her interest in Alfred Olliver's grave is twofold. First, as a long-standing member of a global 'community' of enthusiasts, she is aware of how many people there are with an interest in visiting the graves and memorials of *Titanic* victims.

If his grave were to be properly marked, she believes, it would draw many enthusiasts to the Island, or at least provide another attraction to tourists with even a passing interest in the *Titanic*.

Secondly – it would honour an Islander who underwent a traumatic experience, and participated - albeit perforce - in an event that has become rightly part of the story of our history as a nation. A marker on his last resting place would be right and fitting, and a tangible link to the past.

Mandy works as a compliance and money laundering reporting officer at the Jersey offices of an asset management company. Her interest in the *Titanic* began in 1986 when she read a book on the *Titanic*, 'Triumph and Tragedy', by John Eaton and Charles Haas – the two authors have since become good friends.

Gradually she became more and more involved in the '*Titanic* community', and over the years made many *Titanic* friends around the world, travelled widely and completed a lot of research.

The *Titanic* was not the worst-ever maritime

Mandy Le Boutillier

disaster – there have been others of equal or greater severity. But it was probably the first 'multi-media' disaster: the first time that people could use Marconi's new invention to find out – quickly – the details of an important news story, and the names of those who had been killed and survived.

In fact, the New York Times published three lines about the *Titanic* on its front page, first edition, published at 12.30 am New York time, on Monday 15 April 1912 – a time when the *Titanic* had not yet actually sunk. Under the headline, TITANIC HITS ICEBERG? it stated: 'Montreal, April 14 – The new White Star liner, *Titanic*, is reported in advices received here late to-night to have struck an iceberg.'

'That is quite incredible,' she said, 'as good as anything in our modern days of twenty-four-seven news coverage. The story broke so early because a ship travelling in the opposite direction to the *Titanic*, the *Virginian* picked up her distress signals. She was carrying a cargo of fresh apples. Naturally, she wanted to go to assist the *Titanic*, but she needed to get permission first from her Canadian owners, the Allen Line, to turn around, because the apples would be in danger of getting spoiled if they abandoned their course. A wireless message to the owners was sent accordingly, and this was picked up by a journalist, following a tip-off from one of the Allen Line's staff.

"This sounds like a good story", he must have

The Iceberg

thought, and immediately he passed it on to a friend of his in New York, who passed it on again to the New York Times. Its legendary editor, Carr Van Anda, presumably took the view: "I can't verify this, but I'll take a punt on it," and published three sentences. He got the world exclusive.'

Mandy's research into the *Titanic* story over the years has been considerable. 'Most people who get hooked by the *Titanic* eventually specialise in one part or another of the story. There are some who are just interested in the movies, some who research people from a specific country or profession, and there are those whom the rest of us teasingly call "rivet counters"- they are the people with an interest in the engineering details of the ship. They can tell you how many port holes were on each deck, how many rivets there were to a plate, or details about the electrical system. That's not exactly my own interest – I really don't have a clue about any of that!'

She continued: 'Like all "*Titanic* people", if I know of a town that has a got a *Titanic* memorial, and I happen to be in the vicinity, I go to see it. One day, in 1993, I happened to be near Godalming, in Surrey, so I made a detour to see what I thought was just a plaque. It turned out to be a building – the Phillips Memorial Cloister and Gardens - and in fact it is the largest memorial in the world to a single *Titanic* victim, the senior wireless operator, John George ('Jack') Phillips. It covers over three acres.

'I found the plaque, but discovered it was just the centrepiece of the memorial – a large red-brick cloister, surrounded by an open field of wild flowers, a bowling green, bandstand and a walkway along the River Wey.

'I thought it was a lovely memorial, so I went to the local museum and library to find out more about it, although there wasn't much to find out. However, chatting to Alan High, one of the museum's "friends" who was the volunteer looking after the museum for the day, I found out that he used to live next door to Jack Phillips' sister – one of the many coincidences that happen in *Titanic* World!

'Alan helped me with research and in making

Underway

many local contacts; my knowledge of Jack Phillips and his family grew. Sadly, in 1996, Alan passed away, but the following year – the 85th anniversary of the *Titanic* disaster – the museum and local community organisation "Go Godalming" asked me to assist when they organised a month-long programme that included a memorial service in the cloister. It was a recreation of the cloister's opening ceremony in April 1914.

'As part of the commemoration there was an exhibition in the town's museum. We located an oil painting of Phillips that had been done in 1913 as a gift to the town from the headmaster and past pupils of Godalming Grammar School, which he had attended. It had been in storage in the Borough Hall safe for about 20 years; we arranged for it to be restored and it became the centrepiece of the exhibition.

'We also persuaded a local stonemason to clean and restore (free of charge) the Phillips' family grave. The grave features, somewhat bizarrely, an iceberg-shaped tribute to him from his parents and sisters.

'For the centenary, the Museum's exhibition

co-ordinator and Go Godalming are planning an updated version of the events of 1997, and I am helping them to create a new exhibition. The last one was more about the *Titanic* in general; this new one is more about Jack and his part in the disaster.

'Also, in the past 15 years, so much more new information has been gleaned – often from Godalming people with new information about him and his family – that I now know much more about him than I did when we organised the original exhibit.'

Jack Phillips was just short of his 25th birthday when he boarded the *Titanic*, and celebrated it during the voyage. His father managed the Farncombe branch of Gammon's, a drapery shop in Godalming. He was educated at Godalming Grammar School, leaving at the age of 15 to join the Post Office, where he trained as a telegraphist.

In 1906 he left to be trained at the Marconi Company's Wireless Telegraphy Training School at Seaforth Sands near Liverpool. Upon graduation he received his first post as an operator aboard the White Star liner, *Teutonic,* and afterwards sailed on such famous liners as the *Oceanic* and *Mauretania*.

From 1908 to 1911 he was promoted to an operating post at the Marconi station outside Clifden, on the coast of County Galway, where he served as an operator corresponding with the Marconi station in Glace Bay, Nova Scotia.

During this time he struck up a friendship with an operator at Glace Bay, Walter Gray, who later transferred to the Cape Race Station. By a tragic coincidence he was on duty the night the *Titanic* went down, listening helplessly as his friend sent out his desperate SOS messages.

Jack Phillips returned to sea again in early 1912. Once again, he was on the White Star Line (although the Marconi Company continued to be his employer), and he joined the *Titanic* in March 1912 at Belfast.

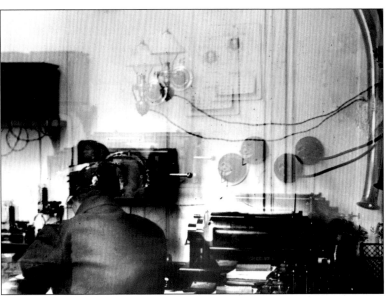
The radio room

The wireless was kept so busy with traffic during the *Titanic*'s voyage that one of the transformers burnt out, and Jack Phillips stayed on duty for over 40 hours, locating and repairing the fault. His actions would prove crucial to the survival of so many when disaster struck later in the voyage.

Around 250 messages were sent during the short duration of the trip until the fateful Sunday night – tiring work, but each message meant extra income for the Marconi Company, which remained his employer.

He was just about to go to bed when the collision occurred, and shortly afterwards Captain Smith arrived in the wireless cabin to order him to send for help.

Thereafter he remained at his post, sending messages constantly to try to obtain help from other ships, until he and his deputy, Harold Bride, were finally released from their duties by Captain Smith. Even then he held on and continued sending until the power finally faltered at 2.17 am, a mere few minutes before the ship went down.

Bride escaped from the wreck on an upturned collapsible lifeboat. Some reports claim Jack Phillips made it to the boat as well, but he was already exhausted before the collision took place, and the effects of the cold caused his death before the rescue by the *Carpathia*.

It is well-known that the *Titanic* received a message from the *Californian's* wireless operator, Cyril Evans, warning that his ship was surrounded by ice and they were stopping as a result. When he received the message from Evans, he replied: 'Shut up! I am busy, I am working Cape Race!'

This has been interpreted as meaning that he was so busy sending the relatively inconsequential messages of paying passengers that he could not be bothered to receive or to hand to the captain such an important message about nearby icebergs.

However, similar warning messages earlier that day had been delivered to the captain, and the ship's lookouts had been warned to be extra vigilant.

Mandy explained: 'Evans, the radio operator of the *Californian*, was quite new to the job, and quite excitable. He was notorious among what was then the very small world of radio operators, where everybody knew everybody, as a chatterbox, for blocking messages, and generally for being annoying.

'He tried to tell Phillips about the ice earlier in the evening, but he failed to use the Master Servicegram, the official ship-to-ship warning, which would have informed him that this to be was an official and important message – pay attention.

'Instead he began his message "I say, old man…" If Jack thought any-thing at all, he may have thought – "Oh no, it's that chatterbox again"! Because the *Californian* was so close to the *Titanic*, Evans' signal blasted Phillips' ears, so he ripped off his headset and sent that famous message: 'Shut up, I'm busy, I'm working Cape Race."

'Evans, on his part, probably thought "Oh well, I've tried to tell him". He was coming to the end of his shift, so he turned off his radio and went to bed – so he heard none of the subsequent messages from Phillips imploring help from other ships.

'Evans had actually been warned about his behaviour that very same voyage. There was a Marconi inspector travelling on the *Olympic* called Gilbert Balfour, who told Evans to stop jamming people and to stop unnecessary chatter. Evans was a well-known chatterer, and operators' sending style was as distinctive as a hand-writing, so as soon as Jack Phillips received the first few words of Evans' message, he would have known who it was distracting him while he was so busy.

'I can understand why people might think that Jack Phillips' reply to Evans was an opportunity lost, but given our knowledge about Evans, I think Phillips can be forgiven.'

She added: 'The ironic thing about the *Titanic* is that it was a horrible tragedy, of course, and so many people were lost, but out of that tragedy has come a wonderful community of friends, and so much enjoyment gained from research and meeting people and travelling around together.

'I do research holidays with groups of friends from around the world. We meet up, we share information and research and we look for – in some cases arrange for – the cleaning and restoration of memorial stones.

'"Fun" is the wrong word, but it's all about remembering the lost 1,600, and perpetuating the memory of what happened.

John George ('Jack') Phillips and the monument dedicated to him

OTHER CHANNEL ISLAND CONNECTIONS

(V)

THE ENTHUSIAST

God himself could not sink this ship!

Unknown Titanic crewmember to embarking passenger, Mrs Sylvia Caldwell.

Alfie Barrett, operations and logistics assistant at the Jersey Tourism section of the Economic Development Department, was an 11-year-old, living with his parents in London's East End, when the *Titanic*, so to speak, first sailed into his life.

'I was out one day with my mother, walking down the street near our home,' he recalled, 'and my mother stopped to talk to a woman – I started being irritable because of all this boring adult talk, until my mother gave me a clip round the earhole – parents were stricter in those days!

'When we finally walked on, she told me that she had been speaking to a very brave woman – someone who had survived the *Titanic*.

"What's that?" "Ask your father!" she said.

'So I asked my dad, and he told me about the ship that sank on its maiden voyage. About six years after that, I was coming home from work, and I stopped at a second-hand bookshop in Ilford – I used to buy sports books.

I went in and saw a book with a cover illustration of a sinking ship and a lifeboat - it was Walter Lord's famous book, *A Night to Remember.* After that I was hooked.'

The *Titanic* survivor to whom his mother was speaking was Eva Hart – she lived four doors down from the Barrett family's home.

Eva had been born in 1905 in Ilford; and in early 1912 her father decided to take his family and emigrate to Winnipeg, Manitoba, where he planned to open a tobacconist's shop. She was seven years old when she and her parents boarded the *Titanic* as second-class passengers at Southampton.

Alfie Barrett

Her mother had a premonition that some sort of catastrophe would hit the ship – to call a ship 'unsinkable' was tempting providence.

On the night of the collision she was sleeping. Her father woke up his wife and daughter, and, wrapping Eva in a blanket, carried her up to the deck. It was very cold, and another passenger, who was helping to free the boats, wrapped his own coat around her. That was Guernseyman, Joseph Duquemin.

Eva's father placed his wife and Eva in Lifeboat No.14 and told Eva to 'hold mummy's hand and be a good girl.' It was the last time she would ever see him.

Soon after being rescued by the *Carpathia* and arriving in New York, Eva and her mother returned to England. Eva had constant nightmares for years: 'I saw that ship sink,' she said in 1993. 'I saw it, I heard it, and nobody could possibly forget it. I can remember the colours, the sounds, everything. The worst thing I can remember is the screaming - and then the silence that followed.'

When salvaging efforts began in 1987, Eva was quick to note that the *Titanic* was a grave site and should be treated as such. She often decried the "insensitivity and greed" and labelled the salvers "fortune hunters, vultures, pirates, and grave robbers."

In 1994, she wrote an autobiography, '*Shadow of the Titanic - A Survivor's Story',* in which she described her experiences aboard the ship and the lasting implications of its sinking.

In her later years she became a Justice of the

Peace, and on one occasion travelled to Guernsey to visit the family of Joseph Duquemin. She died in February 1996 at her home in Chadwell Heath at the age of 91.

Over the decades, Alfie Barrett has amassed an extensive library of books about the *Titanic* or books which mention it, in addition to the files he has downloaded from the Internet. Some of the books are very rare, out of print or hard to get hold of.

The number includes 'specialist interest' subjects, such as details of the Irish or the Canadians aboard the *Titanic*, and of course, the controversy over whether the 'ship that stood still', in sight of the *Titanic* and perhaps nine miles away from it, but never came to its assistance, was the *Californian* or some other boat – a subject that is still hotly contested 100 years later. He expects, in the centenary year of the *Titanic*'s sinking, that many more books and websites will become available.

'Everybody knows that the *Titanic* was sunk by an iceberg, but few of the survivors actually saw it

or have left a description of it,' he said. 'Perhaps the only Channel Islander was Jerseyman Alfred Olliver, who was a member of the crew - a quartermaster who was on duty at the time of the collision.

'There are so many different theories about what was to blame for the sinking... was it the Captain's fault for going too fast? Was it Ismay's fault – did he demand that it should go faster so as to make a speed record for the crossing? Was a correct watch kept? Was it because wireless warnings about icebergs from other ships were not passed to the captain, because the wireless operator was too busy sending passengers' messages and earning money for Marconi? I suppose lots of separate things – perhaps some of them minor in themselves - contributed to the disaster.

'It is like the words of the old rhyme: "For want of a nail, a shoe was lost; for want of a shoe, a horse was lost..." A combination of minor mishaps, combined with some sloppy seamanship, in aggregate, contributed to a major disaster.'

A cross section of the Titanic and Olympic

Smoke room

OTHER CHANNEL ISLAND CONNECTIONS

(VI)
THE WITNESS

'Titanic, name and thing, will stand as a monument and warning to human presumption.

- The Bishop of Winchester, preaching in Southampton, 1912.

Rosalind ('Roz') Makin passed away in Jersey, aged 105, in January 2006. She was very much in command of all her faculties remembers her son, Michael Lanyon, the now retired director of the Jersey Airport.

When Mrs Makin was a little girl, her father was a member of the Coast Guard and worked at Calshot Spit, close to Southampton. Each Sunday afternoon he would take her for a walk in the area and then regularly went to visit a friend of his who lived in a large house called 'Eaglehurst'.

She remembered that the man was very friendly, but spoke with a very strong accent and, being so young, she could not pronounce his name. 'Don't worry,' he told her, 'just call me Julie.'

It was only years later that she discovered that her father's friend was Guglielmo Marconi.

At the age of just 11, Roz had no idea who Marconi was or the significance of the 'science experiments' that he liked to show her father, but living so close to Southampton, she was used to seeing large liners come and go.

One liner, however, stuck forever in her memory. In her later years, she recalled a breezy Easter Monday in 1912 when she decided to fly her kite with some friends. As they tried to do this, they were distracted by the sight of the *Titanic* making her way out of Southampton on her maiden voyage.

'It was so enormous and so close – we could see the faces of the people on deck,' she said. 'I

Photo: Mrs Roz Makin, at her 100th Birthday party, holding a telegram of congratulations from Queen Elizabeth. (Mrs P Lanyon – Le Boutillier collection)

can still see their faces.....'

A couple of months later, on 18 June 1912, Marconi gave evidence to the Court of Inquiry into the loss of the *Titanic* regarding the marine telegraphy's functions and the procedures for emergencies at sea.

Britain's postmaster-general, Herbert Samuel, in court, referred to the *Titanic* disaster: 'Those who have been saved, have been saved through one man, Mr. Marconi...and his marvelous invention.'

OTHER CHANNEL ISLAND CONNECTIONS

(VII)
THE GUERNSEY MEMORIALS

Think of it! A few more boats, a few more planks of wood nailed together in a particular way at a trifling cost, and all those men and women whom the world can so ill-afford to lose would be with us to-day, there would be no mourning in thousands of homes which now are desolate, and these words need not have been written'

- from 'The Loss of the S.S. Titanic, its Story and its Lessons' (1912) by Lawrence Beesley (survivor).

In Guernsey, there is a plaque to all the people with Guernsey connections who sailed on the *Titanic*. It is located at Guernsey's Shipwreck Museum at Fort Grey, Rocquaine Bay.

You don't just have to be keenly interested in shipwrecks to enjoy a visit this museum. The stunning backdrop of the bay, the fort's outline, which has given it the local nickname of 'the cup and saucer', and the walk across the causeway, especially at high tide, makes an enjoyable excursion in itself. The view of the rocks out at sea illustrates very effectively the threat to ships and shipping along the west coast of the Island.

The fort is one of a series of towers built in 1804 as part of a defensive system to protect Guernsey from Napoleon. It replaced an old, ruined castle, the Chateau de Rocquaine, which had occupied the site until then.

In the 20th Century, it was manned during both World Wars, and served as a German anti-aircraft battery during the Occupation. In the post-war years, it fell into disuse other than being used as a fishermen's store. Its restoration and conversion began in 1970, and the completed museum was first opened to the public in 1976. It is now home to a museum - a branch of Guernsey Museums and Galleries - that houses a collection of maritime artifacts and information relating to shipwrecks around the treacherous west coast of Guernsey.

It features wrecks from the time of *HMS Sprightly,* which foundered on the Hanois reef in 1777, to the loss of the *Prosperity* with 16 lives in 1974. It includes displays on shipwrecks, diving, lighthouses, navigation, archaeology and sea rescues.

The plaque to the Guernsey people who sailed on the *Titanic* is prominently displayed, and lists 18 people. That number includes Rosalie Bidois, although it is has now been established that her connection is with Jersey rather than with Guernsey. The display in the museum records the names and fate of all the unfortunate travellers.

It is, to date, the only memorial in the Island to all its *Titanic* travellers. The regular curator there, Jenny Ridley, also has a family connection with the *Titanic*: her grandfather, Joseph Walker, was a plumber working on the *Titanic* during its construction at Harland and Woolf in Belfast. At the time that the ship was finished and launched, the workmen had an opportunity to inspect the new ship, together with their families. She recalls that her grandmother, Jeanette, had such a premonition of disaster that she refused to go on board.

There are two other memorials to individual *Titanic* victims in Guernsey: one to Albert Denbuoy in St Sampson's Churchyard, and one to Clifford Parker in St Andrew's Churchyard. Both these memorials are showing signs of age.

'Private memorials' as they might be called - treasured artefacts, paintings or photos or photos – are kept by descendants who still live in Guernsey today. Among the present-day generation of '*Titanic* families' are Hilda Carpentier and her brothers, great niece and great nephews of Laurence Gavey, Malcolm Woodland, great nephew of the stewardess Anne Martin, the descendants of Edward Wheadon, including Deidre Bell, Suzie Vowles and Martyn Dorey, and Roy and Elizabeth Northey, who have researched the life of Roy's great aunt, Emily Rugg.

Capelles Building Stores, which was for at least three generations the family business of the Duquemin family, has now been sold. Gerald Duquemin, the younger brother of the Joseph Duquemin who survived the *Titanic*, was succeeded by his son, Lawson; now Lawson and his sister, Phyllis Byrnes, are in retirement.

All the names mentioned above have kindly provided material that has helped the author; there are certainly other families and further descendants whose names are as yet unknown to him.

At the time of writing, the centenary of the *Titanic* is getting closer, and with this in mind, one of the descendants of the victims has signalled his intention of funding another plaque or information board – possibly at the Castle Cornet Shipping Museum. The States of Guernsey Culture and Leisure Board is considering the proposal at the time of writing.

ENVOI

'It was another thought that visited Brother Juniper: "Why did this happen to those five?" If there were any plan in the Universe at all, if there were any pattern in a human life, surely it could be discovered mysteriously latent in those lives so suddenly cut off. Either we live by accident and die by accident, or we live by plan and die by plan.'

Thornton Wilder, 'The Bridge of San Louis Rey'

'To my mind, the world of today awoke April 15th, 1912'

Jack Thayer, 17-year-old passenger on the Titanic, writing in 1940.

The book, *'The Bridge of San Louis Rey'*, is one of the classics of 20th Century literature. It explores the themes of life and death, chance and God, faith and unbelief, and tends to be quoted, or referred to, at any occasion when, for no apparent reason, happy and productive lives are cut off and when questions arise: why *them?* Is life and death blind chance? Is there some reason and order that might be discernable to explain the tragedy?

And so, a century ago, people asked much the same questions after the *Titanic* disaster.

Death (it was a jolt for many people to discover) could come just as easily and as unexpectedly for a Guggenheim or an Astor as for the men who cleaned their shoes or stoked a steamer's engines.

There may be many answers to the questions: 'Why do we remember, so vividly and in such great detail, the sinking of this particular ship a century ago? There have been, after all, other marine disasters of equal or even greater magnitude. The sinking of *The Empress of Ireland* in May 1914, for example, is now barely remembered in comparison, despite the loss of over 1,000 people on board, many of them children.

Why today are there still books being written about the *Titanic*, societies in existence to study it and meetings and conventions to discuss it? What, in short, is the popularity of this particular incident that makes its name instantly recognisable and as commonly used as a metaphor?'

After all, any Member of the Jersey or Guernsey States who wishes to signal his opposition to some measure that he finds uncongenial will signify its utter futility by describing it as being as useful as 'arranging the deckchairs on the *Titanic.*' There are indeed some Members whom one might suspect know of no other metaphor, so frequently do they employ it.

And it is used frequently as a metaphor for anything, be it measure, institution, or anything else that continues, full speed ahead and oblivious to danger, to crash into some obstacle that the Great and the Good could easily have perceived. The European Union on a macro-scale, or States reform on an insular scale, are often characterised in this way: measures that will, it seems, so self-evidently bring such great benefit that they are practically - unsinkable. The very use of the word 'unsinkable' is enough to bring the *Titanic* to mind or to score a debating point.

As has often been said, it was the faith in the so-called 'unsinkability' of the *Titanic* that seemed to suggest human hubris, and a challenge offered to Fate that was taken up with catastrophic effect. In some ways the *Titanic* story is like an Ancient Greek tragedy.

But in addition, the *Titanic*'s story is the modern equivalent of a mediaeval fresco on a church wall showing kings and beggar men, equally, being abruptly removed from the settled nature of their lives, their ambitions and expectations, and finding themselves of an instant borne by angels to Heaven or being cast by demons into Hell.

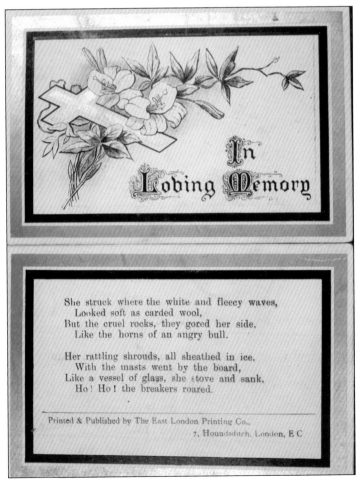

Memorial service, St Luke's, Jersey April 1912
(John Ovenden Collection)

Leaving Southampton

The luxury of the first class accommodation, the superb quality of the restaurant food, and the gilded social life of its passengers came to an unpremeditated and abrupt end, just as did the lives of the poor emigrants in steerage. Ambitions, business proposals, holiday plans, excited anticipation of a new start in a new country… all the proposals of self-confident humanity were overruled by a higher disposition – and thus a warning to us all.

The *Titanic* was far more than a ship, and much more than a modern means of travel that, as we all know too well, transports with minimum convenience and comfort its passengers from a place of departure to a place of arrival. It was a symbol of status, and of exclusivity, and those passengers who paid to travel on the maiden voyage on the *Titanic* in order to be seen and to be noted as being 'with the best people' certainly achieved their ambition – if not exactly in the way they thought, or might really have wanted. The passenger list is still easily obtainable on the Internet, and available for anyone to inspect, a century later.

And that is one of the attractions of the *Titanic* story: the comfortable, even luxurious, life of its passengers came tumbling down – their faith in watertight compartments had proved to be worthless, in the same way as was their faith in the continuing and orderly progress of familiar civilised life.

So the *Titanic* has become a metaphor for the sudden end of Edwardian life and Edwardian certainties, a presage of a dark and troubled century coming, and an end to the belief that the continued path of mankind is inevitably onward and upward to ever greater technological triumphs, to greater happiness and to greater material progress.

For some, the *Titanic* disaster has been seen as a warning to the Western World, and to Britain in particular, to cease its insatiable lust for imperial

Some of the lucky ones

power and commercial dominance. As Kipling put it in 1897, in words that, after the disaster, might have seemed prophetic:

If, drunk with sight of power, we loose
Wild tongues that have not Thee in awe—
.....
'For heathen heart that puts her trust
In reeking tube and iron shard--
All valiant dust that builds on dust,
And guarding, calls not Thee to guard--
For frantic boast and foolish word,
Thy mercy on Thy people, Lord.'

But the warning was disregarded, and so a war came more terrible than any before it, and so did the end of Britain as a pre-eminent world power. Then came further war, and the end of Empire and the long slow retreat to bathos – until in our own time, Captain Smith's reputed last words to 'Be British' might be understood to mean merely an invitation to go on social networking sites, spy on one another with hidden cameras and to shop seven days a week.

The author, sitting up late at night at the computer, is doubtless over-imaginative in sensing others reading the screen from behind his shoulders, a press of other bodies looking on, and mutely asking the question: 'Why?' Why them, and not others? They were probably happy enough with their mundane lives, with their plans for a future that was suddenly snatched from them. They did not want to be wrenched painfully away from this Vale of Tears - they only wanted to reach New York.

But maybe there is no answer. The only meaning for the *Titanic* disaster might be (according to some theories) that when, in the face of the iceberg, the order was given 'hard a-port', the wheel was turned the wrong way, and thus some 1,700 people met their deaths prematurely and needlessly – no divine warning, no moral judgment, just a titanic marine traffic accident.

The last picture taken of the Titanic as she leaves Queenstown, Ireland 12th of April 1912